CARNAL RHETORIC

Jerusalem, Plate 99, by William Blake. Yale Center for
British Art, Paul Mellon Collection.

CARNAL RHETORIC

Milton's Iconoclasm and the Poetics of Desire

Lana Cable

Duke University Press   Durham and London   1995

© 1995 Duke University Press

All rights reserved

Printed in the United States of America on acid-free paper ∞

Designed by Cherie Holma Westmoreland

Typeset in Trump Mediaeval with Adobe copperplate display

Chapter 5 is based on "Milton's Iconoclastic Truth," in *Politics, Poetics, and Heremeneutics in Milton's Prose*, David Loewenstein and James Grantham Turner, eds., © Cambridge University Press 1990. Reprinted with the permission of Cambridge University Press. Portions of chapter 3 first appeared in "Coupling Logic and Milton's Doctrine of Divorce," *Milton Studies XV*, James D. Simmonds, ed., published in 1981 by the University of Pittsburgh Press. Reprinted by permission of the publisher. Chapter 2 is based on "Shuffling Up Such a God," *Milton Studies XXI*, James D. Simmonds, ed., published in 1986 by the University of Pittsburgh Press. Reprinted by permission of the publisher.

Library of Congress Cataloging-in-Publication Data appear on the last printed page of this book.

·(⟺)·

To E. M.

For while I sit with thee, I seem in Heav'n,
And sweeter thy discourse is to my eare
Then Fruits of Palm-tree pleasantest to thirst . . . .
(*Paradise Lost* VIII, 210–12)

CONTENTS

·(⟷)·

ACKNOWLEDGMENTS

The debts of this book are many. I would not have undertaken this kind of study without the intellectual stimulus of Stanley Fish, whose inspired humanity and purity of engagement with his subject make his teaching a beneficent entangling: I am eternally grateful to him. And without the faithful support of my friends and colleagues at the University at Albany, this book could never have been completed. Among these supporters I am most deeply obliged to Sandra K. Fischer, whose meticulous reading of my work under very difficult circumstances remains a model of scholarly responsibility and professional grace. Seconding and continuing her efforts have been two other mainstays: Richard Goldman, with his wisdom and wit; and Warren Ginsberg, with his intellectual strength and perceptive counseling. In addition to these friends and colleagues Harry Staley, Jeffrey Berman, Martha Rozett, Robert Donovan, Deborah Dorfman, Randy Craig, Judith Barlow, Helen Elam, Tom Smith, Carolyn Yalkut, Jennifer Fleischner, George Hastings, Iliana Semmler, Sarah Blacher Cohen, Hugh Maclean, Walter Knotts, and M. E. Grenander and her late husband Jim Corbett all deserve special mention as having heartened and sustained me at a time when my project had fallen on evil days.

Portions of the manuscript have also greatly benefited from critical comments and lively encouragements at various stages of writing by Jonathan Crewe, J. G. A. Pocock, Jerome Schneewind, Milad Douahi,

Acknowledgments

David Loewenstein, James Turner, James Simmonds, Arthur F. Kinney, James Egan, and my friends Ellen Mankoff and Tim Hofmeister. To all, I extend my heartfelt thanks. I wish also to thank Joan Bennett for her positive response to my ideas on *Samson Agonistes*, and with her I wish to thank Michael Lieb, Joseph Wittreich, John Shawcross, and the participants in the 1992 Arizona Milton Institute for their interest in and support of my work. I thank also the National Endowment of the Humanities and Peter Medine for providing the opportunity for me to participate in the Institute. The cogent remarks of two anonymous reviewers for Duke University Press proved extremely useful to me, and the editorial staff at the press has been unfailingly courteous and helpful. Reynolds Smith and Jean Brady guided me through various stages of the production process, and Marie Blanchard's tactful copyediting brought welcome rule to an often troublesome text. Needless to say, whatever faults remain in the book are entirely my own responsibility.

Several other lasting obligations remain to be mentioned. I wish here to record my appreciation of Dr. Glyn Thomas, whose precise articulations years ago at the University of Wyoming first awakened me to the richness of affective detail in literature. My most unrepayable debt is expressed by my dedication of this book to Eshragh Motahar, a sociable spirit who, having discovered the magnificence of Milton's language, has the blessed grace to let it speak for itself. My own compulsion to speak for it, however, could not have been fulfilled without Eshi's wisdom, patience, spontaneous generosity, and computer expertise. And, finally, I want to express my deepest and most long-standing gratitude to my mother, Dorothe Wood Cable, from whom I learned about the power and beauty of metaphor, and to my father, Norman Vance Cable Sr., from whom I learned about the power of the desire for truth.

CARNAL RHETORIC

·(⟺)·

INTRODUCTION

C ritical interest in Milton's iconoclasm has gained force in re-
cent years from the increased attention that has been paid to his
polemical writings and the resultant reinterpretations of his poetry. In
contrast to traditional readings of the poetry that emphasize Milton's
classicism and thus his affirmation of seemingly eternal human values,
readings informed by Milton's temporal polemical concerns provide
surprising insights into the participation of all his writings in dis-
courses specific to early modernism. Nowhere is such participation
more apparent than in the iconoclastic impetus that drives arguments
both in Milton's poetry and in his prose. The subtle negotiations of
the new historicist critics who interweave the poetry and the prose
are especially helpful toward understanding that impetus: with imagi-
nation and great erudition, the new historicists draw Milton's icono-
clastic motifs into the fluid political, social, religious, aesthetic, and
philosophical discourses that manifest early modernism's radically
iconoclastic pattern.[1]

Not enough attention has been given to the specifically linguistic
aspect of the iconoclasm discernible in Milton's writing, however. This
aspect is crucial because it is on the affective level of linguistic imme-
diacy that the workings of Milton's iconoclasm most intimately may
be traced. To account for iconoclasm in the imagination of a writer—
or even just to examine it closely—requires that we probe iconoclastic

activity not only in ideas and forms and argumentative structures, but in the workings of language itself, in the linguistic substance of the imagination. It is on the affective level of linguistic immediacy that the arguments and ideas of a writer like Milton gain the reader's assent. To discover the dynamics of that assent, and of the writer's pursuit of it, we need a means of understanding and acknowledging the kind of cognitive validity that affective language is instinctively granted by the iconoclastic writer. The very idea that affective language might in fact lay claim to any kind of cognitive validity would of course be disputed by a strict rationalist. But as my opening inquiries into "semantic fallacy" and "iconological fallacy" in metaphor theory will show, the rationalist analysis evades much of what we actually experience in the linguistic construct: specifically, it evades language's sensory or "carnal" dimension. That this dimension of language is essential to Milton's writing is increasingly being treated as axiomatic. Yet because his religious faith simultaneously spurns carnal reliance (*fiducia carnalis*) and also validates it as a plastic creative medium, Milton's affective language presents a challenge to any who would know just what kinds of claims such language makes.[2] A means of assessing those claims is therefore provided by the theoretical foundation on which the present study is based, the iconoclastic metaphor theory of "carnal rhetoric."

As is suggested by my emphasis on the assent of the reader to linguistic affect, *Carnal Rhetoric* shares with reader-response theory the critical strategy of breaking through formal and generic barriers by concentrating on affective stylistics. But in contrast to reader-response, *Carnal Rhetoric* does not generate the fiction of the nonexistent text, a phenomenon that is subject to as much abuse as are formalist and generic categories that falsely alienate, for instance, Milton's "imaginative" poetry from his "reasoned" prose.[3] Thus, while my own approach to Milton's language is clearly informed by reader-response theory, I realign my inquiry by focusing not on the reader but on the intrinsic nature of affective language, and on the affinities between such language and the imaginative appeal of that most Miltonic yet analytically elusive trait, iconoclasm. Ernest Gilman has shown how the creative power of poets like Spenser, Quarles, Donne, and Milton is released by the clash between the iconic plenitude of the Renaissance imagination and the Reformist conception of a language purified of affective intent. The iconoclastic instinct of these poets confronts their language with "the choice of polluting itself by coupling with its own idolatrous desires, or of rising up as the weapon of the warfaring Christian to cleanse the temple of the heart and throw down the high places of the imagination."[4] But whereas Gilman's interest in the language of these poets lies in the specifically Reformist clash between sensory image and doctrinally chastened word, my own concern begins with inquiry into the iconoclastic activity of metaphor that marks the creative impetus behind *all* literary art—an impetus by force of which iconic high places are thrown down precisely to *liberate* imaginative desire in a propulsive thrust toward the unknown. It is in metaphor, where linguistic affect and the iconoclastic instinct coalesce, that we can gain insights into the creative process that will be answerable both to Milton's own iconoclastic poetics and to his longing for creative union with an indeterminate ideal. By seeking to understand on the most elemental linguistic level the requisites and intentions of affective language, of images and metaphor, we can equip ourselves to consider language as a medium capable of supporting all of the demands Milton places on it—a medium actually capable of transforming and redeeming human life in the mortal world.

In the interest of such an understanding, then, the long theoretical chapter that opens this study reorients our approach to affective language by critiquing the current state of metaphor theory. From that critique emerges an iconoclastic theory of metaphor that can account for metaphor's emotional and psychological as well as sensory and semantic dimensions. What this enriched account of metaphor provides is a mechanism for recognizing the *cognitive* worth of language that is otherwise too easily devalued as mere rhetorical flourish (Milton's allegedly "scurrilous" polemical passages come to mind), or else that is treated as belonging to a realm other than our own—a realm which, though lofty, must be acknowledged as unreal (as in his more "visionary" millennialist passages). This enriched account of metaphor can give us a specialized insight into what is going on when Milton constructs a metaphoric passage. It enables us to adopt a critical disposition that, without relinquishing the rigorous articulations of logical analysis, nevertheless grants to affective language a cognitive validity akin to that which Milton himself grants it at his most intense and heightened levels of expression.

We need such a critical disposition, because to come to terms with Milton's literary iconoclasm is to comprehend *rationally* the thoroughness with which Milton commits to his nonrational affective language the enormous and unending task of discovering Truth. In practical terms for Milton, this meant perpetually contriving with language to invent Truth while at the same time demonstrating that Truth lies ever beyond the powers of mortal invention. The deeply paradoxical nature of this commitment is not always overtly acknowledged by Milton in his writings. But his commitment is discernible, manifesting itself as an exploration of what his language can do, what he can make it bear, what it can sustain. This exploration, which we ourselves witness, is not necessarily a pragmatic or self-consciously developed theory of creativity such as the Romantic poets worked out, a quasi-scientific critical system for explaining and justifying the writer's own imaginative output. Rather, what is revealed by the present study's presumptive scrutiny of metaphoric passages from Milton's prose (in Chapters 2–5) is the vital interplay between Milton's iconoclastic impulse and his imaginative impetus: the dynamic clash of destructive and constructive energies that is evoked by the popular phrase for Milton's artistic power, his "creative iconoclasm."

I trace this interplay from some of its earliest appearances in the antiprelatical tracts, and follow its evolution through the divorce tracts into something not unlike a deliberately theorized aesthetic and philosophical practice by Milton in *Areopagitica* and *Eikonoklastes*. The passages I work with have been selected for the clarity with which they mark discernible stages in Milton's thinking about and practice with the affective resources of metaphoric language. The primary object of my forays into Milton's polemical works is therefore not to offer a new reading of this or that prose tract for its own sake. My purpose is rather to discover what the affective language in these tracts reveals about iconoclastic thinking, as it bears upon Milton's imagination and upon his sense of what constitutes truth in his own linguistic practice. These explorations result in a picture of creative truth-seeking as necessarily, and by definition, an iconoclastic activity.

From Milton's affective polemics, then, iconoclastic metaphor theory derives an abstract picture of iconoclastic truth-seeking as an exalted human activity. We fleetingly witness a more concrete form of such activity in the archangel Michael's devastating critique of iconic imaginings about God's place in the Garden of Eden. God lives in every part of creation, Michael reminds the nostalgic and fallen, Paradise-adoring Adam: "not this rock only" (*PL* XI.336). And if "this rock" can divest the sensory richness of God's heaven on earth, the highest accomplishments of mankind can suffer from the perceptual corrections made by an undazzled mind. In *Paradise Regained* the Savior at once credits and debunks all outward valuations of human learning: "Think not but that I know these things, or think / I know them not; not therefore am I short / Of knowing what I ought" (*PR* IV.286–88). But these suggestive glimpses of the iconoclastic nature of truth-seeking acquire full dramatic expression only when Milton constructs the figure of his iconoclastic hero Samson. Thus the shift of focus in my final chapter from Milton's prose to his poetic tragedy, while formally discontinuous, is thematically logical and conceptually indispensable. As Milton's embodiment of the mortally burdened, perceptually limited yet devoted truth-seeker, Samson dramatically reifies and fulfills metaphor's iconoclastic requisites. The imaginative dynamic of destruction and creation that metaphor simultaneously feeds on and generates is also the reality that Samson lives out, and it is the truth in which Samson dies.

An argument that finds metaphor, Milton's polemics and poetics, and Milton's Nazarite hero all linked by a commitment to creative iconoclasm must necessarily incorporate diverse analytical strategies. A brief summary of these will help to clarify the relationship of each phase of my argument to the next, as well as its relevance to the whole. I begin my study of metaphor by breaking out of strict disciplinary boundaries, to engage relevant explorations from the fields of philosophy, linguistics, and aesthetics in addition to literature. This approach brings immediately to the foreground the troublesome issues of metaphoric affect versus meaning; poetry's "truth-content"; and the problematic relations between the verbal and the pictorial that remain problematic even apart from the specific doctrinal conflicts of the English reform period. Ways in which metaphor theory discourse is hampered come into play in my discussions of *semantic fallacy*—untoward de-

mands for discursive "meaning"; and *iconological fallacy*—the percep-
tual slant caused by dominance of the visual in metaphor discourse.
Analysis of the iconological fallacy leads to W. J. T. Mitchell's observa-
tions on the symbiotic relationship between iconology and iconoclasm.
These I develop by drawing on Jakobson's discussion of split reference
and Husserl's speculations on the nature of doubt. Through critique
of Paul Ricoeur's schematic account of the metaphoric process, and of
Phillip Stambovsky's phenomenological account of depictive imagery,
I establish the necessary direct psychic connection between the icono-
clastic impulse and the way metaphor actually works.

The resulting iconoclastic theory of metaphor provides a model
for understanding Milton's linguistic vehemence as integral to his
creativity on a level simultaneously philosophical and sensory. This
theory provides a frame of reference and an analytical tool for *Carnal
Rhetoric*'s subsequent exploration of Milton's creative iconoclasm in
the language of his polemical prose and, ultimately, in the dramatic
realization of his iconoclastic hero Samson.

Chapter 2 examines directly the affective impetus of crucial pas-
sages in Milton's early polemical prose. As will Milton's Samson, the
writer of the antiprelatical tracts is forced to abandon cherished pre-
conceptions about the sanctity of his consecrated gifts before he can
fulfill his purpose. But the difficulty of that abandonment for Milton
shows in the rhetorical disjunctions of his early polemics. Entering his
poetic talents into what he initially sees as the profane arena of reli-
gious controversy, Milton writes a prose whose affective impetus splits
away from its rational progression. Yet the richly sensuous metaphoric
arguments in these tracts actually feed on and derive their energy from
the images of those whom he attacks. The antiprelatical imagery thus
displays outright the propulsive impetus of metaphor's iconoclastic
strategy.

Turning in Chapter 3 to *The Doctrine and Discipline of Divorce*, I
demonstrate how Milton's empyreal image of ideal coupling exercises
over the argument a rhetorical control whose affective energy draws
on the universal and elemental claims of the body and sexual regen-
eration. The divorce tracts show coupling dynamics to move beyond
their expected illustrative and thematic role to empower the very syn-
tactic structures of the argument. But the generative potential of the

empyreal coupling ideal is itself troubled by the homoerotic implications of the Eros/Anteros myth, a sign in the divorce tracts of Milton's participation in the conflictual gender dialectic of traditional aesthetics discourse. The seductive dualisms of empyreal coupling thus create for the monistic Milton an ontological dilemma that will force him ultimately to demolish even his idealistic coupling image as another instance whereby the passionately desired image, like Adam's image of paradisal union with Eve, may be erroneously mistaken for the higher reality of divine union toward which the image can only provide a momentary apprehensional means.

Chapter 4 demonstrates how *Areopagitica*'s images carry out imagination's program of creative iconoclasm—the device for perfect freedom for which iconoclastic metaphor theory provides a model. *Areopagitica*'s images elude our own imaginative grasp in a denial of reification that argues not the delusiveness of sensory affect but rather its creative necessity. The pressure Stanley Fish finds in *Areopagitica* to "drive us from the letter,"[5] to drive us from our instinct to grasp and thereby falsify truth in all its forms, can actually be extended beyond Milton's ostensible preoccupation with truth to his underlying concern for the impetus of imaginative freedom. The images of *Areopagitica* demonstrate carnal rhetoric's inadequacy to truth; but at the same time, their protean energy celebrates and enacts the *transformative desire* of carnal rhetoric, its unremitting *re-creative* impetus to reach beyond whatever is known. Through the ruling metaphor of the book that is our life, the iconoclastic activity of *Areopagitica*'s imagery provides a model for the individual imaginative progressivism that is required for our own independent self-authorship.

Chapter 5 addresses itself specifically to the *psychology* of creative iconoclasm, as manifested by Milton's fully developed iconoclastic poetics in the antimonarchical tract *Eikonoklastes*. Here Milton's argument simultaneously critiques and exploits the insight that illusions are the realities of the mind and are the true source of its power. Hence, iconoclastic violence lies not merely or perhaps even most radically in the artist's destruction of the old icon (as if the icon were the object or a victim) but rather in the seizing, manipulating, and redefining of elemental constructs in people's imaginations—beliefs, perceptions, convictions, habits, secure notions that apprehend themselves in and through the icon. In Stuart political iconology Milton saw a crass reflection of the no less illusionistic power of all carnal rhetoric, including his own.

But the theory of creative iconoclasm receives its most dramatic representation in the paradigmatic career of Milton's tragic hero Samson. Joseph Wittreich's historical recontextualization of *Samson Agonistes* directs us newly to attend to "the personal ramifications of this poem" for a poet whose detractors had identified him with the blind and defeated Samson.[6] At the same time, the fact that a very different Samson, heroic and divinely inspired, had earlier in the seventeenth century been regarded as a "patron saint" to the revolutionary cause testifies to the contradictory responses generated by iconoclasts. These conflicting historical responses to Samson are reflected in the current critical debate between regenerationist and antiregenerationist readings of Milton's iconoclastic hero. For Milton, however, it is precisely the unresolvable paradox of such contradictory responses to Samson that validates a particular and highly evolved conceptual truth in the Nazarite's iconoclastic action. For most interpreters of his iconoclasm, blind Samson is surrounded by idols that he must learn to see clearly if he is to destroy them and liberate himself. By contrast, I treat Samson as himself the tragedy's prime maker and worshipper of idols, one who, without understanding how or why, deeply senses himself as a rooted idolater—of his heroic calling, of his magnificent hair, of God's "holy secret," of his own betrayal of that secret—and one who knows no way but radically to transform himself by violence. It is Samson's radically private internal shattering of icons for which the violent theatrical display that ends his heroic career is only an outward sign.[7] Not just in the cataclysmic finale, but throughout the entire drama, Samson knows only to destroy a self that is not serving its ultimately incomprehensible God, on the sole unassured hope that a serviceable self might emerge. The carnal rhetoric of Samson's incremental self-destructions thus manifests early modernism's radically iconoclastic pattern of transformative power and transformative desire, the pattern to which metaphor speaks, by which it operates, and beyond which no higher truth either can or perhaps need be affirmed.

1

METAPHOR AND "MEANING"

Toward a Theory of Creative Iconoclasm

The argument of this book proceeds on a genial confidence in the rewards to be gained by taking Milton's metaphors seriously and even literally. This is not to say that a sufficient account of a given metaphoric passage can be derived from semantic analysis of its components.[1] Rather, this argument holds that when John Milton compares moderate Episcopal ministers to cooling stewpots whose rising lukewarm scum "gives a vomit to God himself," we accomplish little by asserting that what Milton *really means* is that the Almighty prefers ministers of strong religious conviction. Such a reading seeks metaphor's "meaning" everywhere but in our experience of the image itself—the reading turns away from the metaphor (in this instance, with apparent embarrassment) rather than dealing with it. In the next chapter we will take a closer critical look at *Of Reformation*'s iconoclastic image of God sick in the kitchen. But for the moment, I wish simply to propose that the analytic process we set in motion when we seek the *real meaning* of metaphoric passages is flawed from its inception. Metaphor is not about "meaning." If we consider how metaphor is used and what it does, we find that its proper milieu is not meaning but affective resonance.[2]

As my phrase "experience of the image" suggests, this study values and uses interpretive procedures derived from reader-response theory —but with significant qualifications. Ordinarily, reader-response treats "meaning" as that which is actually *composed by* affective resonance, as opposed to the traditional idea that meaning *gives rise to* affective resonance. As Stephen Greenblatt reminds us, it is indeed "impossible to take the 'text itself' as the perfect, unsubstitutable, freestanding container of all of its meanings."[3] But the interpretive theory on which such an account of literature is based demands a radical dislocation and redefinition of "meaning" (from its traditional home in the text to a new one in experience) that burdens the reading experience itself with a presumption of endlessly reverberating epistemological implications that it does not necessarily have. If we make such a radical dislocation, intellectual responsibility demands that we ask, "In the shift of meaning from text to experience, what exactly happens to the *meaning* of 'meaning'?" And the way out of that quandary, as Ogden and Richards demonstrated with great erudition and irony seven decades ago, is to recognize that neither philosophers nor other seekers after wisdom should entirely be trusted with the pursuit of "meaning," for the simple reason that the term is inaccurate. Rather than a shared enterprise, pursuit of "meaning" actually consists of a miscellaneous grab bag of inquiries and concerns whose proper domains emerge only when they are given their right names: intention, value, referent, emotion, symbol, and so forth.[4] Today we might extend and refine Ogden and Richards's list of meanings for "meaning," but we would be unwise to completely ignore or forget their precept.

It may be just such critical amnesia that underlies the misunderstanding to which reader-response criticism seems peculiarly subject. If literary "meaning" is a construct of cultures and readers rather than of texts, if "meaning" is truly no other than what "happens . . . in the interaction between the flow of print (or sound) and the actively mediating consciousness of a reader-hearer,"[5] then the reductive interpreter of reader-response theory may logically conclude that there is nothing in any reader's responding consciousness that cannot be claimed as what the literary work "means"—regardless of how variously a culture's or the reader's own mediating skills may happen to be constituted.[6] Thus, to such an interpreter, the literary text can "mean" anything or everything or nothing. This charge has been leveled against structuralist and poststructuralist analysis in general, but the charge more properly should be seen as a reaction against the reductive maneuvers of injudicious deconstructionism—overly hasty renderings of the deconstructionist theory of apprehension that concludes no text can have a fixed meaning. In its popular formulation, reductive deconstructionism's rhetoric of effacing the text (and consequently the author) sets the stage for effacing the entire experience of literary art as well.

Reductive deconstructionism's zero-sum game results from a relentless implementation of what I take to be a casual (though polemically exploitable and therefore potentially vicious) oversimplification of theory, what amounts in practice to a twofold semantic mistake: the uncritical substitution (1) of the term "meaning" for "the reading experience" and (2) of the term "text" for "interpretation of the text."[7] In the present argument, some distinctions will therefore be maintained by the following expedients: first, I will use the term "text" to refer only to the work that the literary artist produces—not the reader, not the reading experience. Next, for the reader's experience or interpretation, I will use "experience" and "interpretation"; and for the reader, the term "reader" will be used. When we turn to the case made by *Areopagitica*, on the other hand, Milton's own evolving conception of the reader as a self-constituting vital text will be seen to have invigorated these terms *for him* in such a way as to fuse readerly activity with the iconoclastic impetus that itself constitutes, as I argue in the present theoretical chapter, the only true "meaning" of metaphor. The term "meaning," however, has come increasingly to operate, for literary criticism in general and for discourse on metaphor in particular, as an epistemological red herring.[8] For that reason, I limit the term "meaning" to as narrowly unambiguous a circuit as I can. When possible, I avoid the term altogether. My reasons for avoiding it—indeed the term's near expendability for a study in affective theory—will become apparent as we proceed.

Meanwhile, I wish to affirm that I am deeply sympathetic to arguments that assume the primacy and centrality of the work of art itself in the artistic experience. My own iconoclastic theory of creativity, indeed, makes and depends upon that very assumption. Also, though neither theory of meaning nor metaphor theory as such is the subject of this book, my analytical procedures throughout reflect the difference between what happens when we pursue the "meaning" of Milton's metaphors and what happens when we explore their affective dimension. A sufficient account of the latter requires that we understand Milton's polemical vehemence as integral to his creative thought. Toward that end, therefore, the interpretive model provided by the present chapter's theory of creative iconoclasm will explore Milton's rhetoric on a level of affective immediacy that places his arguments in a revealing new light.

First, however, explication of the theory itself is in order. This entails a temporary backing off from critical engagement with Milton's writing. But the analytic structures generated by the present theoretical chapter will help to reveal the internal dynamics of creative iconoclasm, a philosophical and artistic predisposition that is usually ascribed to Milton without examining the complex nature of the thing ascribed. Let me begin with a critical hypothesis that for analytical purposes I will treat as axiomatic. I suggest that in the nuances of the metaphoric process itself must lie the outlines of the activity—the operative principles—of the creative imagination. To discover these outlines requires, not surprisingly, an iconoclastic action: the dismantling of certain prevailing conceptions of metaphor and the way it works. I will start by examining certain critical fallacies in our customary assumptions about metaphor, fallacies that derive from the fact that metaphors "show" (the iconological fallacy) as well as "tell" (the semantic fallacy).

THE SEMANTIC FALLACY

Since the verbal icon is an aspect of language, critical analyses of metaphor have a built-in linguistic bias that is often poorly fitted to metaphor's iconic activity. This bias is language's semantic habit. In metaphor discourse, the semantic habit can lead to reductive interpretation according to a pattern I will call *semantic fallacy*. Questions of "meaning" are intrinsic to language, indeed are language's raison d'être. But questions of "meaning" are not necessarily the raison d'être of metaphor. The kinds of questions we routinely ask of metaphor can be asked of nonlinguistic arts, but when we ask them, the art forms themselves tend to subvert and expose the semantic expectations inherent in our linguistic bias. What does Baryshnikov's second leap in the "Romeo and Juliet Pas de Deux" *mean?* What does the double bass solo in Mahler's Symphony No. 1 in D *mean?* What is the *meaning* of those yellow and blue swirls in Van Gogh's night sky? What does that hint of anise in the ragoût *mean?* What is the *meaning* of the patchouli scent in the temple ceremony? Such questions can be asked, but unless they are formulated in a fairly specialized context that anticipates specific technical responses (the second leap cues Baryshnikov's partner to start her spin; I thought I'd try anise because I ran out of cumin), their implicit semantic expectations make the questions seem naive, vague, or pedestrian. Rarely would such questions strike us as opening to critical insight into the work of art, because they so obviously ignore the *affective* dimension—the sensory experience of the dance movement, or of the musical or painterly or gustatory or olfactory detail. Moreover, we know that none of these affective experiences in art can be accounted for with simple analytic formulas: dance may be defined as rhythmic bodily movement, but an identical leap accomplished by the body of an animated cartoon figure—or for that matter by that of another dancer, even if a better one—would not have the same effect as watching Baryshnikov do it. Indeed, watching Baryshnikov do it a second time would not have precisely the same effect as the first, even if the identical balletic movement were to be duplicated on film and viewed sequentially. Art's affective dimension (artistic affect) implicates not just the artwork but also the sensibility of the one who experiences it—the viewing, listening, tasting, scenting, tactilic, affective perceiver. The affective dimension of literary art cannot, of course, be neatly separated from its discursive and thematic dimension. But where sensory and emotional affect in art can be distinguished at all, it can be seen to operate according to its own exigencies, the first of which is that artistic affect strives not to "mean" but, as MacLeish put it, to "be"; and second, that its "being" will never fully yield to doctrinaire analysis.

For the nonlinguistic arts, assumption of these principles is commonplace. Yet when it comes to accounting for the art of metaphor, we narrow our view, subjecting verbal plasticity to the logical rigor of discursive analysis, as if discursive analysis were language's only legitimate function. This is the semantic fallacy. In an interview, fiction writer Anne Beattie once remarked on the apparent unwillingness or inability of critics to perceive the strictures they impose on the verbal medium by their own semantic expectations:

If they look at a Ray-o-gram by Man Ray and they see the objects there, if they see the compass and the doll and the paper clip and so forth, . . . people are willing to feel at ease on some level, and look at that clutter and come to their own conclusions. But if they saw the same details spread out through a narrative, they would want to know, "Exactly why did you put them there?" . . . But how else do you create texture? There's a world out there—how would you keep the world out?[9]

Metaphor's task of building its own world, of keeping other worlds out or inviting them in according to artistic need, requires that it draw on at least as broad a range of sensory experience and perceptive engagement as does any other art, even drawing heterogeneously on other complete art forms (as in our Miltonic paradigm's sardonic invocation of the art of cooking). Yet because metaphor is a verbal medium, we tend either to rigidify its artistic statement by semantic expectation (what does it *mean?*), or we relegate whatever there is in metaphor that does not clearly or unambiguously "mean" to an anomalous realm of poetic mystery (what it means cannot be put into words—either you get it or you don't).

Apart from having roots in linguistic bias, the semantic fallacy in metaphor inquiry is cultivated by an Aristotelian tradition that sees only rationalist discourse as capable of cognitive validity. To such discourse, sensory evidence may be admitted, but only as a source of information, of literal as opposed to figurative significance. Figurative language is treated in the *Poetics* as epistemologically deviant and therefore cognitively inferior.[10] From the rationalist hypothesis follow several inferences. The very notion of a purely rationalist discourse posits a noetic realm of apprehension, understanding based on intellect alone, without reference to sensory and emotional experience. The materials of a purely rationalist discourse, then, would be selected from only those linguistic categories whose affective dimension is lacking or is no longer arousing to us—theoretical abstractions, for instance, or mathematical concepts, or language stripped of all sensory or emotive capacity. But the assumption that there can be such a thing as purely rationalist discourse leaves unexamined questions: How can even a mathematical concept be formulated without some sensory frame of reference (e.g., spatial relationships)? And what guarantee is there that the formulative language, however seemingly nonsensory, may not arouse an affective response in a perceiver? Even apparently nonsensory language depends on a linguistic construct of "dead" metaphor; and even the "pure rationalist" is somehow aroused by that which he deems purely rationalistic. Perceptual arousal is no more or less than the vital link between perception and response to stimulus: cessation of perceptual arousal would be cessation of perceptive life. However grossly or subtly it may be defined and experienced, perceptual arousal is fundamental to intellectual activity—there can be no "noetic" perception without it.

Intellectual grasp free from sensory reference or affective response is thus a contradiction in terms. This is borne out by recent philosophical discussions of metaphor that focus on the truth-bearing capacity of language. Implicit in this theoretical inquiry is the question with which William K. Wimsatt closes *The Verbal Icon:* "What is the formula by which we shall recognize the metaphoric capacities of language and the moral importance of valid linguistic expression without surrendering our conception of truth as a thing beyond language, without yielding to the lead of the idealistic symbolists, the ritualists, and the myth-makers?"[11] The conception of truth as a thing beyond language remains, in contemporary metaphor theory, substantially intact; but inquiry into what goes on when rhetoric constructs what *feels* like truth has added an ontological dimension. Gestures toward idealistic symbolism, ritual, and myth-making still abound, but these are not fully yielded to. Similarly, judicious formulations like "truth-effect" and "truth-claim" moderate the practical demands made on "Truth" without denying legitimacy to the perfectionist aims of those who inquire into or aspire toward it. As the processes of logical thought, of cognition, and of understanding are found to be inseparable from affective language, metaphor theorists frame their accounts in affective terms that do not affirm, yet also carefully do not disallow, an ontological concept like absolute truth.

This ontological balancing act in theory is necessitated, of course, by the parallel balancing act of poetry. Milton's invocation of the Heavenly Muse is perhaps the most famous testimony to the delicacy of that balance: "Hail, holy Light, offspring of Heav'n first born,/Or of th'Eternal Coeternal beam/May I express thee unblam'd?"[12] Embracing poetry's paradoxical demand to express the inexpressible, Milton's phrases anticipate the careful scrutiny by metaphor theory of the interaction between claims of inspiration and manifest evidence of art. This involves examining the relations between not only linguistic tenor and vehicle (Richards's still fully current terms), but also between the abstract and the concrete in experience and feeling. Such a broad-based examination implicates multiple levels of consciousness in a perceptive and representational field roughly circumscribed by Empson's broad definition of "ambiguity."[13] Typically, metaphor is seen no longer as a mixture of disparates, or as a comparison between them, but as a *psychic tensional process* of response to disparates that involves subverting, suspending, sacrificing, or even destroying the ordinary direct reference of language in order to assert a greater truth that conventional reference would deny.

The violence suggested by this reading of metaphoric activity is made explicit in the formulations of critics like Sigurd Burckhardt and Martin Foss, for whom semantic content is precisely what metaphor militates against. The function of poetic devices is "to release words in some measure from their bondage to meaning, their purely referential role," says Burckhardt, to "drive a wedge between words and their meanings, lessen as much as possible their designatory force and thereby inhibit our all too ready flight from them to the things they point to."[14] Broadening metaphor's field of operations, Martin Foss finds the critical action "not so much in the single word but in the process of speech itself . . . the metaphorical move towards extension of knowledge is . . . to draw [familiar terms] into the disturbing current of a problematic drive"; it is "the intentional process to which the terms are sacrificed, and it is their mutual destruction in this process out of which a new and strange insight arises. . . . In blasting the symbols and shattering their customary meaning the dynamic process of the searching, striving, penetrating mind takes the lead and restores the truth of its predominant importance."[15] Foss's use of the word "destruction" for metaphor's intentional process strikes Philip Wheelwright as overstatement,[16] yet he finds Foss's term "sacrifice" appropriate to describe what happens in metaphor to direct reference. The new awareness generated by metaphor's sacrifice of reference, Wheelwright sees not as an affirmation of truth (nor of the "predominant importance" of the "penetrating mind"—more on this shortly), but as a tensive interplay of promising contingencies.[17] Articulate *insufficiency* has a peculiar value of its own when it comes to meeting the demands of truth: "If we cannot hope ever to be perfectly right, we can perhaps find both enlightenment and refreshment by changing, from time to time, our ways of being wrong."[18]

But the terms of Wheelwright's formulation suggest an activity more purposive than that suggested by a mere pursuit of enlightening and refreshing variety. Implicit in a campaign of striving toward *right* by constantly changing ways of being *wrong* is the idea that old ways, known ways, are by definition flawed; that sacrificing old ways in the interest of new ones—even if they are still wrong—is more consistent with the demands of truth than would be no movement at all. What matters in metaphor, then, is not so much a given metaphor's semantic content as the metaphor's capacity for subversion of semantic content. This kind of thinking, whether applied to metaphoric or any other action, must be recognized as essentially iconoclastic. In order to consider metaphor as an iconoclastic medium, however, we must turn from examining the semantic aspects to examining the iconological aspects of metaphor theory.

THE ICONOLOGICAL FALLACY

As shown by the work of Wheelwright, Foss, Wimsatt, and others, metaphor's affective dimension, and the determinative relations between linguistic affect and our conceptions of truth, have enjoyed a good deal of serious critical attention despite rationalist skepticism about the veridical standards such inquiry upholds. Wheelwright's recognition of linguistic affect expresses an analytical openness shared by many metaphor theorists. Poetic truth is that which engages our "fullest imaginative response," says Wheelwright: "where an appropriate emotion is not aroused the full insight is not awakened."[19] But while this validates on some level the claims to truth of affective language, Wheelwright's terms raise more questions than they answer. Are some emotional arousals more "appropriate" than others? How is such appropriateness determined? Is "appropriate emotion" the same thing as "imaginative response"? What exactly is the relation of imagination to emotion, and just how does either one become involved in the reading experience? And finally, how does the qualifying adjective "poetic" modify, restrict, enhance, or otherwise change the idea of "truth"?

Central to these issues is the correlative dynamics that links language, thought, and feeling. In practice, metaphor discourse rearticulates this triad as a dichotomy, which makes metaphor analysis easier to manage but reductive. The elusive term "thought" habitually gives way to more accessible inquiries into the remaining two members of the triad—inquiries, that is, into the relations between "language" and "feeling." Language and feeling, in turn, are normally reinterpreted as the relations in metaphor between "words" and "pictures." So it happens that, to analyze metaphor's affective dimension, metaphor theorists withdraw not just from the evanescence of thought, but also from the full spectrum of concrete sensory experience to become sensory binarists, as if only sound and sight really counted. Metaphors, we learn from Aristotle via Sir Philip Sidney, are speaking pictures; therefore the relations between words and pictorial images become the object of our investigation. To facilitate inquiry into affective language, we expand our taxonomy of verbal experience by introducing terms drawn from visual experience; but this broadening in turn imposes subtle restrictions on the ways we think and talk about metaphor. When we refer in theoretical discussions even to nonvisual metaphors, we employ the term "imagery," as if verbal representations of smells, sounds, tactile sensations, or tastes had first to be thought of as pictures in order to be discussed.[20] It is natural, of course, for our analytic vocabulary to rely on the highly evolved terminology that defines our primary discriminating faculty, eyesight: if bloodhounds wrote poetry, olfactory metaphors would no doubt rule bloodhoundian theoretical discourse. All the same, our tendency to favor the visual in our theoretical discourse on metaphor adds a perceptual slant to our already established semantic bias, a slant I will call the *iconological fallacy*.

Like most critical fallacies, the iconological fallacy provides insight into how we think and feel about literary art, particularly the art of metaphor, and ultimately insight into our most elusive and sublime processes of thought. For as Wimsatt's query suggests, inextricable from critical inquiry into the nature of metaphor is philosophical inquiry into the nature of truth. Surrounding both these discourses, and linking them historically on many levels, is a common theme of deep anxiety over the role played in human cognition by the visual image. It is an anxiety that, when understood in a religious context, idolatrously parodies the faith which demands of believers that they simultaneously fear God and worship him.[21] To study theory of images, W. J. T. Mitchell has discovered, is everywhere to confront *fear* of images. Mitchell's investigations compel us to recognize the extent to which "iconology" must be seen as "not just the science of icons, but the political psychology of icons, the study of iconophobia, iconophilia, and the struggle between iconoclasm and idolatry."[22] Not surprisingly, ubiquitous fear of images has generated collateral theory for coping with that fear. If a common theme in discourses of literary metaphor and truth is image anxiety, then the treatment for the malady that has evolved within both discourses is theory that centers on the iconoclastic impulse.

For the dominance of iconoclastic theory in the field of iconology, Mitchell offers an undeveloped but provocative explanation—one which, because the visual image pervades both metaphor discourse and truth discourse, makes his explanation pertinent to virtually all discourses in which the image plays a dominant role. Iconoclastic theory, according to Mitchell, enables us "to rationalize the claim that, whatever images are, ideas are something else."[23] The implications here are worth exploring, for by this account, iconoclasm's nemesis is not its ostensible enemy, images per se, but rather the disturbing possibility—to many impermissible—that ideas may themselves be nothing more than projected images. To rationalize the claim that ideas *are* something more than images is actively to counter the Nietzschean concept of "truth" as merely "worn-out metaphor": "a sum of human relations which become poetically and rhetorically intensified, metamorphosed, adorned, and after long usage seem to a nation fixed, canonic and binding; truths are illusions of which one had forgotten that they *are* illusions; worn-out metaphors which have become powerless to affect the senses."[24] When John Milton finds himself entertaining doubtful suppositions of his own about ideas, projected images, and the power of these to affect the senses in his antiprelatical tracts, the implications for his religious enthusiasm are potentially devastating, as will be seen in the concluding arguments of Chapter 2 below. Moreover, the apprehension that ideas may be nothing more than projected images would seem to be intrinsic both to literary iconoclasm and to its critique: first, iconological fallacy shapes an image-dependent discourse; then, recoil from that dependency energizes the iconoclastic impetus. Therefore, notwithstanding the seemingly ungovernable character of the iconoclastic impetus (wherein fresh ways of being wrong apparently provide a tolerable substitute for being right), contemporary iconoclastic metaphor theory also treats ideas—or at least the *idea* of ideas—as sacrosanct.

This predisposition toward sanctity of the idea follows from the iconoclast's sense that reification of ideas—the rendering of ideas into images—inevitably falsifies or deadens them, and therefore the image or reified idea must continually be challenged for the true idea to remain alive.[25] Hence the paradox at the heart of creative iconoclasm, and of iconoclastic theory of metaphor as well: the act of destruction—destruction of image, destruction of reference—not only generates new insight but actually liberates the idea from what would otherwise make it "canonic and binding." This paradox in Milton's polemics is dramatized, as we will see when we turn to *Areopagitica* (Chapter 4 below), by the self-immolating metaphoric constructs of Milton's own defense of the sanctity of the idea.

To the iconoclast, the purity of the idea can be articulated only by pointing to the idea's sensible representation (a necessary, if regrettable, concession to our mortally flawed faculties of understanding), and saying "that, yet not that"—a version of the split reference embodied in Jakobson's paradigmatic example of the Majorca storytellers who begin with the formula *Aixo era y no era* (It was and it was not).[26] This simultaneous affirmation and destruction of reference Jakobson sees as establishing the conditions of ambiguity requisite to poetic function, an ambiguity which entails not only split reference but doubleness on the part of storyteller and audience as well. The paradigm's significance for metaphor, says Paul Ricoeur, is that it "contains *in nuce* all that can be said about metaphorical truth,"[27] a truth that simultaneously must and cannot be represented. For iconoclastic theory of metaphor, Jakobson's paradigm may usefully be extended by means of a variant on the storyteller's preamble, one drawn from Iranian oral tradition: *Yeki boud yeki naboud. Gheir az Khoda hich kas naboud.* (There was one, there wasn't one. Apart from God, there was no one.)[28] Behind or beyond temporal ambiguity's split reference lies the eternal, infinite, absolute which is susceptible of no reference. The ineffable idea expressed as "God" affirms split reference as a construct that serves not only the requisites of ambiguity (there was one, there wasn't one), but serves also as a means of distinguishing the temporal from an absolute that neither ambiguity nor destruction of reference can convey (there was, there wasn't; *nevertheless* God). The sensible, the referential, and the ambiguities of both that result from their cognitive limitations occupy a territory distinct from that of truth, the absolute, the idea.

Yet the second storyteller's preamble fits even the territory reserved for the nonreferential into a dualistic pattern that, at least since the time of Descartes, has channeled discourse of truth and metaphor onto any of a number of binary tracks: either/or, is/is not, temporal/eternal, true/false, appearance/reality. This reading of the iconoclastic perspective on ideas thus brings Mitchell's observation ("whatever images are, ideas are something else") into line with the Platonic tradition that depreciates the imitative and delusory world of appearances. An example of this is the master duality of image versus idea, which forms the central track along which pictorialist aesthetics discourse—the *ut pictura poesis* tradition—distributes miscellaneous elements of artistic expression and experience between the faculties of eye and ear.[29] Following in this received tradition, by which Leonardo conceives painting as "mute poesy" and poetry as "blind painting," Locke's theory of mind transmutes verbal images (appeal to the eye—poetry) to images of fancy (wit, resemblance); and it transmutes discursive language (appeal to the ear—prose) to images of reason (judgment, difference). Along this same dualistic trajectory, aesthetics discourse from Burke and Lessing to contemporary Marxist theory may be discerned carrying out elaborations on the central image/idea conflict through parallel conflicts. The ramifying binary terms of pictorial versus verbal, and "spatial" versus "temporal" forms of art, Mitchell finds ultimately to polarize along gendered lines that separate the "feminine" beautiful from the "masculine" sublime.[30] Thus, deprecation of the sensory and visible in aesthetics discourse makes a sexual inference (images are feminine, ideas are masculine) that further explicates, and even exposes as invidious, the critical theorist's impulse to keep ideas sacrosanct. How these sexual implications in aesthetics discourse bear on the present study will become clear later in connection with individual literary works, specifically Milton's divorce tracts and *Samson Agonistes.*

My immediate concern, however, lies with establishing an even more fundamental principle for iconoclastic theory of metaphor. I propose an alternative to the conventional assumption that the destruction of reference which sanctifies ideas must necessarily or exclusively signify devaluation of sensory experience. There can also be a purely *creative* impulse behind the urge to treat ideas as sacrosanct, one that neither implies deprecation of the senses nor leads to rejection of sensory reality and evidence. This impulse derives from the nature of doubt, as theorized by Edmund Husserl. Characterizing the Cartesian "attempt to doubt everything" as simply "a device of method," Husserl situates doubt "in the realm of our *perfect freedom.* We can *attempt to doubt* anything and everything, however convinced we may be concerning what we doubt, even though the evidence which seals our assurance is completely adequate."[31] This view of doubt as an intellectual device for perfect freedom, a device that needs neither to deny nor to devalue reference, provides a mechanism for pragmatically derailing metaphor analysis from the deterministic Cartesian dualist track. Instead of dividing sensory evidence into opposing categories—either/ or, is/is not, true/false, appearance/reality, and so forth—we may suspend or "bracket" sensory evidence to entertain doubt according to the Husserlian model: we doubt evidence on principle, and without rejecting it, as a means of enabling perfect mental and imaginative freedom. This suspension of the known for the sake of the unknown, for the sake of perfect freedom, is *epoché,* a term based on the Greek εποχη, epokhe—abstention.[32] Such a conception of doubt (most particularly the will to doubt for the sake of perfect freedom) must be accorded psychological validity if we are to understand the iconoclastic impulse, for it is only in the context of a credible psychology of the iconoclastic impulse that a theory of creative iconoclasm fully applicable to Milton can evolve.

METAPHOR AND RICOEUR'S PSYCHOLOGIES OF
IMAGINATION AND FEELING

We may now recall Martin Foss's argument for what he terms metaphor's "intentional process," the means by which metaphor draws familiar terms "into the disturbing current of a problematic drive" in order to extend knowledge and give rise to "new and strange insight." Up to this point, Foss's formulation may be seen as drawing on established interaction theories of figurative language: metaphor estranges the familiar through tensional juxtapositions with the unfamiliar or improbable, thus compelling new insight. But Foss's inference as to what empowers metaphor's "problematic drive" introduces to the intentional process a new element: "In blasting the symbols and shattering their customary meaning the dynamic process of the searching, striving, penetrating mind takes the lead and restores the truth of its predominant importance."[33] According to this reading, metaphor's "truth" is not an elusive ideal sought, nor even a subjective vision imposed. It is instead a signifier for the penetrating mind itself, for the predominance of the mind's *own* importance. On the face of it, the "truth" that metaphor's iconoclasm thus affirms has only limited artistic worth, since neither metaphors, nor ideas, nor literary experience can very well be its primary object: the "blasting" and "shattering" of customary reference make a spectacular display of egoistic energy and little else.

Yet the celebration of radical individual will that Foss's metaphor theory evokes comes closer than does conventional aesthetic theory to isolating and identifying the psychological impetus behind creative iconoclasm. While the penetrating mind's own predominant importance might in itself make a tiresome poetic subject, its predominance in creative activity unquestionably fuels the impetus toward perfect freedom. The radical will to doubt for the sake of perfect freedom is essential to creative iconoclasm and to iconoclastic theory of metaphor. It is essential because only in the space provided by doubt— only in the space carved out by the will's assertion of the truth of its own importance as predominant over certainty and reference—only in that space can new being, new understanding, new insight, or creation take shape.

And it is in that space also, in the space created by split reference, by doubt for the sake of perfect freedom, by *epoché*, that iconoclastic theory of metaphor begins to coalesce with the psychology of creative iconoclasm that may so abundantly be recognized in Milton. A preliminary sketch for the analytics whereby such a coalescence might be accounted for has been drawn by Paul Ricoeur.[34] Describing the metaphoric process as a combination of three distinct operations, Ricoeur discerns the pattern of split reference simultaneously in the distinct but operationally parallel activities of cognition, imagination, and feeling. All three of these components of literary experience employ the bracketing or suspension of reference that is *epoché*, and all three are necessary to complete the imaginative activity that Ricoeur calls *predicative assimilation*. Through this activity, the imagination is able "to produce new kinds by assimilation and to produce them not *above* the differences as in the concept, but in spite of and through the differences" (146). In terms of our storyteller paradigm, imagination is able by predicative assimilation to produce from the cognitive differences between "there was" and "there wasn't" not just a concept that would accommodate the contradiction (for example, *ambiguous reference*), but a "new kind" in spite of and through the contradiction (*nevertheless, God*). Predicative assimilation is thus metaphor's "productive and projective function" (152), which can only be acknowledged by clearly distinguishing that function from the merely representational function usually attributed to figurative language. In the image we have not a *single* act of representation, but a *dual* act of suspension and predication—and this dual act is carried out simultaneously by cognition (metaphor's semantic aspect), imagination (its iconic aspect), and feeling (its emotional aspect).

Ricoeur's predicative assimilation is valuable because it recognizes that we cannot have a sufficient semantic theory of metaphor—that is, a theory that would account for metaphor's truth-claims or "insight"— without also accounting for metaphor's psychological features, those features that create "ontological vehemence" in the poetic experience, "the *ecstatic* moment of language—language going beyond itself."[35] Metaphor "compels us to explore the borderline between the verbal and the non-verbal. The process of schematization and that of the bound images aroused and controlled by schematization obtain precisely on that borderline between a semantics of metaphorical utterances and a psychology of imagination" (149). By including *feeling* among the three phases or levels of metaphor's predicative activity, Ricoeur demonstrates the necessity for theory to grant *cognitive* legitimacy to linguistic *affect*.

There remain difficulties, however, in Ricoeur's account of metaphor's schematizing activity. He rightly faults "bad psychology of imagination" for failing to recognize imagination's constructive (predicative) role: "imagination is conceived as a residue of perception" (153). So long as metaphor theory sees imagination only as a means of *re*collecting and mentally *re*producing perceived images, imagination's unique productive and creative capacities are left out of the metaphoric process. Yet Ricoeur's analysis of imagination's productivity leaves confusion as to just what "imagination" consists of. He treats imagination on the one hand as that depictive capacity which schematizes and displays images in order to project "new possibilities of redescribing the world" (152). On the other hand, "all *epoché* is the work of imagination. Imagination *is epoché*" (152); it carries out *all* projection of new possibility for *all three* of metaphor's activities—cognition, imagination, and feeling. Perhaps as a consequence of this extension of activity, the term "imagination" in Ricoeur's argument becomes interchangeable with "image":

As Sartre emphasized, to imagine is to address oneself to what is not. More radically, to imagine is to make oneself absent to the whole of things. Yet I do not want to elaborate further this thesis of the negativity proper to the image. What I do want to underscore is the solidarity between the *epoché* and the capacity to project new possibilities. Image as absence is the negative side of image as fiction. (152)

With Ricoeur's terminological shift from "imagination" to "image," the *capacity for* imaginative projection and the *new possibility projected* blur into one.

A related uncertainty of attribution disturbs Ricoeur's critique of the other "bad psychology" in metaphor theory, a psychology of feeling which leads us to confuse feeling with emotion. To maintain the necessary distinctions, Ricoeur emphasizes the "specific kinship with language" enjoyed by feelings as opposed to emotions, a kinship expressed in the phrase "poetic feelings" (154). Yet to assist this distinction he attributes to emotion the curiously linguistic concept of literality: "Feelings are negative, suspensive experiences in relation to the literal emotions of everyday life. When we read, we do not literally feel fear or anger" (155). The phrase "literal emotions" may not seem particularly odd until we ask what its implied opposite, "figurative emotions," might be like. But more important than such a test is the practical difficulty of maintaining Ricoeur's distinction between feeling and emotion. This becomes apparent as he outlines the procedure whereby "feeling" participates in the schematizing activity of predicative assimilation. Since feelings, too, discriminate (as does visual imagination) between like and unlike, "poetic feelings," he says, "imply a kind of *epoché* of our bodily emotions. . . . Just as poetic language denies the first-order reference of descriptive discourse to ordinary objects of our concern, feelings deny the first-order feelings which tie us to these first-order objects of reference" (155). Ricoeur's introduction of "first-order feelings" (to be denied by other, presumably poetic, "feelings") may itself suggest lexical discomfort with the notion that feeling can be treated as intrinsically different from emotion. To clarify Ricoeur's point: first-order feelings (emotions) belong to a first-order world (the everyday world full of ordinary objects of reference), and that first-order world is touched linguistically by descriptive reference or discourse alone, whereas poetry and poetic feeling operate to deny or suspend that first-order world and its discourse or reference. By this account, then, if feelings or emotions are generated by a poetic text instead of by the experiences of our own lives, they must be regarded as second-order. This second-order reference we must recognize as ontologically primary, however: "For, in another respect, it constitutes the primordial reference to the extent that it suggests, reveals, unconceals—or whatever you say—the deep structures of reality to which we are related as mortals who are born into this world and who *dwell* in it for a while" (151). Ricoeur's allusion to the "deep structures of reality" accessible only to poetic reference hints at an ontological longing similar to that voiced in Wimsatt's call for metaphor theory that does not surrender our conception of truth as a thing beyond language. It echoes as well the urge Mitchell has documented, the urge to "rationalize the claim that, whatever images are, ideas are something else." This ontological longing that unobtrusively yet unmistakably weaves in and out of contemporary metaphor theory sometimes presents itself, as it does in Ricoeur, as a kind of rationalist's loophole for God. That such a provision should so often be felt desirable or necessary in *metaphor* theory (particularly metaphor theory that depends on iconoclastic impulse) does more than simply corroborate my hypothesis that the principles of the metaphoric process and the operative principles of the imagination are the same. It also reveals the radically logocentric connection that contemporary theory is attempting to forge between human creativity and truth.

To the subject of ontological longing this study will have many occasions to return, but I wish for the moment to draw attention to the analytical maneuver whereby Ricoeur divides feelings and reference into first and second orders, and then finds it necessary to reverse the valuations those categories imply by asserting a higher reality that makes *second*-order feelings and reference *primordial*. As we will see in connection with *The Doctrine and Discipline of Divorce*, this is exactly the logical procedure followed by John Milton for a similar cause: the first-order feelings that belong to a first-order world are proven inadequate to truth by the preemptive second-order (yet primordial) metaphoric structures with which Milton suspends first-order reference.

But in Ricoeur's case, and also for purposes of metaphor theory, whether the second-order classification of poetic feelings actually places them on a level "higher" or "lower" than first-order reality is irrelevant. This is because in either instance the same analytical problem arises: Ricoeur's clear-cut differentiation between poetic feeling and "literal" feeling is invalid because its premises are psychologically unsound. Both Ricoeur's psychology of imagination and his psychology of feeling assume a fundamental disjunction between experience generated within the life of the mind ("poetic feelings") and experience generated within the life of the body. "Life of the body" would seem to be the only available way to interpret Ricoeur's phrase "literal emotions"—phenomena that appear to draw on physical sensation: "To the extent that in emotion we are, so to speak, under the spell of our body, we are delivered to mental states with little intentionality, as though in emotion we 'lived' our body in a more intense way" (153–54). This interpretation posits a class of feelings (generated by physical sensation) whose very identity depends on their contrast with feelings that draw on a different order of reality, that of imaginative experience, or poetry. In other words, even as Ricoeur's theory tries to bridge the gap between mind or ideas and matter (the "instantaneous grasping of the new congruence is 'felt' as well as 'seen' " [154]), his psychology of feeling nevertheless depends heavily on a dualistic Cartesian model. As a result, his conception of sensory reality (first-order objects of reference, everyday life) becomes a sort of impeditive matrix from which a very different order of reality (that of ideas) must extricate itself: "Imagination *is epoché*. . . . To imagine is to make oneself absent to the whole of things" (152). By assuming and maintaining such a concept of sensory reality, Ricoeur underrates the directness of exchange between sense and idea: he overlooks the fact that our sensory perceptions may actually be shaped by our ideas, and vice versa. In fact, in the experience of our daily lives we tend to see primarily what we expect to see (in which case our sensory perceptions are shaped by our ideas) until something causes us to see differently, or even to see that we were mistaken (in which case our ideas are shaped by our sensory perceptions).

Moreover, Ricoeur's schema renders artistic experience in terms that are too rationalistic for metaphor's acknowledged ambiguity, too reductively dichotomous: literal/figurative, absent/present, is/is not, true/false. How do we apply such terms to sensory experience in reading? to a verbal evocation, say, of the smell of a ripe peach? According to Ricoeur's theory, my imagination of the peach's scent is *epoché* of the faint whiff of computer plastic and desk lamp heat that I am "literally" experiencing as I write these words. But in fact, these "literal" scents do not have to be suspended for the imaginative one to be experienced. (Indeed, imagining the peach scent is what brought to my attention the office scents that I had not particularly noticed until then.) Attention of the mind to experience of the senses is often more multiform and palpable, and at the same time more elusive, than Ricoeur's schema can account for. The steps that constitute predicative assimilation help to explicate the complex intentional operations of metaphor. But without greater recognition given to sensory immediacy in imaginative experience, Ricoeur's formula for identifying imagination with *epoché* resembles not so much a new psychological synthesis of cognition, imagination, and feeling as it does Coleridge's willing suspension of disbelief.

The overriding difficulty with Ricoeur's predicative assimilation lies in its understanding of literary experience as an imaginative activity that is distinct in kind and fully separable from the imaginative activity of nonliterary experience. This is an understanding shared both by the two "bad" psychologies of imagination and feeling, and by Ricoeur's efforts to correct them. A more psychologically credible account of metaphor's dependence on imagination and feeling would have to recognize that these two are functioning in tandem all the time, whether occasioned by literary experience or by some other kind of experience. It would also recognize that there is no way of neatly separating the activity of the imagination from the activity of sensory awareness—that the shaping of one's imaginative consciousness involves drawing variously and even simultaneously on sense perceptions both immediate and remembered; on understanding and knowledge; on beliefs, aspirations, opinions, and prejudices; on needs and purposes both present and long range; on all the infinite detail contained in exactly that realm to which Ricoeur claims imagination makes us absent, "the whole of things." We may of course exercise considerable control over which elements in the whole of things we allow to influence our imaginative experience: here is where, for instance, category requisites like "needs and purposes" may gain the upper hand. But we are forced to recognize how critical an influence "the whole of things" truly exercises over our imaginative life when our experience of a given text, or of any work of art, differs with each time we return to it. Even more, we are forced to recognize the interdependence of literary and extraliterary imagination when our imaginative experience becomes a determining influence on our participation in "the whole of things"—when our imaginative experience actually changes our ways of doing and being in the world.

Ironically, the project of formulating a psychologically credible account of metaphor's affective dimension is only complicated by the assumption that the imagination's schematizing activity can indeed be adequately traced—that metaphor's operation is determined or controlled by the finite verbal construct. Certainly, if verbal affect is to be granted cognitive legitimacy—if metaphor theory is not to lapse once again into a gesture toward mystery (i.e., "what it means cannot be put into words"), we have to acknowledge that a substantial degree of affective control is indeed exercised by the verbal construct. As I have maintained from the beginning of this chapter, an assumption of the primacy and centrality of the work of art is essential to an iconoclastic theory of creativity.

But not all of the affective power that is generated by the verbal construct is necessarily contained within the parameters of what we call "literary experience." Indeed, the affective dimension of literary experience regularly makes an artistic mission of breaking out of those parameters. That, after all, is the iconoclastic element in imaginative activity. If Ricoeur's predicative assimilation falls short of charting literary affect, the shortfall must be attributed not to a failure of subtlety in his analysis but to the intrinsic unchartability of affect. What is needed is not an ever more exacting analysis of metaphor's schematic predication, but rather a theoretical mechanism for recognizing and accommodating that dimension of literary experience for which there can never be a schematic account. It is the unchartable affective territory of metaphor toward which Ricoeur's terms "ontological vehemence" and "ecstatic moment of language" point, and which an iconoclastic theory of metaphor might help to explain without pretending to trace.

METAPHOR AND THE PSYCHOLOGY OF
CREATIVE ICONOCLASM

I have referred to theory's ontological balancing act in dealing with poetic truth, a truth whose habit is less to proclaim itself than to invoke in its reader affective assent—to invoke, as it were, the reader's fervent witness. To speak of this ontological bearing of poetry as if it were exclusively a literary phenomenon is misleading, of course. All art has such a bearing; all art invokes affective assent, and fervent witness is an important part of what we seek in artistic experience. With that caveat in mind, then, what we have yet to account for in metaphor theory is the nature of affective assent in literary experience—metaphor's "greater truth" that conventional discursive formulations would circumscribe, the sense that if it *feels* strong, it must be *true*. Wary of ontological longing, however, my concern is not to argue that what metaphor achieves actually is a greater truth; rather, it is to suggest how the achievement *works*, regardless of whether the thing achieved has anything to do with "truth." Certainly *something* important happens: poetry—including (but not only) the poetry in polemics—has extraordinary concrete, real-life, "first-order" effects on individual human beings, on groups, on nations. What a vitalistic metaphor theory must account for is why and how this can happen, what it is in metaphor itself that causes literary experience to spill out of what Milton calls "the quiet and still air of delightful studies" and into our real lives—and vice versa.

To attempt such an account, I will begin by making what might seem a perverse claim: metaphor gets its ontological effect not by anything it presents, compares, demonstrates, or "displays in a depicting mode."[36] Metaphor does these things, to be sure, but its ontological effect derives rather from what all this display, demonstration, analysis, and so forth *does not do* because it *cannot provide*. When we talk about metaphoric tension (tensional theories are many and accurate), it is what metaphor does not do and cannot do that creates the tension we refer to. Or more precisely, it is what metaphor cannot do that causes us to feel metaphor's schematizing juxtapositions as a tensional experience. Metaphoric juxtaposition can arouse us to tensive new awareness; but it cannot repay us for what that new awareness costs.

That there are costs to the new awareness induced by metaphor is an aspect of literary experience that theory tends to overlook, even though we know that our experience of any art is capable of drawing deeply on sometimes unrecognized emotional and intellectual resources. Consider the psychological event that must take place for the suspensive activity of *epoché* to "drive a wedge between words and their meanings . . . and thereby inhibit our all too ready flight from them to the things they point to."[37] Of course, we could choose less dramatically graphic terms than does Burckhardt for metaphor's disruption of conventional reference; but without question it does disrupt. Without question also, metaphor's semantic dissociation and divestiture for the sake of imaginative predication is carried out, not among words on a page, but in the mind of a reader. Therefore, what gets dissociated and divested are not merely lexical meanings but also, and more compellingly, the ways people think and feel in response to language. Lively metaphor makes an assault on intellectual and emotional complacency—not always violent, but certainly always on some level disturbing. When we attack "complacency" (merely to apply the term is to vilify), what we really attack is the particular satisfaction someone else derives from knowing what he knows. Our putative aim in the attack, of course, is to heighten, broaden, complicate, or intensify his knowing, but our procedure is nevertheless to expropriate his ways and kinds of knowing for our own purposes.

This is the procedure of metaphor. Ways and kinds of knowing are expropriated by metaphor to be shaped into an evocation of what the metaphor-maker would have known. Nor is the thing he'd have known a specific lesson: there may be poetry in sermons, and lectures in poetry, but a poem is neither a pulpit nor a classroom. Metaphor's ways of knowing require affective assent, fervent witness, yet witness guided by intentions that are not necessarily clear. The function of poetic feeling, says Ricoeur, "is to abolish the distance between knower and known without canceling the cognitive structure of thought and the intentional distance which it implies. Feeling is not contrary to thought. It is thought made ours" (154). Feeling enables us to *experience* metaphor's predication as well as think it; yet by maintaining intentional distance, metaphor assures that what is "made ours" is still under metaphor's cognitive and intentional control. Thus thought may be "made ours," but it is still assimilated as *thought*, as predication—not quite "ours" in the way that unmediated experience is ours. Furthermore, what the metaphor-maker would have *affectively* known—that is, felt and experienced—cannot be formulated in objective terms. We gain access to it not by way of instruction but rather as an unsettling consequence of aroused dissatisfaction with the known (ordinary reference), coupled with a provoked urge toward satisfaction in an untried imaginative realm that offers no guarantees and barely a roadmap. What the metaphor-maker offers is not a new and different satisfaction in exchange for the old complacency, but (at most) an unreifiable suggestion of what that satisfaction might look and feel like.[38] Disruption of the old complacency first leaves a vacuum both cognitive and affective—what we call aesthetic anticipation, or literary (and usually ambiguous) expectation. Then, ostensibly to fill the vacuum, the fresh kind of knowing that is provided by the metaphor may offer pleasure, or shock, or thrill of discovery. But what it cannot offer (and has no intention of offering) is assured *gratification* of the kind it had disrupted in the first place for the sake of its own assertion. If we recognize the conditions of security, of satisfaction, of comfort in the familiar as affective human needs that are basic and legitimate, though indeterminate (i.e., your survival mechanism is my status quo),[39] then it is gratification of these particular affective needs that metaphor withholds or denies even as it posits an alternative vision.

Moreover, that alternative vision itself is not, and cannot be, fully realized by the metaphor. Why? Because metaphor's visionary impetus—its affective energy—depends on exactly those variables in human need and desire that make the character of your complacency different from mine. In response to metaphor's disruptive *epoché*, it is the unknowable detail and quality of our individual cognitive and affective investment in complacency that generates aesthetic expectation and subsequent affective assent. The measure of our disturbance is the measure of our response. Over these, metaphor can exercise only the most limited selective control. Were the quality of our investment—the terms of our complacency—fully known or knowable by the metaphor-maker, or by ourselves, it would be too susceptible to rational understanding for its disruption to disturb us. The metaphor itself would be disarmed by such complete knowledge and thereby made a predictable convention. This is not to say that we cannot be deeply disturbed by disruption of that which we fully understand in rational terms. Of course we can. But while such an understanding may well be upset, it is not going to be seriously upset *by metaphor*. What makes metaphor work affectively is its ability to disturb and play on that which cannot be reduced to purely rational formulae: beliefs, feelings, prejudices, forgotten associations, repressed anxieties, vague aspirations, subconscious desires, unarticulated needs—the entire individual and collective reservoir of our affective resources.

Furthermore, the indeterminacy of these affective resources does not by itself constitute a practical creative impediment to the metaphor-maker. Within a fairly loosely defined range, virtually *any* response attests to metaphor's *affective* power. I emphasize the qualifying term "affective" for metaphor's power because I'm fully aware that my case for indeterminacy opens iconoclastic metaphor theory to a valid criticism: no art, not even an art of arousing imprecisely defined feelings, can itself afford to neglect precision. And iconoclastic metaphor theory as articulated thus far acknowledges great precision in metaphor's *predicative* function. But as metaphoric predication cannot fully or finally be separated from metaphoric affect, the role of indeterminacy cannot be ignored. If we acknowledge that metaphor's power in addition to being precise is also in some respect *anarchic*—and iconoclastic theory can hardly do less—then the principle of indeterminate affect must be included in our account. It must be included because the anarchic element that is affective indeterminacy both *constitutes* transformative *power* and *is constituted by* transformative *desire*. This conflation of transformative power and transformative desire is exactly the iconoclastic impulse that links writer to reader and provides the means whereby metaphor can carry out its program of creative iconoclasm. The writer desires transformation and has the power to effect it in art; the reader desires transformation and has the power to will it in himself. Metaphor makes both writer and reader loci of transformation through acts of creative iconoclasm.

The case for metaphor's capacity to transform the reader is skillfully presented by Phillip Stambovsky. The narrativizing phenomenology of Stambovsky's "depictive imagery" involves the reader in a *dramatic* construction of literary experience: "imagery renders perceived relationships, or (less abstractly) thoughts and feelings, in a symbolic, presentationally immediate form, and in doing so makes them directly assimilable in the perceiver's experience by dramatizing them in whatever aesthetic (or synesthetic) mode the presentational imagery takes."[40] Because the reader's construction of literary experience is thus made a *performative* rather than a merely reconstitutive act, the assimilation of metaphor becomes an irreducible cognitive function, an epistemological primitive that "occurs on the plane of prereflective, phenomenological awareness in which the meaningful is a matter of *presence* rather than of *predication*" (107). More than just "thought made ours," assimilated metaphor in Stambovsky's account becomes assimilated experience; it acquires the perceptual immediacy of intuitive understanding. On this prereflective plane of metaphoric operation depends all of metaphor's unlimited transformative power:

The degree to which a literary metaphor's thematic meaning takes place pre-reflectively, depictively (in what we might call its operational context), determines the extent to which its transformative power is realized. And just as virtually no bounds exist to the possible refinement of human experience and sensibility, so there are none to limit metaphor's power to transform us by being our means of assimilating novel and ever more richly discriminated data of awareness. (103)

Metaphor's limitless power to transform, however, is expressed here in terms that restrict the transformation itself to a carefully circumscribed field of experience. The phrases "refinement of human experience and sensibility" and "ever more richly discriminated data of awareness" hint toward the exact nature of that field. Stambovsky's commitment to the *literariness* of metaphoric affect defines transformation of the self through metaphor as the development of artistic taste and cultural discernment, aims specific to the interests of aestheticism:

This transformative power of metaphor in literature is an expression of the creative, the self-transcending (or ecstatic) dimension of literary reading. The experiencing of literary art is as such ecstatic, mimetic in the performative pre-Platonic sense. . . . By his complementary participation in the literary enterprise, the reader celebrates artistic vision in the only way that the communicative endeavor of the artist is ever actively celebrated. (103)

Celebratory self-transcendence by the reader, and the reader's refinement of sensibility toward aesthetic union with the artist and the work of art, constitute affective witness of a kind assumed by virtually all of the metaphor theorists so far discussed. Celebration of artistic vision is consistent with Foss's "new and strange insight," with Wheelwright's tensive contingencies, with Ricoeur's predication and the ecstatic moment of language, language going beyond itself. All, like Stambovsky, would *contain* metaphor's transformative activity within the confines of "the literary experience."

As a result, such metaphor theory unrealistically isolates "literary experience" from life. Celebratory accounts of literary experience assume that the author writes in order to provide the reader with materials for constructing the aesthetically transcendent, but temporally finite, self-limiting act that we call the literary experience. According to this analysis, for the literary experience to be valid, all extraliterary reference must be excluded. Moreover, to extract elements from the experience is to strip them of their aesthetic verity:

Insofar as any discernible object is conceptually suggestive or emotively evocative in a given literary context, the suggestions or evocations are, for literary experience, *intrinsic* to that object. To abstract a literary-experiential entity . . . from the feelings and thoughts it conveys and is associated with in its thematic context is to engage in something completely different than the enactive envisaging that is literary experience. (67)

The apparent reasonableness of this position hides several difficulties. We do of course regularly extrapolate artistic elements and apply them out of context, and normally (though not necessarily), we realize that in so doing we engage in something different from "the enactive envisaging that is the literary experience." In such a case, what we are doing is deliberately expropriating elements from the literary context for our own use, in effect reversing metaphor's affective expropriation. But when Thomas Carew quotes a portion of one of his own erotic poems in the intimacy of a lady's chamber, is what he does "completely different" from "enactive envisaging" or not? Would it be more or less so if he quoted the entire poem? And what of the *lady's* experience of the poem? Or, when a reader thoroughly absorbs and is deeply affected by a work of literature, his mind may be changed by it to the extent that his entire life proceeds on a different course—he may, in Blake's terms, "become what he beholds." Would we then refrain from calling such an experience "enactive envisaging"? The myriad ways we may live in, with, and through literary art suggest how difficult an exclusionary account of literary experience can be to sustain.

Moreover, we also interpolate into literary experience variables that cannot be controlled by or explained in terms of the work of art itself. I have already discussed metaphor's dependence on our affective resources: "enactive envisaging" cannot occur in a vacuum. Our imaginative construction of literary art obviously draws on perceptual and constructive skills developed in previous artistic and nonartistic experience. Like the author, the reader synthesizes the fresh and strange from fragments—even fragmentation—of the familiar. The resources of familiarity to the author may through the literary experience "commune" with the resources of familiarity to the reader, but as the two fields of resource cannot possibly be identical, the individual literary experience cannot be predetermined. Thus the individual literary experience is "intrinsic" only to itself, not to "any discernible object" in the work of art that "conceptually suggests" or "emotively evokes" the experience. Stambovsky's "enactive envisaging" predicates a homogeneity of readers and readings, a definitiveness in the literary experience that satisfies the terms of structural aesthetics but that fails to recognize how casually aesthetic and experiential boundaries are disregarded by actual imaginative life.

Stambovsky's emphasis on metaphoric affect as an exclusively literary or aesthetic experience, and his adjunct concern for celebrating the "communicative endeavor" of the artist, lead him to turn away from what seems to me his most pregnant insight. This has to do not with the undeniable claims of either aestheticism or communication, but with the claims made by the process of transformation. If self-transcendence is interpreted only as infinite refinement of aesthetic sensibility, the reader might never get out of the library. But Stambovsky hints at the possibility of a transformation more profound:

> A "presenting" of thematic meaning, literary metaphor is a seminal dynamic in the transformation of the wherefore of conscious apprehension into the very condition of consciousness. Put another way, metaphor is the principal epistemic means by which we transform the experience of what we do—which in literary reading involves going beyond ourselves—into that of what we are. (103)

If metaphoric transformation were to serve only an aesthetic imperative, it would be incapable of fully realizing the epistemic role of transforming "the experience of what we do . . . into that of what we are." The activity of "going beyond ourselves" would remain its own end, a heightening of aesthetic refinement that would entail transformation of degree, but not of kind. But in Stambovsky's formulation, "going beyond ourselves" suggests a means toward achieving a different end—conceivably, even an end alien to aestheticist "refinement of . . . sensibility," an end of significant *change*. Metaphoric transformation, "going beyond ourselves" in its fullest account, thus becomes the means whereby we may indeed "become what we behold."

Tracing the critical steps in the process of metaphoric transformation, Ricoeur describes imagination as "[that] stage in the production of genres where generic kinship has not reached the level of conceptual peace and rest but remains caught in the war between distance and proximity, between remoteness and nearness. . . . In the metaphoric process the movement toward the genus is arrested by the resistance of the difference and, as it were, intercepted by the figure of the rhetoric."[41] The assimilation that is *intercepted* by metaphor, the "conceptual peace and rest" that metaphor forestalls or withholds from us, is exactly that security and satisfaction in the known that I have labeled our "complacency." When the reader *constructs* the literary experience, his need for conceptual peace and rest requires as well that he ultimately *reconstruct* the affective and cognitive complacency that metaphor's iconoclastic activity has disrupted. But the disruption itself makes impossible a mere return to status quo ante. Beyond aesthetic celebration, complete assimilation of artistic experience compels us to change the conditions on which peace and rest had formerly depended in such a way as to accommodate the new conceptualization. The conditions that will permit us peace and rest on the new terms may be internal conditions of thought or understanding or appreciation: that is, we find ourselves newly awakened and prepared to change our terms of engagement with the world—we learn, we change *ourselves*. Or, the required new conditions for conceptual peace and rest may implicate external reality, conditions as we perceive them to exist in the world: that is, we find ourselves newly disturbed by or alienated from present external conditions, and thus we are prompted to change *the world*. Obviously clear-cut distinctions between changing ourselves and changing the world cannot be maintained, for in either case, as a necessary first step, we must reconstruct our conceptual imaginations. Only this reconstruction enables us to achieve the conditions that will allow new experience to be fully assimilated, to exist in conceptual peace and rest. Thus, regardless of the specifics in our response to metaphor—regardless of how we assimilate our experience—as beings imaginatively reconstructed through the metaphoric process, we are *changed*.

In an important sense, metaphor's iconoclastic capacity for radical transformation actually embraces rather than denies the celebratory account of literary experience. By depicting the reader's ecstatic self-transcendence as a completion of the author's communicative effort, Stambovsky implies that the creative endeavor reaches fulfillment in the reader's celebratory response, an idea supported by his reference to the words of Maurice Blanchot: "Reading . . . is a creative act: 'more creative' than 'creation'—'although it produces nothing'" (65). But if the active celebration of the artist's communicative endeavor must be a transformation that results in a changed responder, then the artistic vision of the creative iconoclast is a thing not to be celebrated, but to be lived. Or rather, living the vision is the only true celebration of iconoclastic art. As depicted by Blanchot, the celebratory account recollects aestheticism's "art for art's sake"—a reductive formulation that creative iconoclasm would have to see as sterile. To the degree that transformative power and transformative desire motivate any artist, a partaker's living the vision would be the only true celebration of any artist's work—a proposition which puts into question the very notion of aestheticist art. Perhaps most important, given the infinity of living visions that the transformative constructions of art may give rise to, the communicative endeavor of the iconoclastic artist can never be said to be complete or absolutely fulfilled: continually, art begets art. Far from producing "nothing," ecstatic self-transcendence is for creative iconoclasm the essential generative act. The celebratory conflation of power and desire, in the transformative act that unites artist with partaker of art, actually generates new being.

The new being generated owes its character to art, artist, and partaker of art, all three cooperative iconoclasts in the present account. In a televisual culture where media makeovers proliferate, where discriminating between image and substance seems not so much a difficult enterprise as an irrelevant one, we may too easily take for granted the radical reconstruction of consciousness incurred by the process of self-transformation. As the present argument suggests, however, self-transformation and reconstruction of consciousness is not an extravagance accessible only to media celebrities and political figures, nor is it an isolable political or social expedient, an activity intrinsically different from ordinary individual imaginative life. Our susceptibility to the image and our mistrust of it—the paradoxical fear of and passion for images that the iconoclastic impulse both stimulates and relieves—

bears all the uncanny familiarity that we might expect from a mirror of the workings of our minds. It is precisely that uncanny familiarity with which the process of self-construction strikes us that makes us so skeptical of images, so fearful of them, and yet so attracted to them and compelled by them: transformative power impelled by transformative desire beckons from without to a kindred force within. Reconstruction of consciousness is radical, but it is also universal. To a greater or lesser degree we each remake ourselves with every new experience: iconoclastic self-creation is a dynamic constant of everyday individual imaginative life. And imaginative life, for the reasons already set forth, cannot be separated from real life. What we do in our self-transforming imaginations is that which makes us what we are.

REFORMIST ICONOCLASM
AND THE ART OF CARNAL RHETORIC

The connection between transforming imagination and the impetus toward perfect freedom should by now be fairly clear. Their iconoclastic procedures are identical with each other, and also with those of metaphor. Their aims may or may not be identical, of course: conceivably, transformative power and transformative desire could coalesce in an impetus not toward perfect freedom but toward perfect bondage. That is a possibility of greater concern to psychological analysis than to metaphor theory—although, for a culture demonstrably manipulated by televisual imagery, the psychopolitical implications of such a possibility demand that we at least keep it in mind. But for the present study, the transformative power and desire that unite art, artist, and partaker of art in the iconoclastic impulse lead to focus on the interests of perfect freedom that can be seen to motivate much of the iconoclastic activity during the English Reform period. Focus here on the interests of perfect freedom does not mean disregard for the myriad ways in which popular iconoclastic impulses of fifteenth-, sixteenth-, and seventeenth-century England were in fact exploited by powers whose interests actually lay more in bondage than in freedom. Neither would I argue that creative iconoclasm's impetus toward perfect freedom diminishes or excuses the acts of wanton destruction that the iconoclastic impulse so often led to. As I have suggested, iconoclasm's creative and destructive energies are deeply interdependent, and the teleology of perfect freedom is, by at least one definition, anarchic. Reified, iconoclasm's creative and destructive impulses may operate simultaneously, or alternately; they are often mistaken for each other; they may ultimately be indistinguishable. By reenacting, in artistic method and in expressive forms of political and religious conviction, the elemental forces of life and death, iconoclasm bears witness to its participation in universal verities without necessarily affirming particular versions of truth. Among iconoclastic artists of the English Reform period, this reenactment played itself out much as discourse in metaphor theory does—as radical ambivalence toward the image, toward what representation can actually accomplish.

This ambivalence was encouraged on a concrete and practical as well as philosophical level by the age's preoccupation, both professional and amateur, with optical experimentation. If the religious reform movement led to devaluation of the image as a representation of spiritual truth, a revolution was also under way in science and technology with respect to the cognitive value of visual perception.[42] Paradoxically, developments in optics that exposed the delusiveness of the visual also lent to visual experience a peculiar mystique of the sort that comes only with actual scientific discovery—a wonderment that is more keen because it does not depend on simplicity or ignorance, but rather causes us to alter our conceptions of tangible reality. Development of telescopic and microscopic lenses opened up new worlds to visual experience, but they also made people acutely aware of the unaided eye's limitations even as they vastly extended the perceptive capacities of the visual organ. Similarly, delight in optical illusion undermined confidence in visual cognition, while linear perspective enabled mathematical theorizing of the myriad ways in which the eye could be fooled. The paradoxical character of perception invigorated by the new optics thus shared with creative iconoclasm the insight that that which teaches us to believe—in this case the visual faculty—can also teach us to doubt, and further, that doubt's positive aspect may be discovery. So, Protestant iconoclastic discourse could count on a secular milieu favorable to engaging the partaker of art in radical ambivalence toward sensory images and visual representations. Self-reflexive representations of the delusive ephemerality of representation therefore became a hallmark of iconoclastic art. Ernest Gilman shows how ambivalence toward the image spurred self-reflexivity in Foxe and the Marian martyrs, Ben Jonson, George Herbert, Quarles, Donne, Milton, and others in addition to Spenser.[43] Ambivalence over the image actually invigorated the creative activity of those whom it most disturbed.

The natural strategy of the iconoclastic artist is to engage the partaker of his art in his own radical ambivalence. The strategy is natural because the iconoclastic impulse is already there in the mind of the partaker, in the transformative power and desire of the responding imagination. It is natural as well because ambivalence recognizes the contradiction between an ideal of perfect freedom and the inescapable limits of being merely human. Parallel to iconoclasm's interdependent creative and destructive forces is the interdependence, in iconoclastic art, of the impetus toward perfect freedom and the acute awareness of mortality. Art conflates the finite with the infinite: positive conviction of art's limitless living visions collides with an equal certainty that all art's visions, however infinite in number and concept, are nevertheless temporal. Mortal apprehension simultaneously piques imagination and chastens it, providing not only a constant theme but also an integral technique in the formation of iconoclastic art.

And mortal apprehension operates on an ontological as well as a perceptual and aesthetic level in such art. For the Renaissance artist, the impossibility of artistic completion or absolute fulfillment of human aesthetic vision conforms with a religious vision of a created universe—a vision in which fallen beings strive continually in the temporal realm, sustained by hope of regaining conceptual peace and rest in the perfect freedom of an eternal divine order. At the same time, however, lurking around the edges of this reciprocally creative human and divine project, and opportunistically advancing at the merest sign of uncertainty either in artistic confidence or in divine faith, is awareness of an alternative, starkly modernist vision. This is the profoundly disturbing awareness that impossibility of artistic fulfillment may also conform with iconoclasm's nihilistic potential—with anarchic destruction and disintegration, not only of art but of the very idea of a creative self. When Spenser's politic Calidore interrupts Colin's visionary song of the Three Graces on Mount Acidale, the disruption leads not only to devastation of the pastoral landscape and unleashing of the Blatant Beast, but to the abandonment half-finished of Spenser's grand plan for *The Faerie Queene.* Iconoclasm's creative and destructive impulses there work, not a transformation toward conceptual peace and rest, but an engulfment of both art and artist in the domain of mutability, where the temporal constitutes the only order. Mortal hindrances to the endeavor of aesthetic vision thus become as determinative to art as is the aesthetic vision itself.

At the same time, mortal apprehension becomes a positive asset, as the iconoclastic artist taps the responder's deepest affective ambivalences. John N. King has demonstrated the rousing ways in which Tudor satirists popularized the Edwardian program of religious and social reform, by exploiting the playgoer's love for visual extravagance on stage, or that of the reader for sensuous and graphic imagery in the written word. A representative sample shows how the latent ontological dimension of the aesthetic can be brought to the surface by manipulation of affective response to imagery. Satirist Luke Shepherd's scurrilous allegorical portrait of Mistress Missa (a personification of the Catholic mass) advances the Protestant image of the Whore of Babylon through a grotesque genealogy that will later be echoed in Spenser's Duessa and in Milton's portrait of Sin in *Paradise Lost.* Mistress Missa, finally done in by English reform, receives a scatological funeral dirge:

> A good mestres missa
> Shal ye go from us thissa?
> Wel yet I muste ye kyssa
> Alacke for payne I pyssa
> To se the mone here Issa
> Because ye muste departe
> It greveth many an herte
> That ye should from them start
> But what then tushe a farte.[44]

By expressing his sorrow in bereavement as a symptom of venereal disease ("alacke for payne I pyssa") contracted from his liaison with Mistress Missa, the speaker conveys more than just vulgar contempt for the dear departed ("But what then tushe a farte"). He also betrays his carnal attachment to her. The affective vigor of Shepherd's raunchy language simultaneously confesses to and discredits the aesthetic and emotional attractions of the recently rejected, but still alluring, old faith. And like the best satire, it also implicates the reader, whose affective pleasure in the travesty betrays an attachment to images of corruption and disease that at least equals and perhaps outweighs his attachment to images of beauty. The feelings of ambivalence generated by this realization, however, fasten themselves not merely to a certain class of images, but to imagery as a whole. Since it leads the reader to take pleasure in representations of the disreputable, the experience of scatalogical and grotesque imagery raises doubts about the validity of entrusting—as human beings naturally tend to entrust—moral and ideological discernment to the offices of affective response. "How is a Christian to know," as Gilman puts it, "whether the pictures in his mind are the marks of his spiritual illumination or the residue of his depravity?"[45] What *feels* true may not, in the final analysis, *be* Truth after all.

The ambivalence generated by artistic exploration of the grotesque is a mainstay of English reform satire, for religious satire's verbal iconoclasm draws on the very wellsprings that help to feed religious conviction in the first place. Reform portraits of religious corruption, whether claimed against individuals or institutions, evoked a world of energetic nastiness in which the proliferation of bodily diseases, overindulgence in food and drink, and sexual perversion became successful metaphors for spiritual evil because the grotesque could manipulate human ambivalence not only toward images of the ugly but toward physicality and death.[46] The grotesque elicits contrary responses of laughter and horror by its frivolous handling of the macabre, for instance, or its comic treatment of the repulsive. It simultaneously compels and grows intolerable by playing upon our emotional vacillation between not just extremes or opposites but mutually exclusive possibilities: ebullient celebration of life can instantly shift, through a potent image of sexuality corrupted, to chilling awareness of death and bodily disintegration, the limitless predicaments of mortal flesh.

But these terms extend beyond the grotesque to artistic evocations of every kind of sensory reality. What Neil Rhodes claims for Aretino-inspired Elizabethan pamphleteers like Thomas Nashe can, without distortion, be applied as well to virtually all writers experimenting with the power of concrete imagery: "the writers are exploring the physicality of language and its ability to work in a solid and visual way . . . a driving of language from the mental to the physical. They represent an incarnative view of language, the word becoming flesh."[47] Word becoming flesh; and the reverse is also true: in the rhetoric of the satiric grotesque, *carnal* rage gets verbalized. The anticreative vision of total disintegration looms, as *saeva indignatio* bespeaks—in addition to moral outrage—the rage of the flesh against the injustice of its own corruption. In Marvell's "Dialogue," the anguished Body cries, "What but a Soul could have the wit / To build me up for Sin so fit?"[48]

Radical ambivalence toward affective images and visionary representations thus weighs an allotment of mortality that implicates creation, creator, and witness in what is created. Even the sharpest senses are flawed on a purely perceptual level; and on a moral or spiritual level, their questionable priorities are readily exposed. In any case, whatever confirmations the senses achieve are ephemeral, and it is the ephemerality of artistic vision and linguistic affect that disturbs and promises the most. Regardless of whether its representations are beautiful or grotesque, false or true, metaphor verbalizes mortal striving after the immortal. In its compulsive leaps between opposing yet interdependent forces of creation and destruction, metaphor invokes the deep cyclical rhythms of nature: out of death comes new life. The impetus toward metaphoric transformation is instinct with a sense of individual mortality, and desire for transcendence, which can barely hope for conceptual peace and rest even in the prospect of immortal fame. The radical ambivalence that denies itself comfort in representable truth must, by the same rule, divest itself of reliance on any assumption of the spirit: all may be carnal illusion. Embrace of metaphor's mortal striving thus becomes, for the iconoclastic artist, the creative equivalent of submission to divine will, with poetic achievement a commensurate form of supervenient grace. For the poet, the word made flesh—the "driving of language from the mental to the physical"—amounts to surrender of transcendent desire to the only expressive mode desire truly commands: an unselfdeluded, frankly mortal art of carnal rhetoric.

CARNAL RHETORIC AND THE POETICS OF DESIRE

Yet as the paradox suggests, surrender to one's own command enables a different kind of liberation, a liberation of the will to self-determination. I have argued that reconstruction of consciousness is radical but universal: iconoclastic self-creation is a dynamic constant of individual imaginative life. The self-transforming imagination that Stephen Greenblatt has traced making figures like Thomas More what they are expresses the drive toward individual autonomy that underlies many forms of Reformation iconoclastic activity.[49] To effect concrete transformation in the world—the world of material reality or the equally real world of the imagination—is to exercise the individual will to perfect freedom. In the expansive despotism of a monarch like Henry VIII, we may discern writ large the drive toward individualism of a collective national will. Expanding on the insights of Jacob Burckhardt and Ernst Cassirer, William Kerrigan and Gordon Braden suggest that Renaissance patronage of the arts "makes possible for the artist a career analogous to [the despotic ruler's] own, one enabled not by inherited assignment but by present skill. Worldly success unpredicted by the traditional roles of medieval society, an exemption from the constraints of one's station, can be won by the exercise of the creative imagination."[50] The imaginative territory of conscious individualism is thus opened and explored, as the iconoclastic temperament discovers opportunities for self-definition made available by the breakdown of deterministic social, political, and religious structures. This is not to deny the determinative force of those structures. It is rather to locate their determinations in what they no longer control: if we were to make an Althusserian reading of the phenomenon, individualism itself would be recognized less as a cause than as a symptom of structural change.[51] The epistemological validity of that phantom Individual of Romanticist criticism, the transcendental subject, is therefore not an issue here. While creative iconoclasm assumes a *desire* for transcendence similar in many respects to that theorized by Coleridge and Eliot, it is the acknowledged *impossibility of attaining* such transcendence that gives creative iconoclasm its character and, ever mindful of mortality, that makes its rhetoric "carnal."

The history of iconoclasm in sixteenth- and seventeenth-century religion and politics is, among other things, a chronicle of struggles for worldly power in which creative iconoclasm may be seen as negotiating and forging new power relations. In this process, the art of metaphor—the art of verbal and visual image, of symbol, of the icon— plays a central role. Because institutional power exercises control over individual imaginations by means of symbol, iconoclastic theory of metaphor offers insight into the imaginative process by which reality- as-discovered, in a spiritually coherent theocentric universe, shifts to reality-as-created, by and for fleshly human beings. The multiple new realities of the Renaissance are the constructs of disparate human agents who find themselves competitive shareholders in a universe where the idea of an absolute (hence objective) center becomes less and less predominant, while at the same time, the idea of the subjective individual, ambiguously authoritative and complexly self-referential, comes into focus. Pico della Mirandola's call for "holy ambition" re- sounds with an urgency tainted by the profane, as he speaks of the exhilarating competitiveness unleashed by prospects of individual au- tonomy: he exhorts his fellow human beings to "compete with the angels in dignity and glory."[52] Today, the scientific objectivity we re- ductively label "positivism" may justly be debunked as an Enlight- enment myth, yet it was a myth constructed in part to check the sense-bound perceptual and interpretive anarchy to which knowledge and society seemed destined if every individual were to respond to Pico's call by becoming his own fleshly deity. The religious wars of the seventeenth century fed on anxiety generated by the cognizable dis- crepancies between God's universe and Man's. With ever broadening implications, Truth was becoming concretely negotiable.

If religious and political conflict drew a testy vigor from anxiety over Truth, so did poetry. I have noted how the epistemological meticu- lousness of modern poetics discourse commonly splits Truth into terms that pass in a skeptical age for its constituent parts. Wary of posi- tivism, critics today speak not of Truth but of "truth-claims," "truth- value," and "truth-effect"—which pieced together, might be said to make up what Truth would look like if we believed in it. Our critical language thus calls self-conscious attention to the fact that it can only metaphorize Truth, not directly present it. The dramatic shift in critical attitudes toward truth's representability is most easily demonstrated by contrasting this contemporary practice with the relevant arguments made by Sir Philip Sidney. Writing for an audience that held metaphorical analyses in higher esteem, Sidney actually validated poetic truth by means of metaphor, casting the poet as a Godlike "maker," and granting the poet's language a status comparable to that given by medieval theorists to "eloquence" in scripture.[53] Nor was this a mere gesture toward style. Since Sidney's metaphor for the poet makes the poet a metaphor for God, the poet by extension can of course metaphorize God's truth.

Yet what actually happens in poetry's metaphoric activity may, as Sidney surely knew, have little to do with God (recall the sanctity of *idea*) or with any so comprehensive notion as absolute Truth. Instead, it has a great deal to do with the radical displacement of center that Sidney here so unconcernedly promulgates: for the authority of God's Word, the poet substitutes the poet's words. This most fundamental act of iconoclasm—the Renaissance poet's displacement of God's truths by his own truths, thus displacement of God by the author himself—is the ultimate claim for the individual impetus toward perfect freedom. The devout poet, of course, sees his individuality not as a displacement of God but as a conduit for divinity, or as a creative instrument in the hands of God. Nevertheless, a common and poignant sign of creative iconoclasm in religious poetry is the restless and uneasy contingency with which the poet surrounds self-reference. Herbert's self-chastizing "So did I weave my self into the sense" ("Jordan," l.14)—or Milton's self-effacing "if all be mine, / Not hers who brings it nightly to my ear" (*PL* IX.46–7)—bears witness to the poet's anxiety over the individual creative impetus toward perfect freedom. Having generated the impetus, the poet discovers that claims inevitably get made by and for the poet's own self, as a by-product of the extraordinary artistic mission of negotiating divine truth.

Ostensibly for Milton, the call of holy ambition compels not so much competition with the angels, or displacement of God's truth (motives he clearly ascribes to Satan), as it does relinquishment of a fully realized autonomous will to the purposes of an unknown will that is God. Milton circumvents the tendency of fleshly individualism to substitute its own temporal agenda for eternal truth by enlisting the entirety of the claims both of the flesh and of the individual will in his negotiations with the divine. The sign of supreme human individualism for Milton is the autonomous will plunging itself fully aware into the appalling perfect freedom of a divine infinity. Instead of competitively striving to be God*like,* the fully realized, autonomous, fleshly individual cancels that metaphor's distantiating similitude. Rather than imitate God, Milton's autonomous individual subsumes the predominance of his own penetrating mind into the truth of God's predominance. It is this unrepresentable fusion with the infinite that alone can bear the definition of perfect freedom. The sustained paradox of a fully autonomous will attuned to perfect subordination in the will of God is the essential Miltonic version of "split reference": there is a will, there isn't a will; apart from God, there is no will. Milton's autonomous individual thus plays out in his particular career exactly the iconoclastic pattern required by the creative exigencies of metaphor. If every poet must himself be a true poem, carnal rhetoric is there to show the way.

The way shown to and by the poet John Milton will be traced in the following chapters through details from his writing that illustrate at work the iconoclastic principles of metaphor and imagination, as set forth in this theoretical chapter. A continuing, though secondary, theme will be the problem of distinguishing between rhetoric that is carnal in service to God and that which is carnal in service to itself. If the task of Milton's carnal rhetoric is in fact to make the willing embrace of metaphor's mortal striving consistent with, and constantly attentive to, an unknowable will that is divine, one would assume that making such a distinction would be critical. By the evidence of the carnal rhetoric in his antiprelatical tracts, as shown in Chapter 2, Milton would seem to agree. But purely in logical terms, there can be no *perceptible* distinction between rhetoric that serves an unknowable divine will and that which serves the demands of mortal flesh. If it is apprehensible to human sense, rhetoric is by definition *all* carnal—representational, temporal, mortally flawed.

Hence the precariousness of the devout poet's iconoclastic impetus. Some of that precariousness, and a more forthright recognition of the mortality of all rhetoric, come into focus as the present study turns, in Chapter 3, from Milton's attacks on the prelates to *The Doctrine and Discipline of Divorce.* Yet the precariousness itself neither invalidates religious devotion nor compromises the cause in the interest of which the iconoclastic action is being taken. As will become clear in subsequent chapters, with the analyses of *Areopagitica* and *Eikonoklastes*, a state of precariousness is the creative iconoclast's acquiescence to mortal contingency, an embrace of the ambivalence of word against flesh that keeps these irreconcilables interdependently suspended in doubt, in *epoché*, for the sake of perfect freedom.

Meanwhile, the task of determining the spiritual status of carnal rhetoric gradually finds its proper place. Discriminating between fleshly commitment to the divine and commitment to the mundane is for the creative iconoclast not a problem in itself but an essential step in the process of self-enlightenment required to implement the drive toward iconoclastic action. Resolution of the dilemma of carnal rhetoric—clear possession of knowledge that the fleshly service either is or is not divine—can in the end be available to none but the iconoclast himself. In the Miltonic canon, this is Samson at the ecstatic moment of his convergence with the iconoclastic act. No longer external to the rhetoric of his creation, Samson becomes what he beholds. The task of discriminating is passed on to the observer, the interpreter, the responder to the iconoclastic act. And what is left by the act to discern is still not truth, but only a sign of the possibility that the act of creative iconoclasm has been true to its *desire* for transcendence and divine union.

But the iconoclastic activity of carnal rhetoric is not limited to the writing of John Milton or of Renaissance poets caught up in anxious reassessments of the relations between the body and soul, or between the individual and the cosmos. The preoccupation of modern metaphor theory with language's ontological dimension suggests that ambivalence over the relation of image to truth is still with us, that we still need for metaphor to carry a burden greater than can be borne by mere words or pictures or any combination of these. If the "curious perspective" of the Renaissance I/eye stubbornly but piously denies itself conceptual peace and rest in illusions about truth,[54] it is a self-denial that the modern metaphor theorist recapitulates with an air of nostalgia. The nostalgia appears in analytical thought that centers on metaphor's ontological vehemence, thought that I have called *ontological longing*, the rationalist's loophole for God. This longing may best be represented by Paul Ricoeur's engagingly rationalistic "wager"—a philosophical bet that if we assume, for the sake of speculation, that there *is* a higher significance to the symbolic world (we may again recall the *idea* of the idea), then we will reap better returns in understanding, in "power of reflection, in the element of coherent discourse" than we will by assuming that symbolic thought is merely a self-referencing "circle of hermeneutics," a redundant structure of mortal language that can *mean* no more than what mortal minds know to *say*.[55]

Both the logic and the spirit of Ricoeur's almost playful proposition have for this writer an enormous appeal. Yet because Ricoeur's account of affective excess insists on *meaning* as the ultimate desideratum in metaphor discourse, I think he inadvertently and needlessly disparages ontological longing. The expansive variableness of imaginative life is as infinite as the variableness of natural life: both are structured and accountable within categories, yet both endlessly burgeon with production of new kinds. Such expansive variableness evokes a reality beyond any meaning of "meaning," and not just because we haven't yet contrived an adequate significatory code. Only the perfect freedom of an *extrasignificatory* reality guarantees full range for the coalescence of transformative power and transformative desire to which iconoclastic theory addresses itself. Modern criticism, in its determination to settle "meaning," may meticulously cleanse its analytical language of ontological faith, but it demonstrably cannot rid itself of ontological longing. Nor must it do so. An alternative measure is provided by the impulse to perfect freedom, which clearly invites theoretical accommodation. In response to this invitation, iconoclastic theory of metaphor insists on, and is concerned with its principle of transformation to sustain, not truth itself—logically impossible without signification—but truth's far more crucial adjunct, imaginative desire.

2

"SHUFFLING UP SUCH A GOD"

The Rhetorical Agon of Milton's

Antiprelatical Tracts

When the public officer bids Samson appear at the feast of Dagon
to display his superhuman strength before the assembled Phil-
istine gentry, Samson growls his indignation:

> Shall I abuse this consecrated gift
> Of strength, again returning with my hair
> After my great transgression, so requite
> Favor renewed, and add a greater sin
> By prostituting holy things to idols;
> A Nazarite in place abominable
> Vaunting my strength in honour to their Dagon?
> (*SA*, ll.1354–60)

Samson's angry retort provides insight into the nature of consecrated
gifts—how greatly they influence their receivers' choice of actions,
and how little they alter their receivers' intrinsic character. The self-
idolizing tribal hero, who once could brag that at his hand "a thousand
foreskins fell" (l.144), still regards his consecrated gift of strength as
a "holy thing" that he would not "abuse" by "vaunting" it "in place
abominable" and "prostituting" it "to idols." Fascinated by his strength,
the Nazarite strongman Samson ascribes greater sanctity to the re-
newed gift itself than to God's "favor renewed": he would shield his

strength from profane exposure, "a greater sin" than ingratitude for "favor renewed."

Such is the way of consecrated gifts. The consecrated gift ever puts its awed receiver at the mercy of his own mere mortal capacity to deal with it. The English Nazarite John Milton knew well the onerous privilege of consecrated gifts. Like Samson, he had known from youth that he was destined to national greatness. He had spent his early years perfecting his poetic talents—the holy things allotted him, according to his conviction, by a purposeful God. But the heroic vision of poetic achievement that Milton had entertained since childhood was severely tested early in his career by his being drawn into polemical battle. Pamphlet warfare against Milton's contemporary Philistines, the Anglican prelates, required that Milton abuse his consecrated gifts by prostituting those holy things to the idol of an already vulgar temporal controversy that was further tainted by the conditions of the marketplace. He was "put from beholding the bright countenance of truth in the quiet and still air of delightful studies to come into the dim reflexion of hollow antiquities sold by the seeming bulk, and there be fain to club quotations."[1] Like Samson in his strength, the youthful Milton in his poetic ability would have preferred to champion God's truth in an arena truly worthy of his consecrated gifts, one unsullied by the profane.

The task of distinguishing between sacred and profane use of consecrated gifts was particularly difficult for Milton because of the elusiveness of exactly that truth to which his gifts were consecrated. His allusions to Truth in the antiprelatical tracts are girded with a demure reticence very like the Lady's in *A Mask Presented at Ludlow Castle,* when she primly declines to reveal "the sage / And serious doctrine of Virginity" to Comus's unworthy ears. Yet if Milton's polemical audience, like Comus, is not fit to hear itself convinced, his untainted poetic readership is hardly better prepared: "those especially of soft and delicious temper" would presumably come unstrung at the sinews to hear truth, for they "will not so much as look upon Truth herselfe, unlesse they see her elegantly drest" (817–18). Regardless of what it might be, or for whom it might be dressed, "truth" here is clearly something other than the sort of mundane factual business Milton now finds himself compelled to engage in. But at the same time, he is so compelled precisely because of his convictions about what is or is not "true." Thus, in a personal as well as artistic sense, Milton's argumentative purpose and his poetic mission in his early polemical writings operate ambiguously at odds. He writes as if to say that any verbal activity—including polemics—can be either factual or true, but not both at once. Because Milton can neither separate nor reconcile his apparently contradictory aims, the antiprelatical tracts record a rhetorical agon from which no one—not profane fact, not sacred Truth, not even Milton—emerges as victor.

THE SENSORY TRUTH OF TEEMING METAPHOR

Briefly stated, the antiprelatical tracts show Milton shifting back and forth between two rhetorics—that of the temporal world of men and events, the world of polemical activity and "clubbing quotations"; and that of the metaphoric realm of moral Truth, a realm manifested through the free use of imagery. The language of the temporal world is factual, historical, rationally apprehensible, and affectively neutral. It is with this language, and within this world, that Milton claims to construct his argument. Here, accounts of English political events, Reformation history, or the church fathers convey a plethora of busy activities—persons engaged in quarrels and coronations and councils, in suits and dispensations and missions. But Milton's temporal world comes to us largely unshaped by the kind of interpretive intelligence that would give it depth and significance: its details are abundant, but unmemorable. The language of Milton's metaphoric moral realm, on the other hand, produces images that are unforgettable. These images develop from his assumptions of a higher reality, one that is eternal, suprarational, functionally (though not finally) dualistic, theocentric. In such a realm, "meaning" comes not from rational and empirical interpretation, not from historical analysis, but from relationship to God.

Milton's practice of referring moral judgment to God in the antiprelatical tracts is what determines his lifelong polemical stance—his pretense, as Keith Stavely puts it, "that Armageddon has come."[2] For this reason, Milton's rhetorical effectiveness depends largely on a readership that is predisposed to agree with him. Stanley Fish's characterization of *Reason of Church Government* applies to all the anti-prelatical tracts in this respect: "Milton stands alone, or with those of his audience who, like him, are 'eye-brightened' and the prose continues to pressure the reader to enroll himself in that number. . . . It does not provoke the self of the reader to change, merely to acknowledge his position in the polarities it continually uncovers."[3] Readers who find themselves uncomfortable with the vehemence of Milton's affective language understandably resent the rhetorical pressure of this moral realm, the pressure to see to it that they are "implicitly included" among "the elect people of God."[4] But, of course, moral meaning is not the same thing as rhetorical effectiveness—a point less clear perhaps to Milton than to his readers, and one to which we will be returning from many angles. Contrary to the claims made by Milton's moral realm, it is not in fact relationship to God that gives these images their rhetorical authority. It is not their theocentricity but their sensuousness that powers Milton's moral images. They are so pungent, so memorable in contrast to the rational argument that they gain rhetorical ascendancy over it without actually engaging in it. Their effect is to obscure and ultimately to overwhelm the argument rather than enhance it.

For example, watch what happens to the temporal claims of rational discourse in this typical passage from *Of Reformation.* Milton is arguing that the worldly precedence of bishops is not supported by evidence from church fathers. He establishes his rational mode of argument through scrupulous marshaling of historical testimony.

Now for Episcopall dignity, what it was, see out of *Ignatius,* who in his Epistle to those of *Trallis* confesseth *that the Presbyters, are his fellow Counsellers, and fellow benchers.* And *Cyprian* in many places, as in the 6. 41. 52. Epist. speaking of *Presbyters,* calls them his *Compresbyters,* as if he deem'd himselfe no other, whenas by the same place it appeares he was a Bishop, he calls them Brethren. (546)

For a few sentences, Milton sustains the historical level of argument, although he varies it by interpolating the objection of a supposed disputant and immediately answering it:

But that will be thought his meeknesse: yea, but the *Presbyters* and Deacons writing to him think they doe him honour enough when they phrase him no higher than Brother *Cyprian,* and deare *Cyprian* in the 26. Epist.

With the next sentence, Milton still maintains the historical level of argument, but his apparent commitment to that level becomes impaired.

For their Authority 'tis evident not to have bin single, but depending on the counsel of the *Presbyters*, as from *Ignatius* was erewhile alledg'd; and the same *Cyprian* acknowledges as much in the 6 Epist. and addes therto that he had determin'd from his entrance into the Office of Bishop to doe nothing without the consent of his people, and so in the 31. Epist, for it were tedious to course through all his writings which are so full of the like assertions.

The proof from Ignatius "erewhile alleg'd" is Milton's own of just two sentences past, but by casting the allusion into an impersonal passive construction ("as . . . was . . . alleg'd"), he begins to distance himself from the act of citing scholarly evidence. In the phrases that follow, detachment wanes into sheer boredom, as his treatment of patristic testimony disintegrates. What had earlier seemed worthy of minute examination ("Cyprian . . . speaking of *Presbyters*, calls them his *Compresbyters*, as if he deemed himself no other") now is reduced to a kind of shorthand or ditto: "and so in the 31. Epist, for it were tedious to course through all his writings." A case could be made here for a strategical Milton who deliberately subverts the trappings of historical evidence, ultimately to lay that "hors load of citations and fathers" at the prelatical doorstep. But that is not what's going on. Milton's well-known apologetic can be taken quite seriously:

I should not chuse this manner of writing wherin knowing my self inferior to my self, led by the genial power of nature to another task, I have the use, as I may account it, but of my left hand. (808)

The ennui is not a pose: Milton has committed himself to a task and a form of argument which he finds necessary but exceedingly disagreeable, and what we witness in a passage like this is the rumblings of a disgruntled aesthetic sensibility. It is not the technical aspects of prose so much as its attendant presumptions of rational detachment that unnaturally restrict Milton to the use of his left hand: his consecrated gifts want exercise. So, in this instance, Milton permits the requisite historical citations for the case against episcopal dignity finally to wither in scholarly dust. But at the same moment a sign of vigor appears, with the first metaphor in many sentences—an imagerial presentation of Rome as "the womb and center of Apostacy":

It were tedious to course through all his writings which are so full of the like assertions, insomuch that ev'n in the womb and center of Apostacy *Rome* it selfe, there yet remains a glimps of this truth, for the Pope himselfe, as a learned English writer notes well, performeth all Ecclesiasticall jurisdiction as in Consistory amongst his Cardinals, which were originally but the Parish Priests of Rome. (547)

The words "womb and center of Apostacy" momentarily enliven a dry passage. But more importantly, they invoke a radically different level of discourse in which the terms for validating an argument are completely changed. Into a field of scholarly allusions and citations that can be infinitely extended (perhaps without altering the case), Milton suddenly intrudes a moral judgment that is totally independent of such evidence. After all, Rome's identity as apostate can neither be proven nor disproven, only accepted or denied. Striking as it is, however, this moral pronouncement is of secondary importance as a rhetorical gesture. Rome's apostasy is useful here to Milton only as it throws into relief "a glimps of this truth"—the equable consistory of cardinals that recalls the early church "Parish Priests of *Rome.*" The immediate rhetorical import of the image of Rome stems not from Rome's presumed apostasy but from Rome's being presented *metaphorically* as "the womb and center" of apostasy. The intrusion of that metaphor signals Milton's shift away from the rational and historical level of discourse, on which he ostensibly bases his argument against the bishops, while it launches the nonrational, morally resonant, theocentric, and eternal level of discourse. And as we will see, this level of discourse—despite its declared aspiration toward the spiritual, the ideal, and the universal or abstract—is absolutely dependent on language that is sensuous and concrete. It is, of course, the prerogative of imagery to be sensuous. But my point is that in the antiprelatical tracts Milton's moral perceptions and his moral intensity reside entirely in his sensory, affective language, and this language has almost no *rational* connection with the historical entities he discusses—be they fallible princes, timeserving prelates, superstitious monks, or corrupt institutions. This will become clearer as we go along, but for the present it is valuable to watch Milton's affective language take over the passage at hand.

Had Milton called Rome only "the center of Apostacy," his charac-
terization of it would still have remained within the bounds of rational
discourse. That is, one could conceivably agree or disagree with him as
an exponent of partisan opinion. But by adding the metaphor "womb,"
Milton makes of Rome not a temporal location ("center") but a female
primal nurturer, and of her apostasy not a subject for partisan debate
but an entity with a potent life of its own, a life quite distinct from the
temporal life of historical men and places. As a polemical tactic, this
is effective: imagery tends to preclude or outface rational argument.
But that is just the beginning. Once introduced, the organic metaphor
pervades the sentences that follow. Images of the body emerge and
weave among other images in a scenario that burgeons with the copi-
ousness implied by its origin in the word "womb." Significantly, the
connection between the developing images and their original is picto-
rial only, not polemical. The words "womb of Apostacy" can logically
have only negative connotations for Milton, whereas "the mysticall
body" in the ensuing passage is clearly positive. But the sensory visual
affinities between image and image ("womb" and "body") are strong
enough effectually to supersede the nonvisual indictment "Apostacy."
Because subsequent images tend to adhere to the image established,
the "womb" eventually becomes less defined by the term "Apostacy"
than it is enhanced by the visual cue provided through a "glimps of this
truth." In Milton's metaphoric moral realm, in other words, "truth" is
not what you call something, it is what you *feel* and *see.*

This subtle contest between intellectual definition and direct sen-
sory representation ends with the latter in command. From here to
the end of the passage, the veridical claims of historical evidence and
reasoned debate are totally abandoned, while the affective language of
teeming sensoriness fills the polemical arena.[5]

Thus then did the Spirit of unity and meekness inspire, and animate every
joynt, and sinew of the mysticall body, but now the gravest, and worthiest min-
ister, a true Bishop of his fold shall be revil'd, and ruffl'd by an insulting, and
only-canon-wise Prelate, as if he were some slight paltry companion: and the
people of *God* redeem'd, and wash'd with *Christs* blood, and dignify'd with so
many glorious titles of Saints, and sons in the gospel, are now no better reputed
then impure ethnicks, and lay dogs; stones & Pillars, and Crucifixes have now
the honour, and the almes due to *Christs* living members; the Table of Commu-

nion now become a Table of separation stands like an exalted platforme upon
the brow of the quire, fortifi'd with bulwark, and barricado, to keep off the pro-
fane touch of the Laicks, whilst the obscene, and surfeted Priest scruples not to
paw, and mammock the sacramentall bread, as familiarly as his Tavern Bisket.
(547–48)

One notices immediately the way Milton's images seem to multiply
themselves by doubling up at practically every point of syntax.[6] Nouns
pair with other nouns—"unity and meekness," "joint, and sinew,"
"Saints, and sons," "impure ethnicks, and lay dogs," "stones & Pillars,
and crucifixes," "the honour, and the almes," "Table of Communion . . .
Table of separation," "bulwark, and barricado." Verbs and verbals move
in tandem—"inspire, and animate," "revil'd, and ruffl'd," "redeem'd,
and wash'd," "paw, and mammock." Adjectives team up too—"gravest,
and worthiest," "insulting, and only-Canon-wise," "slight paltry," "ob-
scene, and surfeted." All this doubling creates a veritable explosion of
tangible particulars, rapidly crowding the sensory field.

But sheer force of numbers is just one of the ways Milton's affective
language overwhelms the rational argument. In addition to this, the
organic metaphor for the church—generated by the "glimpse of truth"
in the "womb of apostasy"—now develops as "the Spirit of unity and
meekness" that can "inspire, and animate every joynt, and sinew of the
mysticall body." The image of the body transfigures the church, from a
historical institution subject to the accidents of time, place, and human
foibles, to an integral living being founded in eternity and imbued with
truth.[7] Similarly, the body metaphor transforms "the people of *God*,"
whose redemption by "*Christs* blood" makes them into "*Christs* living
members."

The organic metaphor even alters the dimensionality of time. The
syntactic structure "thus then . . . but now" initiates a series of com-
parisons between past and present, but both are released from their
ordinary chronological values by the imagery with which each is char-
acterized. "Then" calls up not the historical past with its patristic
annotators and witnesses, but a seemingly timeless era that thrived be-
fore the spirit of the gospel had been formalized into a canonical text:
"Thus then did the Spirit of unity and meekness inspire, and animate
every joynt, and sinew of the mysticall body." Milton's suprarational
juxtaposition of the evanescent ("Spirit of unity and meekness") with

the explicitly concrete ("every joynt, and sinew") vividly reifies an otherwise intangible abstraction, "the mysticall body" of the primitive church. So reified, "the mysticall body" from the ideal past is kept fresh by successive confirming images—"redeem'd, and wash'd with *Christs* blood," "honour, and the almes due to *Christs* living members"—to operate as a perfect form against which images from a fallen present are tested.[8]

The contrasting vision of the "now" is delineated by increasingly homely, even vulgar particulars: "but now the gravest, and worthiest Minister . . . shall be revil'd, and ruffl'd . . . some slight paltry companion . . . impure ethnicks, and lay dogs; stones & Pillars, and Crucifixes . . . bulwark, and barricado . . . profane touch of the Laicks . . . obscene, and surfeted Priest . . . paw, and mammock . . . as familiarly as his Tavern Bisket." As ideal past alternates with fallen present, a rhythm is established: "then did the spirit . . . but now the gravest," "and the people of *God* redeem'd . . . are now no better reputed," "stones & Pillars, and Crucifixes have now the honour, and the almes." But as if to show how thoroughly temporal "then" and "now" have been redefined as moral "ideal" and "fallen," the alternating rhythms continue beyond all possible temporal connection without any loss of emphasis. In "Table of Communion now become a Table of separation," both terms of the comparison are chronologically in the present: "now" simply announces the immediate unmasking of hypocrisy, as the "exalted platforme" visually converts the "table of Communion" into its moral opposite, "a Table of separation." Then to complete the sentence, there is a climactic imagerial denouement. In the final manifestation of the image "mystical body," the symbolic body of Christ undergoes a mock transubstantiation. As with the table of communion, the true meaning of "the sacramentall bread" is vitiated right before our eyes: the image of "the obscene, and surfeted Priest" pawing and mammocking the sacramental bread visually converts the eucharist into "his Tavern Bisket."

Up to this point, Milton's images have been liberally filling up the scene, and their culmination in the minutely secular graphic detail of the priest's tavern biscuit has an interesting effect. The energetic populousness of all the preceding guarantees that, instead of narrowing the visual field, the single image of the tavern biscuit spontaneously infuses it with broad secularity. As the sacramental bread converts to a

tavern biscuit, so the setting of the church becomes the world epito-
mized by the tavern. Moreover, as the church and the sacrament are
secularized by the prelates, so are the people, whose conversion from
their Christian identity we now see has been in continual progress.
Originally portrayed as the true bishop's "fold," "the people of *God*,"
and "Saints, and sons in the Gospel," they have passed through their
prelatical repute as "impure ethnicks, and lay dogs" to "Laicks" with a
"profane touch." The perceptions and spirit of a secular world therefore
shape the people's conclusions, as signaled by the words that begin the
next sentence, "And thus":

And thus the people vilifi'd and rejected by them, give over the earnest study of
vertue, and godliness as a thing of greater purity then they need, and the search
of divine knowledge as a mystery too high for their capacity's, and only for
churchmen to meddle with, which is that the Prelates desire, that when they
have brought us back to Popish blindnesse we might commit to their dispose
the whole managing of our salvation, for they think it was never faire world
with them since that time. (548)

The people "thus . . . vilifi'd and rejected" are actually changed by
the labels that have been attached to them. Their pastoral simplicity
rescinded, they use cynical tavern wisdom to assess a world grown
morally ambiguous, where "vertue, and godlinesse" and "divine knowl-
edge" have all become as effete and manipulable as communion tables
and sacramental bread, things "only for Churchmen to meddle with."

The measured irony of "greater purity then they need" and "a mys-
tery too high for their capacity's" is both Milton's and the people's,
for irony permits a worldly comprehension that does not embrace. The
people's rejection of and by the bishops registers in the prelates' final
secularizing gesture, "that . . . we might commit to their dispose the
whole managing of our salvation." The commercial language "commit
to their dispose" and "managing" converts "our salvation" to a vendible
commodity. Milton's use of commercial imagery for religion will later
be richly expanded and subtly complicated in *Areopagitica*,[9] but here
the structures of moral accountability remain completely simple. Truth
is what we see. Predictably, therefore, Milton's visually simplistic rep-
resentation of prelatical evil allows for an equally simplistic portrayal
of its cure.

But he that will mould a modern Bishop into a primitive, must yeeld him to be elected by the popular voyce, undiocest, unrevenu'd, unlorded, and leave him nothing but brotherly equality, matchles temperance, frequent fasting, incessant prayer, and preaching, continual watchings, and labours in his Ministery. (548–49)

Milton's reversal of the prelates' secularizing conversions is a material stripping away of external form and substance: the modern bishop must be "undiocest, unrevenu'd, unlorded." In the place of substantial effects, Milton leaves only intangibles: attributes of character— "brotherly equality, matchles temperance"; and disciplinary habits and duties—"frequent fasting, incessant prayer, and preaching, continual watchings, and labours in his Ministery."

With this reassertion of the simplicities of the primitive church, we conclude a representation of the Christian myth on which Milton's moral perspective is premised: an original pristine landscape, here the primitive church, becomes corrupted and falls, then is shown the way of salvation. In purely Christian moral terms the scenario, barring an apocalypse, is complete. But in terms of its affective language, the scenario's return to simplicity is a decided falling off. Milton's stripping away of appearances creates an affective vacuum. Therefore, the final resurgence of prelatical imagery operates as if filling a void—an effect peculiarly enhanced by Milton's sustained syntactic structure:

which what a rich bootie it would be, what a plump endowment to the many-benefice-gaping mouth of a Prelate, what a relish it would give to his canary-sucking, and swan-eating palat, let old Bishop *Mountain* judge for me. (549)

The sensory anticipation raised by withholding completion of the clause "which . . . ," through the teasing hints of "what a rich . . . what a plump . . . what a relish," positively dishes up the antecedent "brotherly . . . ministry" to be engorged by the lip-smacking sibilants and masticating hyphens of "the many-benefice-gaping mouth" and "canary-sucking, and swan-eating palat." By the time we reach the end of the clause "which . . . ," the image of the gourmandizing prelate so precisely suits the pejorative nickname "old Bishop *Mountain*," that this authority whom Milton calls upon to "judge for me" is inescapably caught chomping the evidence.

THE SEDUCER SEDUCED

We may now fairly ask the question raised at the start of this analysis: what has happened to the claims of historical investigation, of rational argument? And the answer, not entirely facetious, is of course that the bishop ate them. For proof, we need only look at the sentence that immediately follows the richly sensory passage we have been studying: "How little therefore those ancient times make for moderne Bishops hath bin plainly discours'd." It has? What plain discourse? What can "therfore" possibly follow from? The gourmandizing scene we have just witnessed? What would it mean to try to draw logical inferences from that? A scenario like the foregoing wreaks havoc with the kind of deductive reasoning Milton invokes by his use of the word "therfore.1' With no more ceremony than the start of a new paragraph, Milton drops an entire level of discourse and resumes on a different plane.

The resulting discontinuity is unsettling in several ways. First, it is disorienting, because there seems to be no connection between what we read now and what has gone immediately before, despite the bald claim made by "therfore." Second, even if we sort out Milton's terms sufficiently to recognize that the "true Bishop" of the scenario might be somehow related to "those ancient times," while the scenario's "canary-sucking" prelate apparently belongs to the "modern bishops," we are still foiled by what follows:

but let them make for them as much as they will, yet why we ought not stand to their arbitrement shall now appear by a threefold corruption which will be found upon them. 1. The best times were spreadingly infected. 2. The best men of those times fouly tainted. 3. The best writings of those men dangerously adulterated. (549)

No help here: once we revert to the rational and historical level of discourse, the terms that had seemed so stable in Milton's imagerial world no longer apply. The vague pronoun references ("let them make for them as much as they will . . . their arbitrement . . . upon them") simply accentuate that fact: morally speaking, the "theys" and "thems" are all one, for in this newly reasserted historical world, even "ancient times" turn out to be unreliable and corrupt. Gone are the facile distinctions, the clear-cut moral types, the giveaway activities and appearances of brotherly laborers versus self-indulgent tavern-biscuit mammockers.

But perhaps most disturbing, in the long run, is an effect few readers of Milton's prose seem willing to admit, although I suspect many have felt it. It is the abrupt loss of reading pleasure. Milton's scenarios are always richly sensuous—the longer he goes, the more graphic he gets. And that's fun, sometimes comic, even captivating. But for that very reason, it is also peculiarly problematic. Milton's images lure us into an aesthetic experience that purports to embody moral truth. The effectiveness of that experience depends on criteria such as visual coherence, richness and suggestiveness of detail, symbolic resonance. All these rhetorical weapons can legitimately be conscripted by the prose artist to serve in the "wars of truth." But here, instead of serving the polemical task, they effectually compete with it. As we are drawn into the scenario by its sensory appeal, we may suppose that we are being given an illustration of the argument we have been reading; but our return to that argument once the scenario is complete shows us how mistaken we were. Repeatedly with Milton's antiprelatical imagery, we are swept up by the affective language, carried with it to a crescendo, and then unceremoniously dumped. No point of contention is illuminated by this maneuver, no comment on the historical citations is made. Instead of using affective language to convey the moral import of a rational argument, Milton actually draws us away from a rational argument which has no apparent moral dimension, only to involve us in a supposedly moral world which has no perceivable rational foundation. Once the affective pressure of Milton's metaphoric moral world reaches its climax, there is nothing left for him to do but to abandon sensory affect and pick up the rational, historical argument where he left off. So, at the conclusion of an exuberant imagerial passage, Milton simply stops; then he resumes his historical argument in precisely the same unruffled tone as had prevailed before his imagery got going: "How little therfore those ancient times make for moderne Bishops hath bin plainly discours'd." Milton gives no sign of recognizing the obvious non sequitur.

Milton's rhetorical inconsistency in the antiprelatical tracts has been variously interpreted. As Thomas Kranidas justly reminds us, Milton writes in the vanguard of a tradition of polemical vehemence derived ultimately from the Book of Revelation.[10] But even if we actually relish Milton's scurrility (and I argue that we do), we are distracted by it from his main argument. Neither does it much help our reading to follow J. Milton French or Edward LeComte in attributing Milton's gross images to satiric convention: rhetorically, even his nonscurrilous "poetic" images disrupt the flow of his argument.[11] Indeed, many readers recall from the antiprelatical tracts little *except* Milton's startling images: regardless of whether their origins are "high" or "low," the images come to vivid life seemingly independent of their argumentative context, which labors grimly, often obscurely, and endlessly behind them.

The divergence between Milton's ostensible rational argument and the affective rhetoric of his imagery has been variously interpreted. K. G. Hamilton sees the rhetorical ascendancy of Milton's figurative language as a failure of dialectic, "a complex but static expression of the strength of his own conviction, rather than either a reasoned statement or an imaginative apprehension of the basis of that conviction."[12] Stanley Fish, on the other hand, turns this supposed rhetorical stasis into a virtue. He finds that intentionally failed dialectic is just one of Milton's demonstrations of the insufficiency of rational processes as against regenerate intuition: "The prose and its forms are continually removing themselves from the reader's path of vision and leaving him face to face with Reality."[13] But a more jaundiced view of Milton's "Reality" is conveyed by Keith Stavely: "A writer whose goal is to see in the prejudices of his audience the human expression of divine wrath has no need for logical procedure or even for elegant rhetorical planning. He need only convince his audience, by the devices of diction, imagery, and syntax . . . that their hostilities do indeed partake of the grandeur of God's wrath."[14] To Stavely, Milton's imagery of wrath serves only to work up a rhetorical frenzy—"to approximate a tone of saintly zeal" that needlessly supersedes Milton's "relatively sober and restrained" critique of "a sociological phenomenon, the behavior patterns of upwardly-mobile clerics."[15]

Although Milton's interest in such clerics was hardly informed by the kinds of concerns we would call "sociological," Stavely makes a valid point. We may find ways of justifying Milton's affective language as such, but that does little to explain his discontinuous rhetorical handling of it. And as to satire theories, Milton may consciously employ satiric techniques, but he is not writing satire, nor does he finally share the aims of the satirist. For instance, he does not, despite certain ringing denunciations, strike the Juvenalian stance of the solitary prophet lashing at the sins of the world. Neither does he formally engage the Horatian mode, and jestingly lampoon his antagonists "all for the grim amusement of his circle."[16] However disillusioned with men and their causes Milton may become, his writings never show him seeking solace in the urbane discourse of the worldly resigned. The sophisticated pose of the Augustan satirist is far too secular, too morally and spiritually detached to suit Milton.

Nevertheless, with the satiric assumptions of French and LeComte, or the historical ones of Kranidas, we may ourselves remain enough detached to enjoy the images for their own sake as artistic and intellectual creations. By joining Fish's highly committed ideal readers, on the other hand, we may ultimately include ourselves among the ranks of the saved. Or, with Stavely we may use modern psychosocial assumptions to expose Milton's supposedly more pretentious millennialist ones. But none of these approaches directly confronts Milton's penchant for purveying affective power as moral truth. Neither do they account for the sudden rhetorical shifts from Milton's imagery back to his rational argument, away from which, whether willingly or reluctantly, we have permitted ourselves to be seduced.

Not that we ought to resist the seduction. In fact, I suggest that our experience with the rhetoric of the antiprelatical tracts is not unlike Milton's own. Writing these tracts is a Milton who, at this stage in his literary career, quite ingenuously equates moral conviction with affective intensity; a Milton who, in his poetic and religious desire to realize Truth as it were "on the pulses," finds the cool rationality of his intended polemical task too enervating for such realization. Rhetorically speaking, the fundamental impulse in the antiprelatical tracts is neither against the prelates nor in favor of the presbyterians, but toward the linguistically and affectively sensuous. For Milton, at this point, *there lies Truth.*[17]

But even if we accept the equating of sensuousness with Truth, there remain rhetorical anomalies in the antiprelatical tracts. Occasionally Milton's impulse toward the sensuous so intrudes upon the rational argument that it inconveniences the author himself. Something like this happens when, in *Of Reformation*, he confronts the historical fact of martyrdom in the persons of Cranmer, Latimer, and Ridley, the bishops whose sufferings had so memorably been narrated in Foxe's Protestant martyrology, *The Actes and Monuments* (1576).[18] Milton's ill-timed pejoratives on the martyrs clash with the inopportune historical facts of their sufferings to produce a virtual tug-of-war for affective precedence.[19] As a responsible historian, Milton must acknowledge the fact of the bishops' martyrdom, which he does. But once this is admitted into the argument, rhetorical difficulties arise. For, almost uniquely among Milton's historical facts, the fact of martyrdom has potential affective power. We find that power operating even in Milton's own attempt at a casual dismissal: "What then? . . . He is not therfore above all possibility of erring, because hee burnes for some Points of Truth." This statement, instead of diminishing, actually elucidates martyrdom's stark drama: the meticulousness of Milton's sarcastic "some Points" contrasts with and intensifies the resonant, graphic "hee burnes." Thus a fact like martyrdom subtly intrudes upon the affective phase of Milton's impeachment of the bishops. In effect, the rhetoric of history actually competes here with the affective appeal of Milton's rhetoric of Truth. So Milton's rhetorical task becomes twofold. He must first of all somehow diffuse the affective power of the bishops' martyrdom. But at the same time, he must also find new terms for dealing with these people, whose recorded history militates against his predisposition to reduce them, by his imagery, to a caricature of their moral failings. This accomplished, he is free to unleash a sensuously compelling display of conviction: the passage on the bishops eventually develops into one of the most stunning scenarios in the tract.

All of this comes about through a complicated series of maneuvers. The passage begins early in *Of Reformation* as Milton's historical investigation finds the bishops personally responsible for the wrongs they have participated in or condoned.

And for the *Bishops*, they were so far from any such worthy Attempts, as that they suffer'd themselves to be the common stales to countenance with their prostituted Gravities every Politick Fetch that was then on foot, as oft as the Potent *Statists* pleas'd to employ them. . . . If a Toleration for *Masse* were to be beg'd of the King for his Sister MARY . . . who but the grave Prelates *Cranmer* and *Ridley* must be sent to extort it from the young King? . . . When the Protectors Brother, Lord *Sudley*, the Admirall through private malice, and mal-engine was to lose his life, no man could bee found fitter than Bishop *Latimer* (like another Doctor Shaw) to divulge in his Sermon the forged Accusations laid to his charge thereby to defame him with the People. (530–33)

Considering that he is arguing here on the historical level, Milton's language is surprisingly vivid ("common stales . . . prostituted Gravities . . . Potent *Statists*"), conferring the kind of affective intensity that characterizes his moral sphere. Indeed, as the investigation continues, we discover that this language and its intensity depend on Milton's narrowly limiting the selection of historical materials. In purely historical terms, such anomalies as time-serving prelates who also happened to become martyrs are humanly credible. But this kind of ambiguity makes for indifferent imagery. Conversely, Milton's facile caricature of the bishops as "common stales" with prostituted gravities" cannot sustain the contradictory extra dimension implied by their martyrdom. Therefore, as soon as the bishops' martyrdom is admitted onto the scene, Milton hastens to explain it away with a digression on the meaning of martyrdom. By the end of this digression, Cranmer, Latimer, and Ridley have been transformed from corrupt and powerful historical figures into mere puppets, while the entire burden of moral culpability is shifted from the bishops to a rhetorically more convenient abstraction—"episcopacy."[20]

The shift of responsibility begins with the first mention of the bishops' martyrdom: "But it will be said, these men were martyrs." With the instinctive immediacy of a defensive reflex, Milton makes a sharp retort: "what then?" Then, the digressive redefinition gets under way: "Though every true Christian will be a *Martyr* when he is called to it; not presently does it follow that everyone suffering for Religion, is without exception." As Milton mounts his supporting arguments against inclusive ascriptions of martyrdom as a concept, the historical martyrdoms of Cranmer, Latimer, and Ridley recede from the argumentative frame:

Saint Paul writes, that *A man may give his Body to be burnt . . . yet not have Charitie:* He is not therfore above all possibility of erring, because hee burnes for some Points of Truth.

Witness the Arians and Pelagians which were slaine by the Heathen for

Christs sake; yet we take both these for no true friends of Christ. If the *Martyrs* (saith *Cyprian* in his 30. Epistle) decree one thing, and the *Gospel* another, either the *Martyrs* must lose their Crowne by not observing the *Gospel* for which they are Martyrs; or the Majestie of the *Gospel* must be broken and lie flat, if it can be overtopt by the *novelty* of any other *Decree*. (533–35)

Milton impugns martyrdom on doctrinally valid grounds: martyrs do not make Truth, they only witness it. And as the passage continues, he makes it clear that it is only man's idolatry that would limit Truth to such "ignominious bondage," the witness of the historical martyr. But martyrdom's proper place in Christian doctrine is in this instance only a secondary concern. More pressing is Milton's need to weaken the affective impact of the martyrdom of Cranmer, Latimer, and Ridley. Therefore, instead of simply dismissing the bishops' martyrdom as he had seemed about to do ("what then?"), Milton awkwardly belabors the issue. He attenuates martyrdom's emotional appeal by conjuring up the disreputable Arians and Pelagians, by reductively labeling martyrdom a "novelty," and then by quoting Gospel—and also, interestingly, Cyprian, who was himself a bishop, and a martyr. Finally (somewhat desperately?) Milton undercuts the presumed sanctity of the martyr's witness (the Greek stem μαρτυρ means "witness") by arrogating *to himself* the ultimate Witness:

And heerewithall I invoke the *Immortall* DEITIE *Reveler* and *Judge* of Secrets, That wherever I have in this BOOKE plainely and roundly (though worthily and truly) laid open the faults and blemishes of *Fathers, Martyrs,* or Christian *Emperors;* or have otherwise inveighed against Error and Superstition with vehement Expressions: I have done it, neither out of malice, nor list to speak evill, nor any vaine-glory; but of meere necessity, to vindicate the spotlesse *Truth* from an ignominious bondage, whose native worth is now become of such low esteeme, that shee is like to finde small credit with us for what she can say, unlesse shee can bring a Ticket from *Cranmer, Latimer,* and *Ridley;* or prove her selfe a retainer to *Constantine,* and weare his *badge.* More tolerable it were for the *Church* of GOD that all these Names were utterly abolisht, like the *Brazen Serpent;* then that mens fond opinion should thus idolize them, and the Heavenly *Truth* be thus captivated. (535)

Aside from overriding the authority of the martyrs' witness, Milton's linguistic act of invocation automatically subverts whatever vestige may remain of the morally neutral terms of historical argument. Any words that are to be witnessed by "the *Immortall* DEITIE *Reveler* and *Judge* of Secrets" will necessarily conform to the moral polarities of a theocentric universe. Conveniently, this shift of rhetorical level also facilitates for Milton the kind of "surgical" procedure that is ordinarily the prerogative of the satirist: he can now "[lay] open the faults and blemishes of *Fathers, Martyrs,* or Christian *Emperors.*" That is, moral errors will henceforth be treated as if they were the bishops' corporeal flaws, abscesses rather than integral qualities of character. This is the sort of physical assault on a moral problem that provides an almost visceral satisfaction in the metaphoric realm of moral truth, while in Milton's historical realm it would be ludicrous. Here, the "surgery" is made possible because the invocation simply cancels the claims of the historical realm. We see no longer a world of men and events, but of abstractions. Error and Superstition are the new objects of Milton's wrath, while the bishops become mere traffickers in spiritual commodities: "Truth . . . is like to finde small credit with us for what she can say, unlesse shee can bring a Ticket from *Cranmer, Latimer,* and *Ridley.*" By the final sentence of the paragraph, these three have been reduced to no more than verbal signs of themselves, "Names": "More tolerable it were for the Church of GOD that all these Names were utterly abolisht, like the *Brazen Serpent;* then that mens fond opinion should thus idolize them, and the Heavenly *Truth* be thus captivated." Already distanced as off-stage ticket dispensers, the bishops are now fairly obliterated by the prominent and opposing images of the Brazen Serpent, and Heavenly Truth in captivity.

With the end of the digression on martyrdom the historical argument resumes. As it does, we find it divested of all its troublesome affective properties, whether good or evil. This reassertion of moral neutrality in the historical realm not only conserves affective resources for the imagery that lies ahead, but for Milton's purposes it now sufficiently dissociates the bishops from the affectively compelling epithets they had acquired ("prostituted Gravities," etc.) in the rather less strategical earlier passage. This makes them presently available to new, quite contrary definitions in Milton's realm of Truth.[21] Moral and affective reconfigurations now firmly in place, Milton actually announces ("Now to proceed") that he can once again take up his dealings with the bishops:

Now to proceed, whatsoever the *Bishops* were, it seemes they themselves were unsatisfi'd in matters of *Religion*, as they then stood, by that Commission granted to 8. *Bishops*, 8. other *Divines*, 8. *Civilians*, 8. *Common Lawyers*, to frame *Ecclesiasticall Constitutions;* which no wonder if it came to nothing; for (as *Hayward* relates) both their Professions and their Ends were different. Lastly, we all know by Examples, that exact *Reformation* is not perfited at the first push, and those unweildy Times of *Edward* 6. may hold some Plea by this excuse. (535–36)

The rational detachment Milton now brings to the historical realm virtually absolves the bishops of the moral responsibility he had once been so concerned to lay upon them. "Whatsoever the *Bishops* were" declares, in effect, that neither historical nor moral evidence for or against the bishops has much bearing on the question: it would have been nearly impossible for them to succeed with church reformation anyway—the times were difficult, the task onerous. Only as Milton's rhetoric begins to shift once more from the historical to the moral and affective level do we discover that he has actually redirected his attack. As the paragraph moves forward, historical events become gradually more vague and generalized, while the moral and spiritual dimension expands and polarizes. Accelerated references to *"Episcopacie"* identify and call attention to the new enemy, while the bishops reemerge from their historical obscurity as reconstituted but radically simplified beings.

Now let any reasonable man judge whether that *Kings Reigne* be a fit time from whence to patterne out the Constitution of a *Church Discipline,* much lesse that it should yeeld occasion from whence to foster and establish the continuance of Imperfection with the commendatory subscriptions of *Confessors* and *Martyrs,* to intitle and ingage a glorious *Name* to a grosse *corruption.* It was not *Episcopacie* that wrought in them the Heavenly Fortitude of *Martyrdome;* as little is it that *Martyrdome* can make good *Episcopacie:* But it was *Episcopacie* that led the good and holy Men through the temptation of the *Enemie,* and the snare of this present world to many blame-worthy and opprobrious *Actions.* (536)

From the historically tangible setting defined by morally neutral language—the "constitution of a *Church Discipline*" in the reign of Edward VI—the scene broadens through polarities ("glorious *Name* . . .

grosse *corruption,*" "Heavenly Fortitude . . . temptation of the *Enemie*"|
to a dualistic universe, abstract and morally absolute. "Episcopacy" is
the primary agent now, while the bishops themselves are mindless fol-
lowers, men "good and holy" and capable of fortitude, but apparently
innocent of exercising either individual will or moral choice. Evil acts
are "many," "blameworthy and opprobrious," but unidentified. Sensu-
ous detail, completely severed from the empirical moorings of histori-
cal checks and specificity, finds in this abstract moral realm a freedom
and independent vitality that enable it to build to the startling climax.

And it is still *Episcopacie* that before all our eyes worsens and sluggs the most
learned, and seeming religious of our *Ministers,* who no sooner advanc't to it,
but like a seething pot set to coole, sensibly exhale and reake out the greatest
part of that zeale, and those Gifts which were formerly in them, settling in a
skinny congealment of ease and sloth at the top: and if they keep their Learn-
ing by some potent sway of Nature, 'tis a rare chance; but their *devotion* most
commonly comes to that queazy temper of luke-warmnesse, that gives a Vomit
to GOD himself. (536–37)

"Before all our eyes" is exactly where Milton's affective rhetoric can
flourish.[22] By subordinating the rational claims of the historical argu-
ment to the suprarational claims of his polarized and theocentric moral
universe, Milton once more creates a sensory apprehension of Truth.
Instead of historical bishops engaged in historically verifiable acts,
the sensuous details achieve something closer to what Milton argues
are the products of episcopacy: manipulable, "luke-warm" bishops.
Yet sensuous as are its details, the scene never becomes only these.
It is simultaneously abstract and concrete: *"Episcopacie"* and "before
all our eyes." Reiterated sibilants and rhymes reinforce this simulta-
neity: "seeming religious" and "seething pot," "reake out" and "zeale,"
"skinny congealment" and "ease and sloth." Finally, the most famil-
iarly homely concrete detail is juxtaposed with the most exalted ab-
straction. And that which forces juxtaposition of these extremes is
the image of Milton's episcopized ministers, whose consequent "luke-
warmnesse . . . gives a Vomit to GOD himselfe." This final image elicits
from Milton's readers an interesting complex of responses, as attested
by the range of comments in the critical canon. At once we feel embar-
rassment for a multilevel breach of decorum: it startles every sublime

image we have of God to find him not only in the kitchen but sick there; and it further unnerves expectations of literary propriety for a great poet to create such a scene. At the same time as the image offends, however, it compels with its sensuous pleasurability. It is richly iconoclastic, grossly humorous, memorable. The sense of decorum thus violated is what Milton would identify as the idolatrous decorum of the lukewarm bishops. The scene produces a carnal effect the iconoclast in Milton could only relish.[23]

The image of God vomiting is clearly a *succès de scandale*. More than any other, it is this scene that critics refer to when they protest Milton's scurrility—a fact clearly anticipated by Milton, since he prepares for it with a prefatory disclaimer: "And heerewithall I invoke the *Immortall* DEITIE . . . That wherever I have . . . inveighed against Error and Superstition with vehement Expressions: I have done it . . . of meere necessity, to vindicate the spotlesse *Truth* from an ignominious bondage" (535). This apologetic "invocation"—really an oath—is often (dubiously) cited by critics as Milton's attempt to justify his strong language. Perhaps Milton liked to believe that it *did* justify him, but in any case, the critical reception shows that the expedient failed. Moreover, Milton's single-minded pursuit of linguistic sensuousness in the present passage suggests that he didn't much care whether his readers accepted the self-justification or not. We have seen that he went to a good deal of trouble to make the conditions right for creating the image of God retching over the bishops—that, having prematurely caricatured Cranmer, Latimer, and Ridley in a manner that would prove inconsistent with some of the facts yet to be treated, Milton found himself obliged to reshuffle his moral charges in the interest of an even better caricature. If this is indeed what happened, we may well ask, why did Milton make such an injudicious move in the first place? Why did he proceed with name-calling that he later would only have to retract, or at least cover for? And I think the most plausible answer is that he simply could not resist. His desire was to create what *felt* like Truth, and at the moment he wrote of the bishops' "prostituted gravities," that image fulfilled his desire. As the disjointed argumentative levels of the antiprelatical tracts show, Milton's rhetorical concern in them is often with local effects. When he discovers an occasion for inserting or developing a rich image, he exploits it with little regard for its rhetorical connections before and after. If this results in contradictions, as it does in his treatment of the bishops, so be it. His instinct for forceful expression of conviction leads him indiscriminately to accept forcefulness as a test of validity: if it *feels strong*, it *must* be True.

SAVING CARNAL RHETORIC

Championship of affective Truth entails peculiar risks. If Milton's animus against the bishops is so intense that it spontaneously manufactures occasions to break forth, we might surely expect the same of his passion for the cause he favors. But we cannot. For instance, Milton's effort to portray the millennial certitude of modern-day Saints is as troubled a passage as can be found anywhere in the antiprelatical tracts. It occurs in *Animadversions*, where contentious evocation of a grimy polemical "present age" points up the difficulty of realizing and maintaining millennial vision. In his desire to reify this eternal and theocentric ideal, Milton detaches his argument from its historical context, only to find himself casting about for other ways to explain reformation's failure in the present age.

The problem develops after Milton's opponent in *Animadversions*, the self-styled Humble Remonstrant, tries to dismiss reformist objections to episcopacy as newfangled querulousness: "They cannot name any man in this Nation that ever contradicted *Episcopacie*, till this present Age" (703). A statement like this one challenges the millennialist regarding a point on which, in chiliastic terms, he ought to be strongest: to justify his view of episcopal authority, the millennialist needs only to invoke the authority of divine revelation. In nonchiliastic terms, however, the millennialist turns out to be quite vulnerable: the Remonstrant and his cohorts need only refer to historical fact. With the two sides speaking, then, what amounts to two different languages (the one temporal, the other eternal), the possibilities for coherent argument or rational discourse are curtailed. Therefore, Milton's rebuttal of the Remonstrant's charges must simultaneously engage the terms of the temporal "enemy" (that, after all, is the purpose of the tract), and also operate as if, in the ultimate scheme of things, these terms do not matter.

The contradictoriness of Milton's position is borne out in the ensuing passage. First, he must defend the millenarian reformers against the implication that they themselves, no less than the episcopists, are merely historical and temporal opportunists instead of chosen instruments of God. He begins by situating the episcopal argument among the exhausted and diseased carnal effects of every other putatively "temporal" doctrine:

What an over-worne and bedrid Argument is this, the last refuge ever of old falshood, and therefore a good signe I trust that your Castle cannot hold out long. This was the plea of *Judaisme*, and Idolatry against *Christ* and his *Apostles*, of *Papacie* against Reformation: and perhaps to the frailty of flesh and blood in a man destitute of better enlight'ning, may for some while bee pardonable; for what has fleshly apprehension other to subsist by then Succession, Custome, and Visibility, which onely hold if in his weaknesse and blindnesse he be loath to lose, who can blame? (703)

The pretense of sympathy for a weakened opponent affords the millennialist a rhetorical stance that seems, in the immediate context, to be physically robust and morally confident. From this superior position, Milton then seizes the Remonstrant's term "present age" and employs it as a cutting edge, radically to separate the Remonstrant's realm from that of the millenarians:

But in a *Protestant* Nation that should have thrown off these tatter'd Rudiments long agoe, after the many strivings of Gods Spirit, and our fourscore yeares vexation of him in this our wildernesse since Reformation began, to urge these rotten Principles, and twit us with the present age, which is to us an age of ages wherein God is manifestly come downe among us, to doe some remarkable good to our Church or state, is as if a man should taxe the renovating and re-ingendring Spirit of God with innovation, and that new creature for an upstart noveltie; yea the new Jerusalem, which without your admired linke of succession descends from Heaven, could not scape some such like censure. (703)

Whereas the "present age" for the Remonstrant is simply the current experience of a continuing history, the millennialists' "present age" is a fulfillment of prophecy, an age "*which is to us* an age of ages wherein God is manifestly come downe among us" (my emphasis).

The moral and rhetorical alignment of these two realms Milton makes readily apparent: on the side of the Remonstrant we have falsehood, Judaism, Idolatry, Papacy, flesh and blood frailty, fleshly apprehension, Succession, Custom, Visibility, weaknesse, blindnesse, tatter'd Rudiments, rotten Principles. On the side of the millenarians are Christ and his Apostles, Reformation, Protestant Nation, God's Spirit, God manifest, remarkable good, renovating and re-ingendering Spirit of God, new Jerusalem, Heaven. In an illuminating discussion of *Reason of Church Government*, Stanley Fish shows how the judgment implicit in such opposing lists pressures the reader to align himself with the millenarian reformists. In fact, Fish accommodates the recurrent disjunctions between the two rhetorics of the antiprelatical tracts by brilliantly finessing the tedious historical and rational argument over to the side of the prelates, leaving the spiritual rectitude of Milton's imagery of Truth to be embraced by the self-redeeming reader. Fish's strategy is appropriate, because that is precisely what Milton himself does here.

But the present passage exposes a difficulty with Fish's analysis. The reader may well reject, as Milton does, the cumbersome and static rational argument, but that action does not automatically entail rejection of the prelates: there are, after all, prelates on both of Milton's argumentative levels, and we have seen that the force of their presence depends on the rhetorical use Milton wishes to make of them. In Milton's realm of Truth, in fact, the prelates may be manipulable, but they are definitely not dispensable. The polarized dynamic that vitalizes Milton's metaphoric moral realm in the antiprelatical tracts actively *requires* an enemy. To see why this should be so, we need only read again through the opposing lists gleaned from *Reason of Church Government* and set forth by Stanley Fish. First, on the side of the prelates:

gross, patched, varnished, embellishings, veil, sumptuous, tradition, show, visibility, polluted, idolatrous, Gentilish rites, ceremonies, feather, bravery, hide, deformed, plumes, pomp, flesh, outward, ceremonial law, delusions, particolored, mimic, custom, specious, sophistical, names, fallacy, mask, dividing, schismatical, forked, disfigurement, Egyptian, overcloud, scales, false, glitter, beads, art, sweet, dim, reflection, fleshly wisdom, garb, defaced, overcasting, copes, vestures, gold robes, surplices, adorn, corporeal resemblances, clothing, maskers, gaudy glisterings, delude, carnal, high, sensual, fermentations, worldly, external, flourishes, counterfeit, crafty, artificial, appearance, outward man, skin, defile, ignorance, pride, temples, carpets, tablecloth, slimy, confections, profane, faulty, false-whited, gilded, vanities, dross, scum, luggage, infection, formal outside, greasy, brazen, temporal, oil over, besmear, corrupt, shadow, darkened, obscured.

And now, on the side of the reformists:

plainly, clearness, eternal, invariable, inspired, open, spiritual eye, inward, plain, clear, evident, pure, spiritual, simple, lowly, internal, faith, homogeneous, even, firm, united, truth, steadfastness, perfection, unity, seamless, unchangeable, constancy, light, sacred, illumination, luster, inspiration, revelation, eye-brightening, inward prompting, divine, bright, belief, common sense, simplicity, clear evidence, naked, inward holiness, inward beauty, bareness, lowliness, purity of Doctrine, wisdom of God, glory, enlightened, true knowledge, holy, cleansed, health, purge, God's word.[24]

Of the two lists, we can have little doubt that the second is the one with which we are supposed to align ourselves. But it is the first that is concretely interesting to read. Indeed, the elements of list number two are so spiritual, so abstract and ineffable that their rhetorical effectiveness depends on juxtaposition with their worldly, fleshly opposites in list number one. An exhortation toward list two without an attendant warning away from list one would make pallid oratory. In contrast with the haphazard human and institutional alliances of Milton's historical realm, the self-polarizing elements of his metaphoric moral realm absolutely require one another, both for moral definition and for affective intensity. Thus, to affirm Milton's Truth is really to affirm the polarities that bring it to life—that is, to affirm or give our "fervent witness" to *both* lists. And, as the polarities are formulated largely in sensory rather than in rational terms, the verities they so affirm are not rational but affective. In other words, what the "self-redeeming" reader embraces in the antiprelatical tracts is the entire panoply of sensuous language—here, Milton's Truth *is* his carnal rhetoric.

To some degree, of course, this is Milton's point: it is precisely because our eyes are darkened and our sensibilities are fallen that the Word's only access to us is through our carnal apprehension. But that premise, as we find on returning to *Animadversions*, has a double edge.

If a sensuous apprehension of Truth requires that the reader—or the author—be compelled to enlist himself among the adherents to one side of a set of oppositions, it will clearly be necessary to keep both sides in view. So long as Milton keeps a sharp eye on prelatical evil, his sense of conviction maintains its impetus: whatever it is he believes in, it visibly cannot be *that*. For some Milton scholars, most notably Thomas Kranidas and Kester Svendsen, the strength of Milton's pejorative imagery lies in its capacity to imply its opposite even where the positive vision is wanting: from disease, we are to infer health; from disproportion and disorder, order and unity; and so forth.[25] As a general principle for assessing Milton's moral polarities, this works quite well, although in the local instance we may be hard pressed to imagine the opposite of a bishop-sick God. But as Fish's study shows, we need not speculate about Milton's positive vision—the language is there. It's just that, as we've seen, such language gives us almost nothing to look at. So, sensibilities earth-bound and ever carnal, we are apt to forget.

And in our carnality we are not alone. As Milton works his way into the millennial vision of *Animadversions*, his effort to relinquish the supporting carnal rhetoric of antiprelatical imagery leads him anxiously to appeal for a more and more concrete, sensuously apprehensible response from God. In his contemptuous rejoinder to the Remonstrant ("What an over-worne and bedrid Argument is this"), Milton shows no sign of recognizing that a world bereft of prelates might turn out to be less than stable. But there are hints nevertheless. Between and around the self-polarizing elements that make up the two lists in this passage—falsehood, idolatry, Custome, as against Christ, remarkable good, new Jerusalem—there lie other elements that resist easy alignment. If contrary interpretations of "the present age" measure the moral and rhetorical distance between "you" the Remonstrant and "us" the reformists, who is responsible for "our fourscore years' vexation of him [Gods Spirit] in this our wildernesse"? Does this "our" refer to the same group of people as those who "should have throwne off these tatter'd Rudiments long agoe," the citizens of "a *Protestant* Nation"? Perhaps Milton's shift in pronouns for the Remonstrant ("your Castle . . . his weaknesse and blindnesse . . . your admired linke of succession" should warn us against too rigorous an assignment of responsibilities, but it is hard not to see in "our fourscore years' vexation of him" implicit chastising of the reformers themselves. Indeed, once Milton dismisses the Remonstrant, he turns a more critical eye toward the reformers. But in dismissing the Remonstrant Milton does more than just quit an adversary. He openly abandons the already segregated ("the present age") temporal level of discourse. Polemical debate is reduced to a circuit of petty quarrelsomeness—"If you require a further answer . . . in stead of other answer . . . not caring otherwise to answer this un-Protestantlike Objection"; and the Remonstrant is left solidly in the middle of it: "leaving this Remonstrant and his adherents to their owne designes."

Theoretically, all that should be left to do is evoke the millenarian alternative: the eternal realm of Truth, populated by the enlightened, "every true protested *Brittaine*." At first, it looks like that is exactly what Milton is going to do, as he illuminates "the present age" in terms of the long awaited reform:

in this Age, *Brittains* God hath reform'd his Church after many hundred years of *Popish* corruption; in this Age hee hath freed us from the intolerable yoke of *Prelats,* and *Papall* Discipline; in this age he hath renewed our *Protestation* against all those yet remaining dregs of superstition: Let us all goe every true protested *Brittaine* throughout the 3. *Kingdoms,* and render thanks to God the Father of light, and fountaine of heavenly grace, and to his son CHRIST our Lord; leaving this *Remonstrant* and his adherents to their owne designes. (704)

"*Brittains* God hath reform'd . . . hee hath freed . . . he hath renewed." These lines clearly express the conviction that God is present, working now among the faithful. But it should be noted, too, that these confident lines are spiked with "*Popish* corruption," "the intolerable yoke of *Prelats*," "*Papall* Discipline," and "dregs of superstition." Nevertheless, as the faithful depart to render thanks for God's favor, they leave all this behind. What follows, we might presume, should be the promised hymn of praise. It is not. Instead, there follows a more painstaking rehearsal of these reforming acts of Britain's God, and this time the scene of reform is portrayed without benefit of the easy targets of pope and prelate:

Let us recount even here without delay the patience and long suffering that God hath us'd towards our blindnesse and hardnes time after time. For he being equally neere to his whole Creation of mankind, and of free power to turne his benefick and fatherly regard to what Region or Kingdome he pleases, hath yet ever had this Iland under the speciall indulgent eye of his providence; and pittying us the first of all other Nations, after he had decreed to purifie and renew his Church that lay wallowing in Idolatrous pollutions, sent first to us a healing messenger to touch softly our sores, and carry a gentle hand over our wounds; he knockt once and twice and came againe, opening our drousie eye-lids leasurely by that glimmering light which *Wicklef*, and his followers dispers't, and still taking off by degrees the inveterat scales from our nigh perisht sight, purg'd also our deaf eares, and prepar'd them to attend his second warning trumpet in our Grandsires dayes. How else could they have been able to have receiv'd the sudden assault of his reforming Spirit warring against humane Principles, and carnall sense, the pride of flesh that still cry'd up Antiquity, Custome, Canons, Councels and Lawes, and cry'd down the truth for noveltie, schisme, profanenesse and Sacriledge: when as we that have liv'd so long in abundant light, besides the sunny reflection of all the neighbouring Churches, have yet our hearts rivetted with those old opinions, and so obstructed and benumm'd with the same fleshly reasonings, which in our forefathers soone melted and gave way, against the morning beam of *Reformation*. (704–5)

By the end of this recapitulation of God's works among the faithful, we find that the very faults hitherto charged against the prelates are now brought to bear on the reformers themselves. Now it is "*our* blindnesse and hardnes," *our* nation's church "wallowing in Idolatrous pollutions," the "inveterat scales" cover *our* sight, and *our* ears are deaf. Despite the best examples of neighboring churches, we "have yet *our* hearts rivetted with those old opinions," those same "humane Principles, and carnall sense, the pride of flesh that still cry'd up Antiquity, Custome, Canons, Councels and Lawes"; we yet remain "obstructed and benumm'd with the same fleshly reasonings" (my italics). Fleshly reasonings, old opinions, pride of flesh, human principles—all are "the same." But without the prelates, the rhetorical effects of these charges are not the same. For, it seems, Milton's true protested Britons are favored by a patient and long-suffering God: they are watched by his "speciall indulgent eye"; idolatrous pollutions are transformed by a "healing messenger" into "sores . . . wounds"; it is possible that our nigh perished sight may be due merely to "drousie eye-lids."

But this mitigating of charges, however salvational for the reformers, acts to weaken the impetus of Milton's affective rhetoric. Instead of building toward a display of millennial conviction, such as his attacks on the prelates have always produced, Milton's critique of the reformers leaves his millennial vision practically in shreds. Everywhere else in *Animadversions*, Milton's reference to the reformist "we" implies a cohesive body of like-minded visionaries. But without the prelatical foil, the reformist "we" disintegrates under Milton's own moral scrutiny: if fleshly reasonings gave way so readily in our forefathers, he asks, how can we, benefiting from the light of their example, still remain so hardened? Have we, who are to fulfill their expectations, so much less virtue than they? *Are* we what we claim?

If God hath left undone this whole worke so contrary to flesh and blood, till these times, how should we have yeelded to his heavenly call, had we beene taken, as they were, in the starknes of our ignorance, that yet after all these spirituall preparatives, and purgations have our earthly apprehensions so clamm'd, and furr'd with the old levin. O if we freeze at noone after their earely thaw, let us feare lest the Sunne for ever hide himselfe, and turne his orient steps from our ingratefull Horizon justly condemn'd to be eternally benighted. (705)

What had started out to be a prayer of thanks has evolved through critical self-examination into an increasingly anxious questioning of the reformists' capacities to sustain their millennial expectations. We may recall the triumphant voice with which Milton had initially turned away from his opponent:

If you require a further answer, it will not misbecome a Christian to bee either more magnanimous, or more devout than *Scipio* was, who in stead of other answer to the frivolous accusations of *Petilius* the *Tribune; This day Romans* (saith he) I *fought with* Hanibal *prosperously; let us all go and thank the gods that gave us so great a victory.* (703–4)

But by the time Milton actually begins to frame his address to God, his tone has altered considerably: his prayer takes the form not of praise and gratitude, but of entreaty. By Milton's own analysis, the frivolous accusation of the Remonstrant could be right on target: the millennialists might well be "justly condemn'd to be eternally benighted."

From this prospect, Milton recoils violently: "which dreadfull judgement O thou the ever-begotten light, and perfect Image of the Father, intercede may never come upon us." Then his language begins, at first tentatively ("as we trust thou hast"), then with gradually increasing assurance ("thou hast opened . . . and given us . . . thou hast done justice"), to piece together the fragile elements of his vision of the millennium. But at the same time—as perhaps we might have anticipated—his gradual movement toward positive vision is accompanied by the return of an increasingly palpable, clearly nonreformist enemy:

Which dreadful Judgement O thou the ever-begotten light, and perfect Image of the Father, intercede may never come upon us, as we trust thou hast; for thou hast open'd our difficult and sad times, and given us an unexpected breathing after our long oppressions; thou hast done justice upon those that tyranniz'd over us, while some men waver'd, and admir'd a vaine shadow of wisedome in a tongue nothing slow to utter guile, though thou hast taught us to admire onely that which is good, and to count that onely praise-worthy which is grounded upon thy divine Precepts. Thou hast discover'd the plots, and frustrated the hopes of all the wicked in the Land; and put to shame the persecutors of thy Church; thou hast made our false *Prophets* to be found a lie in the sight of all the people, and chac'd them with sudden confusion and amazement before the redoubled brightnesse of the descending cloud that now covers thy Tabernacle. (705)

With this, the already weakened charges against the reformers are further diffused in the context of "our difficult and sad times," then excused by recalling "our long oppressions" under "those that tyranniz'd over us." A residue of reformist error may be admitted in the words "while some men waver'd . . . though thou hast taught us to admire onely that which is good." But with resurrection of the enemy (oppressors, tyrants, a tongue uttering guile, plotters, "the wicked," "persecutors," "false *Prophets*"), the reformists can once more be unambiguously aligned on the side of God, whose accomplishments can also therefore be celebrated with renewed vigor: "Thou hast discover'd the plots, and frustrated the hopes of all the wicked . . . put to shame the persecutors . . . thou hast made our false *Prophets* to be found a lie . . . chac'd them with sudden confusion and amazement."

In Milton's initial recapitulation of God's works among the English reformers, millennial vision had been threatened by historical fact: recollection of Wycliffe and his followers had put present-day reformers to shame; presumption of God's constant reforming activity had been baffled by the apparent blindness and hardness of protestant hearts. But as the return of an external enemy once more permits moral polarities, historical reality is left behind, and God's works among men may be conceived in more and more absolute terms: from the uncertainty of "while some men wavered," the assertions progress to God's unqualified discovery and frustration of "*all* the wicked in the land," his finding false prophets a lie "in the sight of *all* the people" (my emphasis). Because the absolute terms of a polarized moral realm have been reestablished, Milton's vision is now freed to see what it needs must— a glimpse of the apocalypse, extracted from Revelation:

Who is there that cannot trace thee now in thy beamy walke through the midst of thy Sanctuary, amidst those golden *candlesticks,* which have long suffer'd a dimnesse amongst us through the violence of those that had seiz'd them, and were more taken with the mention of their gold then of their starry light; teaching the doctrine of *Balaam* to cast a stumbling-block before thy servants, commanding them to eat things sacrifiz'd to Idols, and forcing them to fornication. (705–6)

"Who is there that cannot trace thee now"? Clearly the reformers in Milton's historical critique could not; neither could the partisan polemicist who at that point undertook to examine them—"O if we freeze at noone after their earely thaw, let us feare lest the Sunne for ever hide himself." Only in reaction against a well-defined enemy, capable of being charged with the reformists' own failures, can Milton propel his rhetoric toward a vision of Truth.

But even this hard-won vision cannot sustain itself alone—it yearns to be reified. The entire argument of *Animadversions* (as of all the antiprelatical tracts) rests on the implicit assumption that Milton's cause is identical with *God's* cause, that the prelatical enemy is felt by God to be exactly what *Milton* feels it to be. What Milton asks, then, is for God to justify this assumption; he asks God, in other words, for concrete proof that *Milton is right.* And he sees to it that, should Milton turn out to be wrong, God knows very well whose fault that would be:

Come therefore O thou that hast the seven starres in thy right hand, appoint thy chosen *Preists* according to their Orders, and courses of old, to minister before thee, and duely to dresse and powre out the consecrated oyle into thy holy and ever-burning lamps; thou has sent out the spirit of prayer upon thy servants over all the Land to this effect, and stirr'd up their vowes as the sound of many waters about thy Throne. Every one can say that now certainly thou hast visited this land, and has not forgotten the utmost corners of the earth, in a time when men had thought that thou wast gone up from us to the farthest end of the Heavens, and hadst left to doe marvelously among the sons of these last Ages. O perfect, and accomplish thy glorious acts; for men may leave their works unfinisht, but thou art a God, thy nature is perfection; shouldst thou bring us thus far onward from *Egypt* to destroy us in this Wildernesse though wee deserve; yet thy great name would suffer in the rejoycing of thine enemies, and the deluded hope of all thy servants. (706)

With these words Milton makes the most extraordinary claim in the antiprelatical tracts, although it is only a logical implication, given his basic premise. This is the claim that, if Milton's cause is neither more nor less than God's cause, then failure of that cause will make God suffer much the way Milton would. A more transparently self-serving piece of anthropomorphism would be hard to find. Yet Milton seems oblivious to the solecism, and with good reason. This God who must look after his reputation among men is the direct product of Milton's own rhetorical requirements. Only after visualizing God casting down the prelatical enemy can Milton work up a portrait of the cohesiveness and faith of the reformers: "Who is there that cannot trace thee *now* . . . Every one can say that *now* certainly thou hast visited . . ." (my emphasis). Yet God would not, for all that, suffer failure precisely as Milton would. God's case would be worse, since He would have to put up not just with the jubilant enemy but with the resentment of His disappointed followers as well: "thy great name would suffer in the rejoycing of thine enemies, and the deluded hope of all thy servants." Furthermore, the enemy is now no longer "ours" but "thine," for in revitalizing the polarities of his realm of Truth, Milton has shifted the entire responsibility for the English Reformation off from the imperfect shoulders of the reformers and onto God: "men may leave their works unfinisht, but thou art a God, thy nature is perfection." This shifting of responsibility to God leaves the newly unified, though quite ineffectual, reformers with nothing to do but applaud. Interestingly, once the reformers are safely out of enemy clutches, "thine enemies" can again be acknowledged as "our enemies." But even more to the point, God's settlement of "peace in the Church" would at last liberate not only the "thanke-offering" that had earlier been gestured toward but never quite delivered ("Let us all goe every true protested *Brittaine* . . ."); it would liberate as well an artistic instrument that must be played by Milton's right hand as well as his left:

When thou hast settl'd peace in the Church, and righteous judgement in the Kingdome, then shall all thy Saints address their voyces of joy, and triumph to thee, standing on the shoare of that red Sea into which our enemies had almost driven us. And he that now for haste snatches up a plain ungarnish't present as a thanke-offering to thee, which could not bee deferr'd in regard of thy so many late deliverances wrought for us one upon another, may then perhaps take up a Harp, and sing thee an elaborate Song to Generations. (706)

Milton's tentative promise ("may then perhaps") to play the harp and sing a millennial "Song to Generations" hints toward a poetic unattainable in a hectic polemical world. But in the immediate rhetorical context, the elusiveness of that promised music suggests an attitude bordering on the equivocal. Since Milton has just remonstrated with God for neglecting His credit among men, the promise of an elaborate song oddly resembles a bribe. With other antiprelatical tracts, Milton's argument culminates in rewards for the faithful and punishment for the prelatical enemy; but in this unique attempt to derive millenial vision from history, the requisite polarities have broken down.[26] Here, since the reformers end up looking little better than the prelates, the enemy may indeed still triumph, the faithful may still deserve abandonment. But if responsibility for "the present age" is taken out of men's hands, so will be taken Milton's own polemical and rhetorical task—the task of fully *defining* "the present age," whose opposed meanings (historical versus prophetic) he had delineated but could not sustain. Rewards, punishments, millennial vision, rhetorical task—all causes as well as consequences—are in the end left solely to God. In a different rhetorical context, perhaps, such a resolution would be appropriate for an absolute Calvinist God. But that is not the God Milton sets forth in this passage. Here, Milton's God is alternately apparent and elusive, finally provoking Milton to urge him with something like a threat.

When Milton at last defers to God his own task of illuminating the true, the prophetic meaning of "the present age," he implores God to show not just the enemy, but to show, concretely, *visibly*, the faithful as well. Even the Holy Spirit becomes a material entity, actually divisible into portions, as Milton's own yearning for sensory gratification of a spiritual need fills the passage:

In that day it shall no more bee said as in scorne, this or that was never held so till this Present Age, when men have better learnt that the times and seasons passe along under thy feet, to goe and come at thy bidding, and as thou didst dignifie our fathers dayes with many revelations above all the foregoing ages, since thou tookst the flesh; so thou canst vouchsafe to us (though unworthy) as large a portion of thy spirit as thou pleasest; for who shall prejudice thy all-governing will? Seeing the power of thy grace is not past away with the primitive times, as fond and faithless men imagine, but thy Kingdome is now at hand, and thou standing at the dore. Come forth out of thy Royall Chambers, O Prince of all the Kings of the earth, put on the visible roabes of thy imperiall Majesty, take up that unlimited Scepter which thy Almighty Father hath bequeath'd thee; for now the voice of thy Bride calls thee, and all creatures sigh to bee renew'd. (706–7)

Perhaps the wound made by the Remonstrant's charge against the reformists of temporal opportunism can be healed. But the terms of longing in this passage make it clear that it will require a fleshly healing, one apprehensible to the senses: "as thou didst dignifie our fathers dayes with many revelations . . . so thou canst vouchsafe to us . . . as large a portion of thy spirit as thou pleasest." Unlike the sense-bound creative will of the poet, the will of God so completely *is* the idea that there can be no carnal dread, neither of its own reification nor of any remonstrative charge: "who shall prejudice thy all-governing will?" The Will whose desire transformed Word into flesh is now bidden, by an even humbler remonstrant, once again to perform that divine self-transforming act: "put on the visible roabes of thy imperiall Majesty . . . the voice of thy Bride calls thee, and all creatures sigh to bee renew'd."

In the opening paragraphs of his first antiprelatical tract, *Of Reformation*, Milton alludes contemptuously to the superstitious man, the atheist manqué who "all in a pudder shuffles up to himself such a *God*, and such a *worship* as is most agreeable to remedy his feare, which feare of his, as also is his hope, fixt only upon the Flesh, renders likewise the whole faculty of his apprehension, carnall." Clearly, Milton's own fears and hopes lie not in the fleshly dimension dreaded by the man of crude superstition. Rather, the rhetorical ambivalences of the antiprelatical tracts argue a different order of carnal apprehension—an affective intensity capable not only, to use K. G. Hamilton's phrase, of "swamping the argument" but of seducing, deluding, and finally defeating the arguer. For Milton, however, the issue goes beyond mere style. The antiprelatical tracts document the way in which Milton's vision of the millennium depends on a self-generated and self-sustained structure of affective rhetoric. When in *Animadversions* Milton shuffles up such a God as will remedy his own fear and answer to his own hopes, it is one who can remove from his shoulders more than just the unwanted burden of his present battle with the prelates. Milton would be relieved as well of the agonizing possibility that his most fundamental assumptions about God and God's cause may be in error.

But the rhetorical agon of the antiprelatical tracts in another way *liberates* Milton as well. Forced by half-understood convictions to abandon the still air of delightful studies, Milton finds that his struggle against idolatry compels him to smash certain cherished idols of his own. These include his notions not only about the proper setting for "the bright countenance of truth," but also about the proper exercise of his consecrated gifts. The fractured rhetorical planes of the antiprelatical tracts teach Milton two critical lessons about the nature of carnal rhetoric. First, his rhetorical agon exposes the fallacy of Milton's early assumption, shared by many of his readers, that the difference between rhetoric which serves God and that which serves the world and the flesh may be determined by its outward appearance, its carnal dimension. The antiprelatical tracts prove that *all* rhetoric must by definition be carnal—representational, temporal, mortal, finite—in order that it may be apprehended by human sense.

This leads to the second lesson of Milton's rhetorical agon: his drive toward the ideal gets its visionary impetus from the energetic fecundity of his passion for the concrete. Similarly, and tellingly, his conceptions of God and of the possibility of human righteousness gain both delineation and spiritual fervor from their counteraction with luxuriously sensuous conceptions of evil. In his rhetorical practice, indeed, Milton's conceptions of God and righteousness very much depend on his sensuous conceptions of evil. We can view this phenomenon credibly enough as Milton's application of the principle, articulated in *Areopagitica*, that human knowledge of good depends on human knowledge of evil: "that doom which Adam fell into of knowing good and evil; that is to say, of knowing good *by* evil" (my italics).

Furthermore, in light of the creative process elucidated by iconoclastic metaphor theory, Milton's apprehensive glimpse at the possibility of error regarding God and God's cause might be extended. A "shuffled-up" God raises the specter of iconoclasm's nemesis: a presentiment that the idea of God, like any other idea, may be nothing more than a projected image.[27] Arnold Stein's devastating witticism bears repeating here: "All men are created in the image of God, but only Milton was created in the image of Milton's God." In the antiprelatical tracts, we witness how Milton's own struggle with iconoclastic dread generates and continually refuels his image-making impulse. In its most dramatic manifestation in *Animadversions*, fear that the idea (in this instance the idea of the millennium) may be only a projected human image threatens to destroy the idea itself. But threat of such destruction creates instead an affective vacuum which the impetus toward new reification of the idea seeks to fill. And the process is capable of being extended indefinitely. Only thus can the sanctity of the idea be kept alive.

Prior to writing the antiprelatical tracts, Milton's iconoclastic potential had been anticipated in such breaks with literary decorum as the intrusive speech by St. Peter in *Lycidas*, or the routing of the pagan gods in *On the Morning of Christ's Nativity*. But the iconoclastic impetus in such instances was still circumscribed by the poems' formal settings. The rhetorical agon of the antiprelatical tracts, on the other hand, shatters the generic and formal idols that heretofore had held Milton's developing iconoclastic poetics in check. Nevertheless, as the *Animadversions* scenario illustrates, doubt still functions in the antiprelatical tracts as a creative and visionary threat. The principle of doubt as a device for perfect freedom has not yet been assimilated into Milton's rhetorical practice in the first group of polemics, with the result that his affective scenarios betray his uneasiness over their being mere scenarios. When we turn to *Areopagitica*, we will find Milton's scenarios virtually flaunting the precariousness of image-building and image-dependency. Far from being threatened by ephemerality, *Areopagitica*'s images actively pursue their own dissolution, in a rhetoric that prevents images from being mistaken for the ideas that they can only fleetingly represent. But first, an important intermediate step in Milton's developing iconoclastic poetics is taken when he explores more thoroughly, in the course of his argument for divorce, the potential for idolatry risked by one who must necessarily depend on carnal rhetoric.

3

"WAS SHE THY GOD?"

The Coupling Rhetoric of

the Divorce Tracts

The argumentative strategies Milton applies in *The Doctrine and Discipline of Divorce* are quite unparalleled in the prose. He makes the logical underpinnings of a desired change in legal and social practices of 1642 England do service as a principle for God's creation of the universe—and vice versa. He forcibly yokes the words of Old Testament Law with the words of Christ's Gospel, to demonstrate that these manifestly contradictory statements really mean the same thing. He argues that prohibition of divorce actually constitutes the deepest divorce, and that the dissolver of marriage seeks only the best interests of marriage. In *The Doctrine and Discipline of Divorce*, Milton demonstrates that with the affective power of the image of ideal coupling, there is no claim he cannot make, nothing he cannot prove. He aims for what Susanne Woods has called a *"feeling* persuasion," wherein the effort becomes "as much to insinuate an unpopular libertarian position as to argue directly for it" (my italics).[1] So great is Milton's ratiocinative need to defend the profoundly personal subrational and suprarational cause of ideal marital union that, beyond the tract's ostensible case for divorce, rational argumentation itself is brought to serve a new idol. Whereas in the antiprelatical tracts the imagery-driven affective argument overwhelmed or walked away from the rational argument, in *Doctrine and Discipline* the affective dimensions of the image actively *determine* ratiocinative procedure. Carnal rhetoric itself becomes the idol which other argumentative elements are made to serve.

Apart from its conventional ordering elements of classical form and structure, *The Doctrine and Discipline of Divorce* is controlled by an imagerial dictate that operates less like a calculated rhetorical maneuver than like an obsession. This dictate is Milton's empyreal image of compatible sexual union, an image capable of forcing the materials of whatever obstructions may lie in its path—bad marriages, canon law, Christ's strict prohibition of divorce, God's holy word—into a rhetorical pattern that leads inexorably to the desideratum of perfect and transcendent coupling. Furthermore, like the lessons about consecrated gifts that Milton carries away from the antiprelatical tracts, the imagerial dictate of *Doctrine and Discipline* ultimately yields other distinctive moral and artistic returns. When the severe inquiry of the divine Judge lights on fallen Adam in *Paradise Lost*, the Son asks a question whose probing irony is sometimes missed: "Was she thy God, that her thou didst obey / Before his voice . . . ?" (X.145–46) The object of the Son's scrutiny is not Eve or her aspirations to godhead, but Adam's own engrossment in an image of perfect union, an engrossment that Adam's words have just betrayed:

> This woman whom thou madest to be my help,
> And gavest me as thy perfect gift, so good,
> So fit, so acceptable, so divine,
> That from her hand I could suspect no ill,
> And what she did, whatever in it self,
> Her doing seemed to justify the deed;
> She gave me of the tree, and I did eat.
> (*PL* X.137–43)

Adam's willingness to define the deed by the perfection of the doer is intellectual heir to Milton's rhetorical procedure in *The Doctrine and Discipline of Divorce*, where the passionately desired image is allowed to rule the logic of Milton's argument. In *Doctrine and Discipline*, laws both human and divine are marshaled by coupling rhetoric to obey the voice of transformative desire: *whatever in itself* the argument may do, Milton's desired image of empyreal coupling *seems to justify the deed*.

COUPLING RHETORIC AND ITS
TRANSFORMATIONS

Of the transformations worked by the coupling pattern, the most startling is that by which Milton makes words evoke their contraries. A strategy that in most contexts would be recognized as sophistry becomes in *Doctrine and Discipline* the verbal equivalent of the truest coupling, in which each partner implies his or her opposite. We have hints toward such transformation in logical and rhetorical sleights like the telling Miltonisms "hardheartednesse of undivorcing" and "uncircumcision in the soul."[2] Milton's novel grammatical coinages in the divorce tracts have the effect of making palpable verbal entities out of the affective detritus that is left after specific cognizable actions have been denied, suspended, canceled, or otherwise negated. Thus, although "undivorce" denotes no recognizable legal act, hard-hearted "undivorcing" nevertheless *feels* like a positive act of repression. Similarly, the symbolic purification ritual that accompanies religious circumcision intimates no opposing ritual of impurity; nevertheless, "uncircumcision in the soul" *feels* like it confers on the impure soul exactly that—a formal and ceremonious rite of initiation into sin.

But even more dramatically, and without such negation, Milton employs words in such a way as to displace or convert their customary meanings by enlisting them in a higher service, as if words, like souls, could be Christianly regenerated. The verbal conversions begin with his title page. Merely to read the full title of the 1644 edition of *The Doctrine and Discipline of Divorce* is to experience the kind of rhetorical manipulation that characterizes Milton's argument at its most complex. Phrase by phrase, he leads us in: "The Doctrine & Discipline of DIVORCE Restor'd to the good of both SEXES. . . ." The key word is "Restor'd." We do not even need to know why restoration is being advocated to be cued to a critical first principle governing the argument that follows. Divorce, it says, is possessed of a true "doctrine," a right "discipline," an original perfection and correct practice which have fallen into abuse; and the purpose of this tract is to "restore" that "doctrine and discipline" to its original, unfallen state.[3] Moreover, any conventional interpreter would take the word "divorce" to mean the undoing or breaking of a bond—something that could not occur unless a bond had been previously established, hence something which comes into being only secondarily, after certain other acts have been performed. Yet the concept of "divorce" here seems to be granted full realization in the primal order of things. In fact, we eventually find that the concept of divorce has for Milton an existence *prior* to the order of things; that it is, indeed, an operative principle upon which that very order depends. More of that later. For the present, we have enough to deal with on the title page, whose phrases gradually clarify and circumscribe the scope of the tract. The doctrine and discipline of divorce is to be "Restor'd to the good of both SEXES" (all humankind will benefit from it) "From the bondage of CANON LAW, and other mistakes" (the adversary, and the situation—"bondage"—are now identified and pejoratively labeled) "to the true meaning of Scripture" (now the authority, terms, and context for the argument are established) "in the Law and Gospel compar'd" (we can expect some sort of dialectic between the Old and New Testaments).

The second sentence on the title page is even more explicit: "Wherein also are set down the bad consequences of abolishing or condemning of Sin, that which the Law of God allowes, and Christ abolisht not." This sentence is both a warning and a reassurance: if we fail to attend to the argument of the tract, evil will surely follow; but we may also rest secure in the promise that nothing irregular or contrary to the Scriptures is being advocated. Furthermore, we are reading an improved version of the argument: "Now the second time revised and much augmented, in Two BOOKS"; and as readers we share the document with the august "Parlament of *England* with the Assembly." From the pair of scriptural quotations at the bottom of the title page, we may gather that we are to receive fresh, inspired insights as well as established truths: "Every Scribe instructed to the Kingdom of Heav'n, is like the Maister of a house which bringeth out of his treasury things new and old." And we are reminded of the wisdom and responsibility of reading with an open mind: "He that answereth a matter before he heareth it, it is folly and shame to him." By the time the reader has worked his way from the top of the title page to the bottom, his expectations about the tract have been carefully prepared. If initially he was struck by the curious attribution to divorce of primal beneficence, his perplexity is soon more or less allayed by the familiar trappings of polemical discourse: advantages to be gained, allusions to resources and authorities, a putative audience, and scriptural quotations. Unless exceptionally wary, he may overlook the fact that before the tract even begins, the word "divorce" has been used in a manner wholly unorthodox—used to suggest something proper and right in the original scheme of things, something which was once practiced freely and well but is now held in unjust captivity, something which in its pure and natural form is associated not with severance but with order and unity. In short, the word "divorce" has been used in such a way as to imply its opposite.

What we witness on the title page is the first achievement of "the industry of free reasoning" that Milton advocates in *Doctrine and Discipline*'s opening paragraph. From the contradictory energies released by overturning the "abject and servile principles" of ordinary linguistic usage, there emerges a higher truth answerable to the dynamics of perfect union (223–24). It is a truth grounded, Milton argues, in the original perfection of the created universe:

He therefore who by adventuring shall be so happy as with successe to light the way of such an expedient liberty and truth as this, shall restore the much wrong'd and over-sorrow'd state of matrimony, not onely to those mercifull and life-giving remedies of *Moses*, but, as much as may be, to that serene and blisfull condition it was in at the beginning. (239–40)

By what principle or power Milton would hope through divorce to restore marriage to its original unfallen state is not made clear until after his argument is well under way: he does it by finding the doctrine and discipline of divorce to exist *prior* to marriage, prior to man, prior to the world itself. It is this archetypal act of divorce which gives the highest sanction to the principles by which Milton argues: "ev'n by the first and last of all his visible works; when by his divorcing command the world first rose out of Chaos, nor can be renew'd again out of confusion but by the separating of unmeet consorts" (273). Nor is it only in *Doctrine and Discipline* that Milton makes divorce God's original creative act: years later he reasserts its priority. In *Paradise Lost* light is granted, as in the Scriptures, precedence as the first of *things;* but contrary to the Scriptures, God's first *act* is made the separation of adverse elements:

Darknesse profound
Cover'd th' Abyss: but on the watrie calme
His brooding wings the Spirit of God outspred,

> And vital vertue infus'd, and vital warmth
> Throughout the fluid Mass, but downward purg'd
> The black tartareous cold infernal dregs
> Adverse to life: then founded, then conglob'd
> Like things to like, the rest to several place
> Disparted, and between spun out the Air,
> And Earth self-ballanc't on her Center hung.
> (VII.233–43)

The original act of creation in *Paradise Lost* is thus an iconoclastic act of disruption. The infusion of "vital vertue" and "vital warmth" into "the watrie calme" unleashes forces that derive from that engendering violence the power required to shape a "fluid Mass" into a desired vision of order and unity. And at the same time, the infusion itself is a dynamic coupling of the Spirit of God with his own substance. With the primal earthly scene thus made an archetype of creative iconoclasm, Milton merges his redefinition of divorce into the foundation of all that is known and sacred to humankind.

Coupling rhetoric's power to convert to a radical creative principle the breaking of what Milton believed to be a merely social bond may be extended as well to the bond itself—that "yoke of prudent and manly discipline," marriage. Marriage and divorce are indeed so reciprocally intertwined in *Doctrine and Discipline* that they at times seem to signify the same thing. The affective structures by which Milton virtually equates marriage and divorce testify to his expressed conviction that the measure of both is their capacity for promoting the empyreal ideal of perfect union. "Certainly such a one forbidd'n to divorce, is in effect forbidd'n to marry," he argues, in phrases whose lucid affective symmetry glosses over the manifest rational contradiction of this statement (252). Under the dictate of empyreal coupling, it matters little whether the question under debate happens to be one of marriage or of divorce: "Whosoever does most according to peace and love, whether in mariage, or in divorce, he it is that breaks mariage lest" (258). When peace and love define the doer, moral distinctions between the deed of divorce and the deed of marriage all but disappear.

In the ingenious and liberated industry of free reasoning every righteous interpreter, every "Scribe instructed to the Kingdom of Heav'n" may therefore hope to thrive: the industry's resources and mission know no boundaries. Its distinctive trademark, the pattern of coupling logic, can be discerned in the very syntax of *Doctrine and Discipline*, as the industry of free reasoning discovers more and more ways to generate new truths from the tensions between contraries. This may sometimes require only the rhetoric of moderation:

> Christ meant not to be tak'n word for word, but like a wise Physician, administring one excesse against another to reduce us to a perfect mean: Where the Pharises were strict, there Christ seems remisse; where they were too remisse, he saw it needfull to seem most severe. (282–83)

But what may look at first like a purely rational argument for temperance is delivered by a significant affective maneuver. The structural symmetry that we see elsewhere in *Doctrine and Discipline* glossing over logical contradiction can be seen here working a variant on that symmetry, a notably *sensory* effect of rhythmically measured balance that further elucidates the affective resources of Milton's coupling rhetoric. The rhythms of complementary phrasing that bear the impress of empyreal coupling can be scanned: "Where the Pharises were strict, / there Christ seems remisse; // where they were too remisse, / he saw it needfull to seem most severe." Christ's rule of moderation here is really *modulation*, a contrapuntal exercise that operates in a manner similar to that of chiastic structures in Milton's poetry: the reciprocal structure persuades the senses as much as it does the intellect. The empyreal coupling ideal regularly demands that Milton's new truths be expressed in such demonstrably *correlative* terms:

> He who wisely would restrain the reasonable Soul of man within due bounds, must first himself know perfectly, how far the territory and dominion extends of just and honest liberty. *As little must he offer to bind* [/] *that which God hath loos'n'd,* [//] *as to loos'n* [/] *that which he hath bound.* (227, my italics)

Again and again, Milton's truths are formulated in rhythmic, balanced, complementary phrases like these. His need for such reciprocally consummate accounts of truth pervades *Doctrine and Discipline* with a rhetoric that repeatedly finds—or creates, or compels—accord between seeming disparities. The conjunction of opposites regularly serves to achieve a transcendent whole. That such an accord describes as well the dynamics of regenerate sexual union is fundamental to the effectiveness of Milton's argument in the tract.

Balanced periods and parallel structures are of course not unique to *The Doctrine and Discipline of Divorce:* artful coordinate sentences appear often in Milton's prose. But nowhere else in his polemical writings does syntactic structure so directly mirror the logic and purpose of his argument. Nor elsewhere do syntax, logic, and purpose all so felicitously reflect the dominant affective language. Uniquely in *Doctrine and Discipline*, argumentative point and counterpoint make a pleasing rhythmic and logical balance, a complementary antithesis that contributes the bearing of balanced and rational argumentation to the affective image of healthy coupling. At the same time, point and counterpoint also contribute the bearing of dynamic sexual union to the logical processes of reasoned argument.

But there is more than just symmetry, balance, and concord in the syntactic equations of coupling rhetoric. Just as often, Milton's points and counterpoints may awkwardly mismatch, displease, lose balance, and thereby call attention to their alliance with the grotesque anti-image of unhealthy coupling. The balanced versus unbalanced coordinate rhetorical structures may be graphically illustrated by a form of sentence diagram. Here is the balanced structure with which Milton rationalizes Christ's delivery to the Pharisees of only a partial truth:

> for it was seasonable
>> that they should hear
>>> their own unbounded license
>>>> rebuk't,
> but not seasonable
>> for them to hear
>>> a good mans requisit liberty
>>>> explain'd. (307)

The rhythmic equation that sets "a good mans requisit liberty" against "their own unbounded license" assures that the terms of Christ's justice are perfectly balanced. By contrast, Milton delineates his canonical opponents' rationale for justice with a coordinate sentence whose rhythms stumble:

> The Law was harsh
>> to extoll the grace
>>> of the Gospel,

and now the Gospel
by a new affected strictnes of her own,
shall extenuate the grace,
which her self offers. (305)

In this instance, the reasoning of the canonists requires a qualifying extra step, and the unbalancing cadence of the telltale words "by a new affected strictness of her own" makes the step false on a rhythmic, sensory level as well as on a doctrinal or spiritual level. Furthermore, the balanced, logical complement to harsh law extolling the grace of the gospel would presumably be for a mild gospel to perform some comparable act, such as mitigation, toward the harshness of the law. But the gospel in the canonists' terms makes no response at all to the law, acting instead in self-contradictory isolation, "extenuat[ing] the grace, which her self offers." And finally, Milton's gendered personification of the gospel renders the canonical interpreter's repudiation of reciprocity as an image of mincing sexual prudery ("by a new affected strictness of her own"). By visualizing falsely interpreted scriptural doctrine as repudiative sexual conduct, Milton implicitly locates the true grace of the gospel in the only conduct the established imagery makes available: he locates it, that is, in the responsive sexuality conveyed by the empyreal image of ideal coupling. The question posed to Adam by the divine Son may therefore be asked as well of Milton's rhetorical impetus in the divorce argument: "Was she thy god?"

The coordinate sentences of coupling syntax show just how far Milton's impetus toward transcendent union could press the affective rhetorical powers of his governing image. Whereas the rhetorical agon of the antiprelatical tracts polarizes the rational and the affective arguments of the tract, *Doctrine and Discipline* shows that rational and affective instruments cannot be separated—indeed, that they may even be the same instrument. In this respect, *Doctrine and Discipline*'s image of empyreal coupling may be seen as a model for the whole of Milton's carnal rhetoric, a rhetoric that elicits affective assent by tapping the resources of sensory witness.

The use of correlative structures to conflate rational with affective argument becomes particularly strategic in those instances where Milton takes a stand contrary to specific passages of Scripture. He frames his rationale for contravening the letter of the Word in rhythmic paired phrases, whose correlative structure I will here, as elsewhere whenever useful, call attention to by displaying their natural cadences:

> And shall we be more severe in paraphrasing
>> the considerat and tender Gospel,
> then he was in expounding
>> the rigid and peremptory Law?

Having established an *affective* balance in his argumentative procedure, he will now argue for the "spirit of Christ" by using precisely those passages whose literal significance seems most contrary to his position:

I pronounce, the man who shall bind so cruelly a good and gracious ordinance of God, hath not in that the Spirit of Christ. Yet that every text of Scripture seeming opposite may be attended with a due exposition, this other part ensues, and makes account to find no slender arguments for this assertion out of those very Scriptures, which are commonly urged against it. (281–82)

Milton would, in any case, have to address the arguments "commonly urged against" his assertion about "the Spirit of Christ," but his method entails more than systematic, point-by-point refutation. The affective appeal of Milton's coupling dynamics makes possible and seemingly natural the taking of unusually daring, paradoxical argumentative positions:

> He I say who therfore seeks to part,
>> is one who highly honors the maried life,
>>> and would not stain it:
> and the reasons which now move him to divorce,
>> are equall to the best of those
>>> that could first warrant him to marry. (253)

> May it not be fear'd that
>> the not divorcing
>>> of such a helples disagreement,
>> will be the divorcing
>>> of God finally from such a place? (277)

Divorce honors marriage; not to divorce is a greater divorce: extraordinary claims. But because of their rhythmic symmetry, these paradoxes *affectively* declare their adherence to complementary, unifying, transcendent, yet arguably *rational* values that belie their apparent logical contradictions.

Alternatively, the same coupling pattern may articulate a mechanism for judicious and elegant *avoidance* of a clear position—the kind of clear position that the creative iconoclast would see as actually freezing truth, and the industry of free reasoning, in attitudes of idolatry:

> He who wisely would restrain the reasonable Soul of man within due bounds, must first himself know perfectly, how far the territory and dominion extends of just and honest liberty.

> As little must he offer to bind
>> that which God hath loos'n'd,
> as to loos'n
>> that which he hath bound.

> The ignorance and mistake of this high point, hath heapt up one huge half of all the misery that hath bin since *Adam*. (227–28)

Every enterprise must be twofold to be complete; it cannot justly aim at what it intends without giving generous consideration to possible results that it would *not* intend. The ambiguity of the object of Milton's reference to "this high point" is surely deliberate. We are offered a principle ("As little must he offer to bind . . . as to loos'n"), but it is a principle that cannot be applied as a specific rule. In a treatise on divorce, we can assume that man's binding and God's loosening— or man's loosening and God's binding—would refer in general to the practices of marriage and divorce. But it is impossible to tell which practice belongs to which agent or action. Thus the empyreal coupling principle of defining the deed by the doer is reaffirmed: "Whosoever does most according to peace and love, whether in mariage, or in divorce, he it is that breaks mariage lest." By such a logic, neither the "deed of marrying" nor the "deed of divorcing" has a determinate role in the constitution of true marriage. Milton's ideal of empyreal coupling deputizes peace and love as doers *equally* capable of justifying *either* deed.

For his definitive justification of the deed by the doer, Milton turns for his most elevated coupling image to the mystical acts of God.

Milton's primal creation scene in *Paradise Lost* presents a familiar yet etherealized instance of God's seminal virtue: when the "brooding wings" of the Holy Spirit outspread above the waters infuse into them "vital virtue" and "vital warmth," the image suggests an act vaguely sexual. But a more graphic evocation of God as a sexual being appears in the conclusion of *Doctrine and Discipline*'s address to Parliament:

Who so preferrs either Matrimony, or other Ordinance before the good of man and the plain exigence of Charity, let him professe Papist, or Protestant, or what he will, he is no better than a Pharise, and understands not the gospel: whom as a misinterpreter of Christ I openly protest against; and provoke him to the trial of this truth before all the world: and let him bethink him withall how he will soder up the shifting flaws of his ungirt permissions, his venial and unvenial dispenses, wherewith the Law of God pardoning and unpardoning hath bin shamefully branded, for want of heed in glossing, to have eluded and baffl'd out all Faith and chastity from the mariagebed of that holy seed, with politick and judicial adulteries. (233)

Initially in this passage marriage occupies only an inferior temporal and legalistic status as "Matrimony, or other Ordinance." But even as Milton deflates its worldly authority, he elevates the idea of marriage to a higher realm, establishing it as a locus of heavenly truth. By envisioning "that holy seed" which is "the Law of God" as engendered in "the mariagebed" of the Scriptures, Milton places marriage on the highest possible level, while the patrons of matrimonial ordinance become cosmic adulterors, "baffl[ing] out all faith and chastity from the mariagebed of that holy seed." And from this scenario there emerges again, in newly familiarized terms, the paradox that a union of contraries may generate a higher truth. Against the canonists who consider adultery the only legitimate cause for divorce, Milton will later in the tract level the following charge:

> he who affirms adultery
> > to be the highest breach,
> affirms the bed
> > to be the highest of mariage. (269)

Yet to the ineffable workings of the Supreme Being, he now ascribes precisely that copulative act which those modern pharisees idolize, and which Milton himself debunks, as the primary justification for and purpose of marriage.

This shift of significance has been accomplished through a complicated syntactical maneuver. At first "the Law of God" seems to be implicated in the pharisaical practices of "pardon ing and unpardoning," eluding and baffling. Then, after the word "mariagebed," the law of God is identified as "that holy seed" and is thus made the victim of "politick and judicial adulteries." Because of the initially ambiguous status of "the Law of God," and because the qualities of "Faith and chastity" are ordinarily categorized among human virtues, it seems for a moment that the eluding and baffling are suffered by human beings; hence "mariagebed" apparently refers to the corporal union of human marriage. But with the words "holy seed," all these terms must be reassigned godly, spiritual, or scriptural meanings. Nevertheless, since the image of engendering in a marriage bed remains, as an image, insistently *human* (unlike the wings of the Spirit above the calm waters), the effect of this passage is not finally to dislocate our concept of marriage from a worldly, human sphere and reestablish it in a godly one. "Holy seed" is at once germinative animal semen and divine spirit; it participates in both spheres, so both spheres are evoked in this passage simultaneously. Thus, unions of human with human, of the corporal with the spiritual, of humankind with God, and of the spirit of the Word with the letter of the word—all, in their fullest definitions, are one. It is this manifold supreme union, sustained in delicate syntactic balance by the word "mariagebed," that is toppled by the "politick and judicial adulteries" of the misinterpreting pharisees. So, we have marriage and marriage, the deed defined by the doer. The matrimony of the modern pharisees is an adulterous idol which displaces both God and his creatures; whereas matrimony truly defined is not only ordained by God but is of his essence. The empyreal image of compatible sexual union thus synthesizes a rhetorical intercourse that transfuses sensory flesh into divine being.

THE PROBLEM OF RHETORICAL DUALISM

Milton's striking investment of spiritual ideas with erotic metaphor, like his Puritan investment of erotic ideas with spiritual metaphor (as in "due benevolence"), manifests his profound belief in the essential oneness of body and spirit. Indeed, every paired issue dealt with in *Doctrine and Discipline* may be inferred from the universal coupling of the physical with the spiritual that characterizes the human relationship to God. That an essential *oneness* should require affective realization through patterns of *coupling*, however, points to a fundamental and in some respects unresolvable rhetorical dilemma for Milton's divorce argument. Stephen Fallon traces this dilemma to its origins in Milton's metaphysics: "Milton struggles here, as we must struggle, to articulate a monist conception of human nature with a vocabulary colored by dualism."[4] At his most rhetorically effective, Milton is able to manipulate the inevitable conflict between philosophical monism and expressive dualism by attributing dualism to his opponent and offering monism to the gentle spirit. "In his own mind," Fallon argues, "Milton . . . is less torn between monism and dualism than he is intent on separating his audience into wise monists and blind dualists. Milton invokes dualism to blast his contemporaries for acknowledging the body before the spirit in marriage; he invokes monism to hold out to the godly the prospect of an ideal sexual life" (69). Milton's strategy for separating truth from error, and dividing his divorce tract's audience accordingly, resembles his strategy in the antiprelatical tracts, where he had used affective language as a means of sorting out self-serving prelates from eye-brightened reformers. But just as that strategy had foundered when he tried to extricate spiritual vision from carnal affect in the *Animadversions* prayer, so in *The Doctrine and Discipline of Divorce* Milton's monist vision of empyreal union is carnally entangled with a conceptual apparatus that remains stubbornly dualist. His case against canon law in favor of divorce depends substantially on the argument that mental or spiritual incompatibility may be more damaging to marriage than the mere physical impediments of sexual incapacity or adultery:

How vain therefore is it, and how preposterous in the Canon Law to have made such carefull provision against the impediment of carnall performance, and to have had no care about the unconversing inability of minde. . . . Yet wisdom and charity waighing Gods own institution, would think that

> the pining of a sad spirit wedded to loneliness
> should deserve to be free'd,

as well as the impatience of a sensuall desire
so providently reliev'd. (248)

The canonists are charged with severing bodies from souls, but Milton's own appeal for sufferers of mental *as opposed* to physical incompatibility simply reverses the canonists' priorities; it does not dismantle their conceptual or ontological assumptions. "Sensuall desire[s]" and "sad spirit[s]" are not only separated but given different priorities in Milton's formulation: whereas sensual desires may be only "impatient" for relief, sad spirits can actually "deserve to be free'd."

Milton's implicit devaluing of the physical in such constructions is a sign of what Fallon calls the "powerful and dualist drag" of Gnostic influences on Christian metaphysicians (81). The drag is unquestionably there. But I would argue that its weight signifies for Milton not so much a metaphysical burden as it does a necessary rhetorical ballast.[5] In granting priority to sufferers of mental over physical incompatibility, he is not particularly devaluing the physical; he is rather making the case, in a spirit-infused world of matter, for the complete *interdependence* of physical powers and spiritual will.[6] That interdependence is expressible in terms of the rhythmic counterpoise that interprets each dimension of our twofold nature, our physical being and our spiritual being, as a necessary means of articulating the other:

And with all generous persons maried thus it is,
    that where the minde and person pleases aptly,
        there some unaccomplishment of the bodies delight
          may be better born with,
    then when the minde hangs off in an unclosing disproportion,
        though the body be as it ought,
          for there all corporall delight
            will soon become unsavoury and contemptible.
                (II.246)

To "all generous persons maried," minds and persons do please, but bodies, too, can "delight." On the other hand, a mind that "hangs off in an unclosing disproportion" exhibits behavior that looks, in fact, very like that we might expect from a body anxious in its "unaccomplishment." Thus, the ways of the body receive articulation through the spirit, while corporal effects assist in articulating the mind. Like the richly sensory language of the antiprelatical tracts, the intrinsically dualist patterns of the divorce tracts give Milton the syncretic affective materials he needs to make his case for a monism whose *essential* character (but not the way it palpably *looks* or *feels*) can only be intuited by our metaphorizing human sensibilities in terms of what it is not. In Milton's view, without the "powerful dualist drag" neither the problem nor its solution would exist. The ancient storyteller's preamble still holds true: there was one, there wasn't one; apart from the One there was no one.

Nevertheless, in order to get any kind of story going, there will sooner or later have to be *two*. And from the beginning, once there are two, the risks to any conception of absolute certainty are well known. The particular risks for the twofold rhetoric of Milton's divorce argument bore their first tainted fruits in contemporary charges of libertinism. Those rhetorical risks are still bearing similar—newly alluring—fruits. As James Turner sees it, Milton's oscillation between advocacy of voluntary sexuality and dualistic denunciation of the flesh leads to a claim that "the wife's adultery could make her a better companion"—thus implicitly making Milton an advocate of adultery: "At such moments we glimpse, however tantalizingly, a Milton who prides himself on his expansiveness and urbanity (neither 'crabbed' nor 'rustic'), and who projects into marriage an almost libertine fusion of erotic excitement and mental life."[7] Closer examination of the evidence suggests, however, that Milton's marital ideal bears only a superficial resemblance to that of the libertine. The greater companionability that, in *Tetrachordon*, Milton argues might be possible in the aftermath of an adulterous affair, depends entirely on a particular set of conditions:

For this [the past adultery], as it is not felt, nor troubles him who perceaves it not, so beeing perceav'd, may soon be repented, soon amended, soon, if it can be pardon'd, may be redeem'd w[ith] the more ardent love and duty in her who hath the pardon. (674)

By Milton's analysis, the marriage partner wronged by adultery might owe his bliss either to his own ignorance ("as it is not felt, nor troubles him who perceaves it not"), or to his wife's repentance ("beeing perceav'd, may soon be repented, soon amended . . . pardon'd . . . redeem'd"). If a renewed marital happiness characterized by an even "more ardent love and duty" can possibly follow on the ending of an adulterous affair, that happiness in Milton's view clearly derives not from adultery but from repentance and forgiveness. To assume that Milton regards adultery with an urbane libertinism in the interest of erotic excitement is comparable to using the felix culpa argument not as a means of explicating divine grace but as a mechanism to justify the promotion of sin and disobedience, "tempting" God in the manner of Satan in *Paradise Regained.*

Yet the iconoclastic means of generating new truths does tempt us to take the means itself for the truths it desires to generate. *Doctrine and Discipline*'s sexual metaphors, the most obvious signs of Milton's imaginal dictate, can hardly escape being interpreted in some way as signs of Milton's personal attitude toward sex. The reading by Edward LeComte of this imagery not as a rhetorical strategy but as an indicator of Milton's sexual antipathy has been superseded by Turner's related but more thoughtful study; yet Turner still interprets the diseased and perverted sexual images as Milton's general indictment of human physiology.[8] Annabel Patterson sees the same imagery as shaping the tract into the novelistic form of psychobiography, with the story telling the storyteller rather than the reverse.[9] Such readings shed light on Milton's complex personality at least partly because they participate in an iconological fallacy similar to Milton's own, when he subordinates his argument to the affective rule of images. Yet for that very reason, distortions occur. Milton's metaphor for semen, the "quintessence of an excrement," Patterson traces to "a venerable tradition of misogynistic disgust."[10] But to read such an image only as psychologically revealing evidence of Milton's participation in that tradition is not merely to devalue the metaphor's immediate rhetorical function; it is also to ignore the evidence provided by another Miltonic metaphor (one equally available for psychoanalytic interpretation) in which semen becomes "the best substance" of a man's body, "and of his soul too, as some think." Even more sublime, of course, is the instance noted in the preceding section of this chapter, in which rather than being metaphorized, semen becomes itself a metaphor for the divine law, God's "holy seed." All Milton's images of sexual union, whether repulsive or idealized, have an affective bearing. When the rhetorical function of this affective language is acknowledged, it can invert the antipathetic conclusions reached by determined psychoanalytic focus on sexual attitudes. Human physiology is not, as such focus suggests, necessarily degraded by Milton's rhetoric of bestiality and disease. Rather, Milton's rhetoric of bestiality and disease expresses the degradation of human beings whose admissible needs and desires have been reduced by canon law to the demands of their physiology.

But to assert this is of course to return to the problem of rhetorical dualism. It is a problem best witnessed in the allegorical metaphors with which Milton expresses the contrast between true and false couplings: his image of the perverted union of Custom and Error; and his counter-image, the ideal union expressed in the myth of Love and Anteros. In an earlier version of the argument that I make here, I had referred to the union of Custom and Error as a grotesque parody of the Eros/Anteros myth, upon whose "reflection of a coequal and *homogeneal* fire" Milton partly based his own image of perfect and equal coupling.[11] Annabel Patterson has since noted the "peculiar misappropriateness of the Eros/Anteros model" for human marriage. The myth is "literally a tale of passionately incestuous love between brothers . . . whose oddness in this context is only underlined by Milton's disclaimer that 'of matrimoniall love no doubt but that was chiefly meant.' "[12] The oddness of Milton's choice for an ideal coupling image, and the gendered discomfort that Patterson finds betrayed not only by that image but also by Milton's awkward rationalization for using it, are both tied to the same rhetorical dilemma. This is the dilemma of the philosophical monist who must dramatize his argument by exploiting the affective resources of dualism, a practice which translates to a euphemized and gendered aesthetic in *The Doctrine and Discipline of Divorce*. This aesthetic could have developed, as Patterson suggests, from Milton's "effort to conceal from his readers and probably from himself the precise effect on his psyche of the long-delayed induction into heterosexual experience."[13] But submerged autobiography does not by itself account for the awkwardness of Milton's choices in the Eros/Anteros passage.

In Chapter 1 of the present study, I have noted how gender dialectic and the euphemizing tendencies of gender ambiguity permeate the history of Western aesthetics discourse.[14] The Platonic distinction between *eidos* and *eidolon* gives rise to a presumption of fundamental conflict between image and idea. This basic conflict then gets elaborated by gender dialectic, as "masculine" attributes and "feminine" attributes get shuttled back and forth between image and idea, according to the prejudices and argumentative needs of whatever philosophical system is being promoted.[15] For example, John Locke finds feminine "agreeableness" of *resemblance* in the obscurities of poetic imagery, while judgment of *difference* and the "severe rules of truth and reason" characterize the clear "masculine" ideas of prose. Edmund Burke, on the other hand, treats discrimination of *differences*, judgment, and clarity of vision as essential to Beauty and the "feminine" aesthetic mode; while the masculine mode of "power" depends on *resemblance* that actively frustrates clear vision. For Burke, feminine "clarity" (a masculine trait for Locke) produces, in the end, only bathos; it takes "obscure" masculine vision (obscurity is feminine in Locke's view) to produce the terror of the truly sublime. Thus in spite of the sublimity of their shared masculine vision (or perhaps because of its obscurity), superior "strength" in the masculine aesthetic mode and manifest "weakness" in the feminine aesthetic mode are finally the only attributes of gendered aesthetics discourse on which the two philosophers of image and idea can agree.

If the respective gender designations of image and idea are remarkably unstable, however, a more dependable set of alternatives is made available by the tradition that aligns *ideas* with soul or spirit, and *images* with body or flesh. Contrary to Patterson's assumption, when Milton wishes to reify Love's effort toward the spiritual goal of restoring "the almost faded ammunition of his Deity," the polemicist may be less concerned with gender per se than he is with a need to shed some of the carnal affect his negative images of heterosexual coupling have acquired in the course of his argument. As in the antiprelatical tracts, in the divorce tracts it is the graphic, corporeal imagery that the reader—perhaps also the writer—most vividly and memorably experiences. The familiar contrasts between Milton's coupling and anticoupling figures show why. Sexuality in a loveless marriage is reduced to dreary "work of male and female," an "animal or beastish meeting . . . brutish congress," a "sublunary and bestial burning," or "the promiscuous draining of a carnal rage . . . a perilous hazard and

snare" (II.240, 275, 269, 355). The hapless couple becomes "two car-
kasses chain'd unnaturally together; or as it may happ'n, a living soule
bound to a dead corps" (II.326). On the other hand, ideal sexual union
based on peace and mutual love is portrayed as a "human society,"
"kindly and voluntarie . . . *Benevolence*," "choisest home-blessings,"
"cordial and exhilarating cup of solace," "cheerful conversation of man
with woman," "rationall burning," and "pure and more inbred desire
of joyning . . . in conjugall fellowship a fit conversing soul" (II.275,
270, 342, 311, 235, 251). As with the antiprelatical tracts, the images of
ideality are probably the ones we'd choose to live with, but the anti-
pathetic images of destructive union are the ones most difficult to
erase from our carnally responsive imaginations: ideas evanesce under
fleshly persistence. Needless to say, if Milton thought that shifting
from images of heterosexual to homosexual coupling would prevent
this from happening, the strategy was doomed. Rhetorically, a mere
corporeal shift of gender would achieve, instead of copulating bodies of
male and female, only copulating bodies of male and male. Either way,
the rhetoric of bodily coupling insists on its own carnality.

Yet it is questionable whether Milton chose the Eros/Anteros myth
for (conscious or unconscious) reasons of gender in the first place. As
Arnold Stein has shown, Milton's arguments about love may "owe
something to Plato" without necessarily becoming dependent on Pla-
tonic concepts. For example, although Milton would obviously dismiss
the fanciful notion that human beings were originally hermaphroditic,
he for argumentative purposes "needs the suggested relation between
likeness and love which is presented whimsically in the *Symposium*,
and yet is a part of Plato's master-concept of 'sameness.' "[16] The relation
between likeness and love in Milton's handling of the Eros/Anteros
myth resembles not so much what Patterson calls "the mindset of
Adam after the Fall," yearning for an all-male world in the manner
of "Angels without Feminine,"[17] as it does the etherealized, bodiless
union of the angels themselves. If our response as we read the Eros/
Anteros passage includes visualization of copulating boys, that con-
crete image has been fleshed out accordingly by our own imaginations,
not by Milton's rhetoric. Milton creates his Eros/Anteros image of
idealized love in the same kinds of deliberately *incorporeal* terms he
uses to create his other images of godly coupling: "that mystery of joy

and union," that "cordial and exhilerating cup of solace" (II.258, 311). When Eros finds Anteros at last, "he kindles and repairs the almost faded ammunition of his Deity by the reflection of a coequal & *homogeneal* fire" (II.255). This depiction of loving and equal reunion as a mutually reflecting divine flame avoids not only gender distinctions but gender itself, along with every other suggestion of corporeality. It is an avoidance that Fallon has noticed accompanying all Milton's portrayals of spiritual union: "The collapsing of gender distinctions attendant upon this retreat from graphic detail is prophetic of the Spirit who is both cock and hen in the act of creation in *Paradise Lost*, and prophetic even more so of the genderless but physical relations of the epic's angels."[18] What is abrogated by the collapse of gender distinctions in Milton's ideal-love rhetoric is not heterosexuality but *conflictual* difference—the "encroachments of difference" included by Stanley Fish in the curious amalgamation of forces that Milton's carnal rhetoric commissions only to rescind: forces like "woman, sexuality, interpretation."[19] The heterogeneous character of what is rescinded therefore guarantees that no ideology, not "masculinist or any other" is finally gratified by Milton's rhetorical procedure.[20] Milton's argument in *Doctrine and Discipline* would have all conflictual differences submit to nothing more, or less, than what Milton most desires to submit to himself: dissolution of the carnally conflictual and individuated self into the perfect wholeness of ideal union. It is true that the desire for submission articulated by Milton is really "two contradictory things": he wants "to dissolve his ego, and he wants to be the one (the ego) that announces and performs the dissolving; he at once seeks and resists dissolution; or rather, *in* seeking it, he is also (and necessarily) resisting it."[21] But the contradiction expressed by Milton's desire is a response to—indeed, a reverse image of—the paradoxical dynamics of divine generation, whereby unified spirit produces differentiated flesh. In one way or another, the interactive ambiguities that bind ideological and philosophical monism to expressive dualism are thus recapitulated with every creative impulse.

It had been the conflictual differences of inchoate physical matter in the primal creation scene that had first required God's "great divorcing act": "downward purg'd / The black tartareous cold infernal dregs / Adverse to life: then founded, then conglob'd / Like things to like" (*PL* VII.237–40). In the rhetoric of Milton's divorce argument, the "like things" are Eros and Anteros, whose unconflicted complementary union restores Love to godhead. Like Eros and Anteros, Milton's angels in *Paradise Lost* are themselves also gendered; but their highly sensuous, and yet manifestly incorporeal, love unions clearly are not: the angels "obstacle find none / Of membrane, joint, or limb, exclusive bars . . . Total they mix, Union of Pure with Pure / Desiring" (*PL* VIII.624–28). By representing in his angels the paradox of a sensuous love union that is replete both with total fulfillment and with open desire, Milton acknowledges, yet denies lasting force to, the disequalizing conflictual dialectic that has vexed gender distinctions throughout the history of human experience in the fallen world.

ICONOCLASM AND THE RHETORIC OF THE FLESH

Meanwhile, in that fallen world, Milton's antipathetic gendered images stick in our minds, for reasons he would justify on polemical and rhetorical grounds. It is surely true that Milton's case against canon law in the divorce tracts is intimately informed by his experience of mistaken marriage, just as his case against the episcopal hierarchy had been informed by what he had experienced of Anglican church politics. His polemical writing obviously has its personal dimension. But the more important and immediately determining influence on the animus of Milton's image rhetoric is the stance of his polemical opponent. To misconstrue Milton's specific rhetorical target is inescapably to misinterpret his weaponry. For example, the apparent absence of an expressed concern for children leads one reader to ascribe to Milton an attitude of "contemptuous bawdry" on the issue.[22] But the contempt in the *Colasterion* passage that gives rise to this interpretation is clearly not directed toward children. Rather, it is directed toward Milton's polemical opponent, the "Answerer" to *Doctrine and Discipline*, whose ignorance of provisions for children in "the ancient civil Law" shows that such learning "was not in his Tenures" (II.735). For Milton's personal attitude toward children, on the other hand, we might just as easily refer to his statement regarding children of a second marriage:

And because some think the childer'n of a second matrimony succéeding a divorce would not be a holy seed, it hinder'd not the Jews from being so, and why should we not think them more holy then the offspring of a former ill-twisted wedlock, begott'n only out of a bestiall necessitie without any true love or contentment, or joy to their parents, so that in some sense we may call them the *childer'n of wrath* and anguish, which will as little conduce to their sanctifying, as if they had been bastards; for nothing more then disturbance of minde suspends us from approaching to God. (II.259–60)

Milton's appropriation from Ephesians 2:3 of *"childern of wrath"* converts that metaphor for unregenerate humanity to an image of all the evils that spring from "ill-twisted wedlock"—evils experienced as well by the children of those marriages, "begott'n only out of a bestiall necessitie," children whose own "sanctifying" is no better served by the legal bond of marriage than if the parents had not been married at all. But regarding what ought to be the place of children, Milton leaves no doubt in this passage. It is a place prepared for them by "true love" and "contentment," which not only enables their own sanctification but also permits them to be "a joy to their parents." The "weak supposes of Infants" with which Milton charges his polemical opponent in *Colasterion* (II.734–35) are weak precisely because the Answerer ignores substantive causes of misery in children's lives. Legal concern for the flesh that excludes concern for the spirit leads inexorably to degradation of both: "for nothing more then disturbance of minde suspends us from approaching to God." Hence the visceral animus of Milton's rhetoric of the flesh. Since betrayal of the flesh is the only betrayal recognized by canon law as a crime against marriage, it is the fleshly icon that Milton's image-rhetoric must demolish.

Yet the hazards of the iconoclastic rhetorical maneuver can be measured by the critical responses to it. Readers who find themselves attracted to Milton's healthy and beneficent couplings may nevertheless feel that these are etherealized practically out of existence. At the same time, Milton's brutalized fleshly couplings seem at crucial points to constitute the only tangible reality for marital communion. The more harmoniously his marital pairings are conceptualized, the less concretely realizable they seem to be. While we may attribute this predicament to the decorporealization of gender differences, Fallon suggests that such reasoning still fails to set at ease our sense that something remains amiss:

> To balance the many "anatomically correct" images of debased copulation Milton can summon only . . . one from which the distinction of gender is washed away together with the harshness. . . . Although Milton has made "legitimate and good the carnal act," he avoids in the tracts the frank eroticism of *Paradise Lost*, partly for reason of genre, but also because in the 1640s he still finds "something of pollution in it" (II.326). (81)

When carnal weapons are used against a carnal opponent, the prospects for ideal vision get caught in the crossfire. The rhetoric of gender that burdens strategic dualism places a similar burden on the redemptive capacities of the flesh.[23] Arguably, the "frank eroticism" that we might hope to find in the divorce tracts could be missing not, as Fallon argues, because Milton "still finds 'somthing of pollution in it' " but because, as far as Milton is concerned, the rhetoric of an attack on canon law does not warrant celebration of frank eroticism. But critical misinterpretations of Milton's rhetorical choices suggest that his iconoclastic pitching of flesh against flesh may on occasion work too well.

Or it may, on Milton's longer view, work exactly as it should. However elusive in concrete terms, the gratifying symmetries of image and syntax that shape *Doctrine and Discipline*'s rhetoric of ideal union resemble the seductive but illusory vision of earthly perfection that the libertine sensibility, at its most idealistic, actively strove for. It is a vision Milton's carnal rhetoric already knew it could create. His evocation of the "age of gold" in the *Nativity Ode* had shared with libertine idealism the notion that all that is needed to recover a fallen world to its original state of joy and innocent pleasure is our sustained creative repudiation of the outward manifestations of worldly corruption:

> For if such holy song
> Enwrap our fancy long,
>   Time will run back, and fetch the age of gold,
> And speckled vanity
> Will sicken soon and die,
>   And lep'rous sin will melt from earthly mould,
> And hell itself will pass away,
> And leave her dolorous mansions to the peering day.[24]

Under the holy spell of sustained creative vision, or "fancy," evil falls
away and makes space for the regenerate moral order to come. Yet the
affective character of a space thus provided hints toward the possibility
that sustained creative vision alone will not be sufficient to the task
of redemption. Fancy's "holy song" can recollect or "fetch" the age
of gold; but if vanity and sin melt away, their "earthly mould" never-
theless stays in place. When hell disappears from her mansions, her
mansions not only remain, but they remain "dolorous." Moreover, the
light that exposes hell's empty mansions is itself a relentless custo-
dian, "peering day." Over such a landscape, the regenerate moral order
that rises in a single splendid action may at first seem perfectly spon-
taneous:

> Yea Truth, and Justice then
> Will down return to men,
>   Orbed in a rainbow; and like glories wearing
> Mercy will sit between,
> Throned in celestial sheen,
>   With radiant feet the tissued clouds down steering. (141–46)

But the light of peering day had shone harshly on hell's dolorous man-
sions, and the residual effect of that harshness can now be seen to work
on Milton's vision of the golden age as well. The longer his creative
vision is sustained, the more its language betrays the contrived artifice
of its structure:

> And heaven as at some festival,
> Will open wide the gates of her high palace hall. (147–48)

What had started as "holy song" has, by the end of Milton's fantasia
on the reign of Truth, Justice, and Mercy, been reified into little more
than spectacular display. When the next line reveals that "wisest fate
says no" to this youthful evocation of the golden age, Milton's vision
retrospectively reassembles itself as the miscellany of carnal properties
from which its image-making author had appropriated it—the "tissued
clouds" and "celestial sheen" of a "heaven" artfully contrived for the
"festival" masque of some "high palace hall."

A similar fate, as the more mature Milton realized, would neces-
sarily be met by the blissful promise held forth in any libertine, though

empyreal, vision of the flesh. Such a vision was Milton's image of ideal coupling—a vision delineated, and therefore limited, by the affective resources of carnal rhetoric. The pressure toward unified vision in the divorce tracts provides ample evidence that Milton's monism, fully articulated in *De Doctrina Christiana*, had in fact been with him even in 1642. But since *De Doctrina*'s analytical distinctions could strip from Milton's purely theological arguments the affective and persuasive rhetoric that his polemics required, the rhetorical dualism that disturbs the philosophically monistic *Doctrine and Discipline* did not have to interfere with the arguments of the theological tract. Thus an unambiguously monistic Milton could affirm in *De Doctrina* that "the whole man is the soul, and the soul the man: a body, in other words, an individual substance, animated, sensitive, and rational." As Fallon explains, "If all substance is both vital and tangible inseparably, it can nevertheless be spoken of as one or the other in turn."[25] Such distinctions are fully answerable to the doctrinal aims of Milton's theological treatise, for which reason *De Doctrina* is able so methodically to set down Milton's understanding of all that he finds demonstrably knowable of Christianity.

But the *demonstrably* knowable is not all that can or should be known to the creative, self-transforming mind. *De Doctrina*'s intellectual rigor severely constrains what Milton would see as a necessary imaginative treatment of "the whole man [as] the soul, and the soul the man." The affective dimension of "the whole man" is fundamental to the all-inclusive aims of transformative desire—aims whose embrace of the threefold activities of cognition, imagination, and feeling might superficially resemble, but cannot parallel or explicate, *De Doctrina*'s threefold terms for the soul, "an individual substance, animated, sensitive, and rational."[26] For the requisites of transformative desire, the insufficiency of the latter, Aristotelian terms is demonstrated by the metaphoric constructs that vivify nearly every other piece of writing by Milton. Both in his poetry and in his polemics, imaginative solutions to the metaphysical dilemma are actively pursued: that is the function of carnal rhetoric. Yet, as iconoclastic metaphor theory suggests, the imaginative pursuit not only *knows* that sensuous spectacle is artfully contrived, but it also actively *requires* the mortality of linguistic art in order to sustain transformative desire. Because the imaginative pursuit assumes the mortality of all language, imagination's linguistic construct must be fluid, constantly changing. In its mode of operation, therefore, the imaginative linguistic construct must finally resemble neither the rigorously explanatory doctrine of Milton's theological treatise, nor even the desirable yet illusionistic and potentially blinding perfections of his empyreal vision. Instead of these, what the imaginative linguistic construct must operatively resemble is the liquid, endlessly refreshed, streaming fountain of Truth in *Areopagitica.*

Ultimately, Milton's struggle to build a monistic vision from a dualistic language in *The Doctrine and Discipline of Divorce* parallels his rhetorical struggle toward an argumentative image of perfect union between man and wife, between Law and Gospel, between body and soul, between the Word and the flesh, between humanity and God. That he succeeds in making these multiple pairs rhetorically inextricable from one another by the affective dictate of empyreal coupling suggests how close, at this stage in his career, Milton actually was to an Adam who could wish to subsume himself and his entire universe into an icon of perfect union: "Was she thy God?" As the omniscient divine judge of Adam clearly knew, the passionately desired and fleshly image of perfect union is both expressed and critically exposed by the terms of the question itself: not "she," nor "they," nor any other desirable *image* of perfect union can either illustrate or substitute for the temporally unattainable perfect union with God.

For the creative iconoclast in Milton, therefore, an even greater *transformative* desire impels the whole and vital person beyond the carnal image of perfect union toward an iconoclastic response. The gratifying, but potentially self-limiting, affective symmetries of *Doctrine and Discipline*'s idealized mortal vision thus become the greatest stimulus to the iconoclastic activity of Milton's images in *Areopagitica.*

4

"THE IMAGE OF GOD IN THE EYE"

Areopagitica's Truth

For the argument of *Areopagitica*, carnal rhetoric undertakes to persuade readers of the truth of its own expendability. The image-construction that in *The Doctrine and Discipline of Divorce* had been an activity of generating inspired analysis, of imbuing the real with the ideal, becomes in *Areopagitica* an exercise in the temporality of images per se. By their vital activity, rather than by their iconic representations, the images of *Areopagitica* illustrate a principle for the right conduct not just of poetic imagery but as well of every other concern in our lives—material, intellectual, moral, spiritual. By their operation, the images in *Areopagitica* evince a newly matured conception of truth. In *Doctrine and Discipline*, Milton's truth no longer lay sequestered in the still air of the study, nor were the claims of truth exploited, as had occurred in the antiprelatical tracts, to justify Milton's indulgence in powerful sensory language. Truth was, however, consistently expressed there through telling images: throughout the divorce tracts, truth could be recognized by an outward sign, the harmonious coupling. *Areopagitica*, on the other hand, regularly points to the inadequacy of all signs to express the truths they serve. Milton's iconoclastic treatment of images may be summarized, as Ernest Gilman has noted, by application of the Phoenix symbol that Milton invokes toward the end of *Samson Agonistes:* "In a moment of destruction and re-creation like the Phoenix's own, Milton revives an image only to discard it in the service of a higher truth which it cannot represent."[1]

Areopagitica actually asserts a new discontinuity in Milton's use of images—not an accidental discontinuity like that between image and argument in the antiprelatical tracts, but rather, a discontinuity whose activity demonstrates that images are to be used, not rested in. Stanley Fish has argued that if Milton treats printed books as repositories of the highest achievements of the human spirit, he does so for the express purpose of driving his argument *away* from that same laudatory principle.[2] I suggest that the activity of Milton's images in the tract not only illustrates this rhetorical maneuver but actually locates its rationale in the affective domain of transformative desire. This domain is manifested by the activities both of Milton's images and of his argument for humankind. The kinetic images bear witness to something they themselves cannot contain. Similarly, human beings serve the interests of truth only when a desire for truth leads them unceasingly to search beyond whatever they think they have learned of it. For both images and men, this activity is a transformative and re-creative impetus that depends on *affective indeterminacy*, that anarchic element in the imaginative process that links writer to reader through metaphor's iconoclasm. The creative value that we have seen placed on articulate insufficiency by iconoclastic metaphor theory thus applies as well to the aspiring transformations undertaken by human beings, as they strive toward the perfect freedom of the infinite divine.[3] To the creative iconoclast, each step in the process of transformation is valued not, as we might assume, for its evidence that the aspirer is embarked on the *correct* path: that would mean imposing doctrinal judgment on a concern whose programmatic content, as we will see in the debate over "progressivism" in *Areopagitica*, must by its own logic remain indeterminate. Rather than signifying a specific program or agenda, each step indicates to the creative iconoclast that transformation is being undertaken in the interest of imaginative freedom. Much as "reason is but choosing," so ultimately truth is not in itself an objective at all, but only a mode of discovery. *Areopagitica* demonstrates the perspective on truth that Milton will later make explicit in *Eikonoklastes:* "For Truth is properly no more then Contemplation; and her utmost efficiency is but teaching."[4] Furthermore, truth's "efficiency" now supports virtuous engagement with the world, thus rejecting the isolation of truth's ideality in both the antiprelatical tracts and the divorce tracts: "To sequester out of the world into *Atlantick* and *Eutopian* politics, which never can be drawn into use, will not mend our condition; but to ordain wisely as in this world of evil, in the midd'st whereof God hath plac't us unavoidably."[5] Truth is neither to be lamented as lost nor regretted as yet unfound. For, in *Areopagitica*, the only *substantial* "meaning" of truth lies in the activity required by the search itself.

THE SANCTITY OF THE IDEA

We may recall Nietzsche's concept of "truth" as merely worn out metaphor, "a sum of human relations which become poetically and rhetorically intensified, metamorphosed, adorned, and after long usage seem to a nation fixed, canonic, and binding; truths are illusions of which one had forgotten that they *are* illusions."[6] The Milton of *Areopagitica* would have had little quarrel with the underlying premise of this passage—the idea that what we know, we know metaphorically; knowing comes to us, that is, by way of metaphor. He would also have agreed that what we commonly regard as "truths" are ordinarily illusory constructs of our own making. Therefore, against the hardening of these illusions and this metaphoric knowledge into what Nietzsche calls "fixed truths" that become "canonic and binding," *Areopagitica*'s images actively militate. For *Areopagitica*'s images refuse to let us forget that they are illusions; they resist the pressure to convert them into truths by demonstrating their ephemerality. Adequate only to gesture toward truth and, momentarily, to acknowledge truth's existence, the images relinquish all claims to even symbolic possession of truth. Yet their relinquishing activity yields a better understanding of Milton's concept of truth than their power to signify it could ever achieve. For in contrast with the images of either the divorce tracts or the antiprelatical tracts, the images in *Areopagitica* subvert our carnal propensity for grasping at and accepting as true the externals, the incidental appearances, the forms an idea may take, instead of exercising our reason toward a lively comprehension.

For example, the central image of books as men is no sooner expressed than it is metamorphosed, restored, and finally shed, by the fluid thought to which it can give only momentary shape:

I deny not, but that it is of greatest concernment in the Church and Commonwealth, to have a vigilant eye how Bookes demeane themselves, as well as men; and thereafter to confine, imprison, and do sharpest justice on them as malefactors: For Books are not absolutely dead things, but doe contain a potensie of life in them to be as active as that soule was whose progeny they are; nay they do preserve as in a violl the purest efficacie and extraction of that living intellect that bred them. I know they are as lively, and as vigorously productive, as those fabulous Dragons teeth; and being sown up and down, may chance to spring up armed men. (492)

The passage treats books as reasoning men even before the metaphor is fully articulated: the phrase "how Bookes demeane themselves" takes books' volitional capacity for granted. But even as books are confirmed as actors and doers, "as men," they are further recognized as potential wrongdoers, "malefactors," capable of deserving confinement, imprisonment, "sharpest justice." Moreover, the image of books as prisoners is itself never allowed full realization. Milton briefly evokes the corporal malefactor to reify a moral dimension of the written word. But the image is proffered as a transitory vision only; whatever we may learn from it of the potential powers and influences of books, we are not permitted to regard the image itself as truth, or even as a representation of truth. The image gives us only a moment's grasp of an elusive potential danger. If we actually try to hold on to the image—if we dwell on the picture of books as imprisoned malefactors—our grasp converts the image to a visually static absurdity, items of printed matter languishing behind bars.

But the thought to which books-as-prisoners gave a fleeting shape eludes our stultifying grasp by acknowledging, and moving on to explicate, the metaphor itself. It is not the mere corporality but the vitality of men that books can be said to resemble: "For Books are not absolutely dead things, but doe contain a potencie of life in them to be as active as that soule was whose progeny they are." And the vitality itself is more than just lively; the language that attributes sexually generative powers to spirit ("potencie of life . . . soule . . . whose progeny they are") alludes, without succumbing, to the kind of interesting tension between the fleshly and the sublime that Milton had used effectively in *Doctrine and Discipline's* "mariagebed of that holy seed."[7] Yet even this compelling imagerial union is cast aside, used only as a step toward further refinement: "nay they do preserve as in a violl the purest efficacie and extraction of that living intellect that bred them." The generative human image, rarified to a quintessence, then evaporates without notice as it is replaced by a magically generative image from Greek mythology, the legendary soldier-seeds planted by the Phoenician prince Cadmus: "I know they are as lively, and as vigorously productive, as those fabulous Dragons teeth; and being sown up and down, may chance to spring up armed men."

So we come full circle to the original image of books as men; but now they are freshly armed, ready for battle. Is this complexly evolved warfaring image books' true incarnation? Are soldier-books, as Christians militant, preparing to fight the good fight? If so, the thought that created them doesn't seem much to care: books fight battles, it's an available calling, let them do as they will. The thought presses on again, casually discarding the entire books-as-men sequence in favor of books-instead-of-men, books-beyond-men. The violence implicit in "dragon's teeth" and "armed men" is detached from those safely remote mythic, yet serviceably militant, trappings; and it is subsequently turned against both men and books, with books the greater victim:

And yet on the other hand unlesse warinesse be us'd, as good almost kill a Man as kill a good Book; who kills a Man kills a reasonable creature, Gods Image; but hee who destroyes a good Booke, kills reason it selfe, kills the Image of God, as it were in the eye. (492)

Here the violence, although visually apprehensible in "kills a reasonable creature," nevertheless eludes our visual grasp as it moves on to "kills reason it selfe"; and this movement parallels an even more elusive progression from "Gods Image" to "the Image of God . . . in the eye." This latter progression actually requires us to construct an image of the un-imageable—to create for the purpose of our own comprehension a visual prototype for the kind of ceaseless intellectual and spiritual activity Milton has in mind whenever he refers in *Areopagitica* to "truth." Instead of locating truth as Nietzsche does in the illusory and wornout metaphors themselves, Milton locates truth in *the perceptual activity* that metaphors have both the affective power to stimulate and the "vehicular" capacity (to adapt Richards's term) to carry. If "truth is properly no more than contemplation," then reason is truth. But more tellingly, reason is not God's image (i.e., man) but rather the image of God—that is, the dynamic mental concept or idea of God—that only reasoning beings can entertain. As such, it is an image not doctrinally formulated or externally perceived, but an image "in the eye": that beam of inward light that marks the intuitive moment of intellectual or imaginative perception. Our image of God "in the eye" signifies both that toward which we aim—the idea—and our activity of aiming toward it. Yet as reason cannot itself be a thing achieved, but only a means of achieving, so only as it lives "in the eye" can our "image of God," our idea, remain valid and useful—or "true." In our mortal grasp, when the image itself is taken as truth, it becomes canonic and binding. The forgotten illusions that Nietzsche calls "truth" are what Milton would call superstitious idols, graven images, icons. Reason itself, on the other hand—the iconoclastic activity of the seeking mind, the image of God that can live only *in the eye*—this is Milton's image for truth. It is an image that, as it represents imaginative vision, cannot itself be concretely visualized.

To delineate truth's preserve by retaining the image of God solely "in the eye" is to stake out for the affective freedoms of transformative desire the same territory that is so staked out by iconoclastic metaphor theory. Of course, the metaphors "stake out" and "territory" themselves actually misrepresent what they refer to by implying that it is something material, measurable, discrete—exactly the wrong message. Yet the idea is deliverable only by such misleading messengers, for the right message lives not in metaphor but in imaginative vision, "in the eye." The disparity between idea and message or messenger can never be overcome by carnal rhetoric—nor need it be, given carnal rhetoric's self-expending purpose. Both the rhetorical strategies of Milton's imagerial sequences and the theoretical strategies of iconoclastic metaphor analysis accommodate the ontological longing that underlies what I have called the rationalist's loophole for God.[8]

Nevertheless, the concern for the sanctity of the idea that so obviously governs *Areopagitica* makes tracking the metaphors by which Milton actually explores the idea an often disconcerting exercise. It is disconcerting because of what seems to be Milton's casual irreverence in the tract toward his cherished subject, the *idea*, and also toward each of the subject's related manifestations: truth, understanding, and knowledge. The metaphors he uses to delve into his subject actively discourage our drawing from them the kinds of reassuring inferences that their conventional affective associations would otherwise allow.

For instance, Milton's application of the commercial metaphor to "truth" suggests at first glance that he regards the hustle of trade activity as somehow morally or aesthetically beneath the character of the abstract ideals that he values:

Truth and understanding are not such wares as to be monopoliz'd and traded in by tickets and statutes, and standards. We must not think to make a staple commodity of all the knowledge in the Land, to mark and licence it like our broad cloath, and our wooll packs. (535–36)

To suggest that abstractions like truth, understanding, and knowledge conceivably *might* be manipulated as "staple commodities" by the bustling apparatus of trade—tickets, statutes, and standards—seems by its palpable incongruity to elevate such ideas above the mundane exigencies of broadcloth and woolpacks. This would especially seem true since Milton here explicitly warns us against making such a crass mistake. But if we try to extrapolate from or build upon this implication, we will only be tripped up a few pages later, where Milton deplores "the incredible losse, and detriment that this plot of licencing puts us to, more then if som enemy at sea should stop up all our hav'ns, and ports, and creeks, it hinders and retards the importation of our richest Marchandize, Truth" (548). Here, not only is truth *not* a thing apart from or superior to merchandise; it *is* merchandise, and that of the most elite and self-indulgent kind, the foreign-made luxury item. So the merchandising metaphor turns out to be equally valid or invalid for showing how truth is or is not to be regarded. And since it can be used in so many ways, all inconclusive, the metaphor itself makes no independent claims about the nature of truth—that is, about what truth looks like, where we might find it, how we might know it—what, in essence, truth *really* is. In other words, the commercial metaphor declines to pass the kind of judgment that might permit our shifting perceptions about truth to reach the end-point of metaphoric transformation, the point of conceptual peace and rest.[9]

To use images rightly is to have recourse to them, not depend on them. Should we depend on *Areopagitica*'s images, expecting analysis of the images themselves to yield light, they will disappoint us. As instruments of analysis, they serve the flow of ideas about truth; their presence makes no guarantee for a truth of their own. The superficially promising metaphor that treats books as nourishment bears this out. As "food for the mind," printed books could be expected to stimulate intellectual growth. But in *Areopagitica*, the nourishing of minds bears so little resemblance to the nourishing of bodies that the nourishment cliché begins immediately to self-destruct:

> Wholesome meats to a vitiated stomack differ little or nothing from unwholesome; and best books to a naughty mind are not unappliable to occasions of evill. Bad meats will scarce breed good nourishment in the healthiest concoction; but herein the difference is of bad books, that they to a discreet and judicious Reader serve in many respects to discover, to confute, to forewarn, and to illustrate. (512–13)

If good books are like good meats, it is not because of their shared goodness but rather because of the complete *irrelevance* of that goodness. Whatever effects good books might seem to have, these effects derive not from the quality of the books themselves but from the quality of the readers, good or evil, who consume them: "best books to a naughty mind are not unappliable to occasions of evill." Furthermore, the nourishment metaphor provides no convenient negative corollary. If the effects of "wholesome meats" offer no analogous insight into the probable effects of wholesome books, then the deleterious effects of unwholesome meats will enlighten us even less. Indeed, the books-as-nourishment metaphor makes its strongest claim at the very moment the argument forswears it as a comparison: "Bad meats will scarce breed good nourishment . . . but *herein the difference* is of bad books" (my italics). At this point, it is actually the inaptitude rather than the aptitude of the nourishment metaphor that yields insight.

Yet even a negative conclusion about the truth-value of the nourishment metaphor would be mistaken. When, later in the same paragraph, Milton regathers the metaphor, both meats and books are made part of a "universall" diet in which neither goodness nor badness but only temperance is given a significant charge:

> I conceive therefore, that when God did enlarge the universall diet of mans body, saving ever the rules of temperance, he then also, as before, left arbitrary the dyeting and repasting of our minds; as wherein every mature man might have to exercise his owne leading capacity. (513)

With this, the nourishment metaphor abandons its good/bad dichoto-mizing altogether, in order to elaborate upon moderation via the Exo-dus story of manna in the wilderness. The books-as-nourishment meta-phor in and of itself neither provides insight nor offers answers. Rather, it facilitates an exploratory and analytical process that requires us ulti-mately to make our own determinations regarding food for the mind.

The casual self-transformations of *Areopagitica*'s image sequences graphically demonstrate the paradox that lies at the heart of creative iconoclasm and its practice in metaphor. The disruption of reference that inheres in all metaphor construction is forthrightly enacted by *Areopagitica*'s images for the sake of the tract's highest cause, the sanctity of the idea. As a cause, the sanctity of the idea reaches be-yond books (which, as Fish persuasively argues, are in themselves ir-relevant), beyond freedom of expression (however desirable or broadly defined), and even beyond "the constituting of human vertue"—a mis-sion that books of all kinds are eminently qualified, but not foreor-dained, to serve.[10] The principle of the sanctity of the idea reaches beyond, because its domain is the imaginative realm from which all of these lesser concerns derive their being. The undertaking for Milton, for metaphor, and for the image sequences of *Areopagitica* is to im-plement strategies that liberate *the idea* from what would otherwise be canonic and binding. Such an undertaking specifically would guar-antee right of existence to the realm of *indeterminate possibility* on which transformative desire entirely depends.

A prime beneficiary of such a guarantee is clearly the reader, but only that reader who is already committed to the same cause. Com-mon interest in the ineffable "image of God in the eye" bonds images of reader and writer and book, in a rhetoric whose permutation of these reified guarantors works to *preserve indeterminate* the unreified potency of the idea. The dedication of fleshly rhetoric to the undefinable interests of the spirit is nowhere more graphically displayed than when, on behalf of the unreified idea, *Areopagitica*'s images of enforced censorship engage in the same emancipatory activity on the affective level as do the tract's images of uncensored reading. As a censor, "Martin the Fifth, by his bull, not only prohibited, but was the first that excommunicated the reading of heretical books" (502). "Excommunicated the reading" conveys the affective import of the individual reader completely assimilated into the moral, spiritual, and intellectual activity that is his reading. That is to say, the gerund "reading" is made by the punitive action "excommunicated" to *feel* as if "reading" were not an activity engaged in by persons, but itself an independent agent subject to prosecution. This affective import is not delivered by the merely iconic or semantic information provided by the image: the practical target of the excommunication must obviously be the reader, not "reading." Nevertheless, the censorious excommunicator's true aim is to obliterate precisely the kind of imaginative independence that Milton's image of "excommunicated . . . reading" so eloquently delivers by its *inability* to depict. Unreified as it is, "excommunicated . . . reading" thus acquires an affective vitality *outside* the semantic and the iconic, an independent life *beyond* what the image materially presents.

The same holds true, we find, for imaginative independence in writing, as the writer's flesh and the writer's text are depicted interchangeably:

Which cours *Leo* the 10, and his successors follow'd, untill the Councell of Trent, and the Spanish Inquisition engendring together brought forth, or perfeted those Catalogues, and expurging Indexes that rake through the entralls of many an old good Author, with a violation wors then any could be offer'd to his tomb. (503)

The printed catalogues and expurging indexes, as they are themselves fruits of a monstrous copulation ("the Councell of Trent, and the Spanish Inquisition engendring together brought forth"), impart perverse sexual overtones to these censoring activities, suggesting sodomite necrophilia in the violation "rake through the entralls." But beyond vilifying censors, these grotesque images by their very carnality liberate the moral and aesthetic *idea* of "old good authors" from the necrophilic literalism whose "bringing forth" is a rape. The images liberate the idea when they expose how the literalist estimates goodness by the extent to which "old . . Author[s]" may be anatomized and rendered aseptic ("perfeted") in catalogues and indexes. By reifying "old good Author[s]" into the carnal properties of their books and their entrails (thus making these authors physiologically as well as ideologically vulnerable to the censors' "expurgations"), the images depict a censoring act remarkable not only for its moral offensiveness ("a violation wors then . . . to his tomb") but also for its lack of imagination. What the images leave us to "see" can only be seen by an imaginative guarantor of the idea: that what the censors most had feared, and what they therefore had wished to expurgate from "old good Author[s]," was never to be found *there* (neither in bodies nor in books) in the first place.

PROGRESSIVISM AND THE PURSUIT OF
THAT WHICH IS FIXED, CANONIC, AND BINDING

To guarantee right of existence to the realm of indeterminate possibility is radically to deny a status of final arbiter to claims put forward by whatsoever sect, or doctrine, or prevailing consensus. Articulating the primacy of "elective poetics" in Milton's prose, Susanne Woods makes a powerful case for critical recognition that "dialogic engagement with the reader" takes precedence over ideology in the tracts.[11] Milton "relied on his reader's ability to choose beyond current ideological assumptions" by creating "distance between his text and cultural norms . . . in order to invite the reader to take a leap of faith toward redefinition."[12] Woods's argument clearly supports the case for affective indeterminacy: "to invite the reader to take a leap of faith toward redefinition" is a gesture at one with the rhetorical impetus that excites and is excited by transformative desire. Nevertheless, those readers who prefer to believe that *Areopagitica*'s polemic is bound to one or another determinate program find a degree of iconic support for their assumptions in Milton's comparison of Truth to the torn and scattered body of Osiris, with the friends of Truth portrayed as Isis's sad gatherers. To seekers of Milton's determinate program, the Egyptian myth encourages the supposition that truth is a sundered whole that requires only putting together again for all to come out right—for fallen humanity at last to restore order, to regain paradise, to "fetch the age of gold." Yet the Osiris portait, like the festival-masque heaven of the *Nativity Ode*, remains in the end an iconoclastic image. If the "image of God in the eye" is beyond visualization, the image of Truth we get with the Osiris portrait can be visualized only as a dismembered god, a shattered icon whose parts remain incapable of reuniting by human agency.

But the persistent critical tendency to interpret *Areopagitica*'s truth as a previously unified whole that can once again be made whole demands close examination, for this tendency consists with the essential Christian myth of regeneration that the image of Osiris directly illustrates in the tract. As a guide to Milton's determinate program, the Osiris tale leads to the following inferences. First, even if practically unreachable, truth is an aim whose full achievement would—in theory at least—bring to an end the program of relentless striving after it. And second, those elements of truth that the program has already achieved are fixed, absolute, to be held onto and vigilantly guarded against incursions by those who seek to destroy it.

By extension, the programmatic composition of the scattered limbs of Truth may be determined by what seems to operate in *Areopagitica* as fixed, canonic, and binding: scriptural authority, revolutionary republicanism, Protestant ideology. Nigel Smith has recently strengthened the case for reading *Areopagitica*'s program as broadly inclusive and structurally flexible, by demonstrating the multiple influences and contextual parallels that inform Milton's "new theory of ethics" in the tract, a theory manifested by "the exercise of choosing in a virtuous way."[13] Milton's frame of reference for the new ethics includes resources as varied as the intellectual milieu of Hartlib's scientific reformers, the tolerationist principles of Roger Williams, the Natural Law arguments of John Selden, and historical critiques of licentiousness by Paolo Sarpi and Bernardo Davanzati, in addition to the notoriously licentious writings of Aretino. Together, these influences shape not a model to be imitated, but a means of inculcating virtue through exercise of a multiplicity of choices. Yet even if Milton's program for "the collective recovery of lost and scattered divine truth" is conceived as no more determinate than a virtuous education through free choices that will lead to "the better circulation of knowledge," the implication remains that by means of such a program, in some concrete way, "reformed 'truth' may be reconstituted": "Milton envisages a return through virtue to that state of perfection in which nature and governance are harmonized, and true creativity is possible."[14] But this analysis leads to a problem. By locating truth's achievement in the "state of perfection," even a state attained under the virtuous dictate of harmonized governance and nature, Smith leaves truth fixed in an "age of gold" as canonic and binding as it began to seem to a perfect, unfallen Eve at the moment when, despite living in Paradise, she found herself moved by the Nietzschean serpent's sensuous appeal to transformative desire. The problem is not that perfection cannot be achieved; the problem is that, once perfection is achieved, *desire does not want it.*

This point is not wholly lost on proponents of progressivism like John Stuart Mill, with whose libertarian progressivism (despite Willmoore Kendall's caveat over a generation ago) Milton's case for virtuous reform through free exchange of ideas is still indirectly linked.[15] It is so linked primarily because the underlying assumptions of libertarian progressivism are identical to the assumptions that support what program-seeking readers of *Areopagitica* believe to be Milton's advocacy of an achievable truth. In their respective addresses to the requisites of transformative desire, the parallels in progressivist thought between Milton and Mill are almost, but not quite, as revealing as the distinctions.

First, the parallels. The complaint Milton raises in *Areopagitica* against the "heretick in the truth" (543) is exactly the complaint Mill raises in *On Liberty* against "prejudice" and "superstition":

Assuming that the true opinion abides in the mind, but abides as a prejudice, a belief independent of, and proof against, argument—this is not the way in which truth ought to be held by a rational being. This is not knowing the truth. Truth, thus held, is but one superstition the more, accidentally clinging to the words which enunciate a truth.[16]

Mill's "belief independent of, and proof against, argument" recapitulates Milton's "if he beleeve things only because his Pastor sayes so, or the Assembly so determins, without knowing other reason" (543). The affective distinctions between Mill's "prejudice" and Milton's "heresie" measure a shift, spanning more than two centuries, from the religious sphere to the social sphere in the rhetoric of reform. But the shift is less radical than at first it might appear. Milton too, throughout his polemical writings, uses the term "superstitions" to indicate these same phenomena. Whether for heresy, prejudice, or superstition, the purely *rational* process in either Mill's view or Milton's is the same: Mill's "accidentally clinging to the words which enunciate a truth" neatly mirrors Milton's "though his belief be true, yet the very truth he holds, becomes his heresie" (543). And against such accidental, clinging heresy, the only possible defense is the constant testing provided by the libertarian's free circulation of knowledge.

Mill's progressivism shares with the argument for achievable truth the assumption that with this free circulation of knowledge things would surely get better and better. From Mill's rationalist and libertarian perspective, this means that human affairs could gradually reach a point where there is actually nothing left to work on:

As mankind improve, the number of doctrines which are no longer disputed or doubted will be constantly on the increase: and the well-being of mankind may almost be measured by the number and gravity of the truths which have reached the point of being uncontested. ("On Liberty," 168)

Because it quantifies human well-being by the number and gravity of undoubted truths humanity shares, this statement virtually equates happiness in the human condition with self-satisfied stasis. But that would seem to mark the point where Mill's progressivism diverges from Milton's: self-satisfied stasis is precisely the condition against which the iconoclastic impetus militates. Uncontested doctrines are what give rise to Nietzsche's "fixed truths," to Milton's idols.

Mill's solution to this problem, curiously enough, turns out to be less satisfactorily "progressive" than Milton's. This is because Mill's solution slights or ignores the imaginative function of transformative desire, while at the same time remaining helplessly subject to it. In Mill's view, to keep alive the dynamics of debate, once its natural means—dissent and diversity of opinion—have grown obsolete, the progressive society must evolve artificial means:

If opponents of all important truths do not exist, it is indispensable to imagine them, and supply them with the strongest arguments which the most skilful devil's advocate can conjure up. ("On Liberty," 162)

The contrived expediency of Mill's safeguard against ideological stasis—the artificially invented "devil's advocate"—exposes the imaginative impoverishment of his progressivism. Mill's progressivism *must* assume, on a practical level, the possibility of human self-perfection: without this assumption, "progress" becomes an exercise in relativism. By the same logic, however, achievement of the absolute toward which "progress" aims would render human activity itself pointless. Since Mill's progressivism defines itself entirely in terms of concrete and rationally explicable human needs, his vision for a progressive society falters when confronted by ontological longing, the affective and imaginative dimension of inquiry which perpetually resists or escapes satisfactory rational and concrete realization. Ironically, this is the dimension of inquiry that prompts Mill's own anticipatory dread of stasis—a dread replete with the iconoclastic fear that the idea may itself be only a man-made image.[17] Achievable truth in Mill's rationalist and progressive social vision provokes so great a dread of entrapment by human finiteness, that truth's barriers must be breached or overleapt by the affective and imaginative arts of that "most skilful devil's advocate," perfectionism's escape-clause, the clever trickster mechanism needed to keep perfect, achieved truth alive. Unwittingly, Mill's rationalist mechanism acknowledges, without truly accommodating, the force of transformative desire.

But transformative desire does not only combat ideological stasis. As Mill's awkward retreat from perfection suggests, transformative desire may actually *require* the threat of stasis in order for desire to be prompted into existence. And this principle can be extended. Not only stasis but falsehood and error and conceptual inadequacy may be recognized as crucial to transformation. Rather than impediments to be overcome with the prospect that one day, like some dread disease, they will be finally wiped out (yet still, unlike diseases, compel us artfully to reinvent them), these multiple ways of being wrong are useful and necessary steps in an endless process of self-transformation. Like images, like icons, they are also instrumental in prompting the fear that the true idea may be no more than a delusive idol. In this way falsehood, error, and conceptual inadequacy function continually to reopen, on seemingly closeable questions, the dissatisfied inquiry that articulates desire: they actually help to generate the iconoclastic impetus that underlies creativity.

By contrast, an achieved state of "perfection" draws out the full meaning of the word's Latin root: man's "perfected" being is accomplished, performed, completed. "Perfection" leaves mankind with nothing more to do. Mill's own skepticism about the risks posed by "miscellaneous" humanity's will toward self-improvement saves him from dwelling too long on the societal implications of his brand of progressivism. He cannot quite free himself from the conviction that "perfected" mankind, being mortal, would surely mess things up. Implicitly, even his argument for a "devil's advocate" shows that by engaging in the libertarian promotion of progressive and relativist inquiry into truth, Mill knows that he does not really get rid of the absolute; he merely places it in incompetent hands.

That, of course, is where John Milton found he himself had placed it, just before the point in *Animadversions* where he at last manages to wrest his affective vision for English reform from the hands of the reformers and turn the entire absolutist project over to God.[18] In *Areopagitica*, by contrast, he no longer presumes on the basis of the absolute nor, for that matter, any definitive program for the achievement of truth. Indeed, when readers substantially ignore Willmoore Kendall's warning against reading Milton through the libertarian glass of Mill, it is because the principles that link Mill and Milton lie not in their common focus on any determinate social program for discovery of truth, but rather in their common regard for the *primacy of the individual* in the cause of intellectual freedom. According to Kendall's rendition of the libertarian "prevailing doctrine" (which his argument allows to stand for Mill's thought as well), the Free Society consists in an unrelenting search for Truth: "the 'value' at stake is Truth and the process by which truths are arrived at."[19] But the arguments of Mill and Milton both demonstrate a converse formulation: that the True Society consists in an unrelenting maintenance of Freedoms. And in this cause, it is Milton, not Mill, whose argument for individual freedom may be the more radically "progressive."

Milton's individualism is potentially more radical because he attributes oppression of the imagination to ideology itself: not just those particular ideological forerunners of modern progressivism that were being experimented with during the English reform period, but the working phenomena of programmable ideology in general—that is, any program for concrete achievement of truth. What *Areopagitica*'s Milton has come to recognize is that ideologies suppress imaginative freedom not because they exclude *other* ideologies: were that the case, then Mill's libertarian remedy of allowing free play to every conceivable doctrine would suffice. But it does not suffice, because it is the nature of all ideologies to harden into idols, to become fixed, canonic, and binding. The ideology Milton most notably sees as having reached this point is Roman Catholicism. The terms in which he critiques that ideology are worth studying for the *nonideological* light they shed on what Milton actually declares to be intolerable:

I mean not tolerated Popery, and open superstition, which *as it extirpats all religions and civill supremacies, so it self should be extirpat*, provided first that all charitable and compassionat means be us'd to win and regain the weak and the misled: that also which is *impious or evil absolutely either against faith or maners* no law can possibly permit, that intends not to unlaw it self. (565, my italics)

What is declared intolerable in this passage is not Catholic doctrine, is not *this* ideology as against *that* ideology, that is, Popery as against Presbyterianism. What is intolerable is rather the operation of any ideology or "open superstition" that would "extirpat" those guarantors of individual freedom on which imaginative self-transformation would actually depend. Public guarantors of imaginative freedom, in Milton's view, would necessarily include freedom of religious worship, maintenance of civil supremacy, and defense against assaults by whatever force would be "impious or evil absolutely" against faith or manners. Under the category "manners," as we find in a passage to which I will return in the next section, Milton lists "all recreations and pastimes, all that is delightfull to man" (523). That which must be defended from assault, then, is not any particular ideology but the full range of sensory, intellectual, spiritual, and imaginative experience. By institutionalizing orthodoxy, the Roman church reduces truth to precisely the sort of programmatic ideology and rote discipline that *Areopagitica* argues it is not—something to be fixed, literalized, obeyed, and followed without thought. Such a practice Milton regards not merely as a conflicting ideology, but as an active denial of the basic principle of intellectual discovery, a repudiation of the need for precisely the kind of imaginative and spiritual activity he writes *Areopagitica* to defend. To institutionalize truth is to contradict the vital principle on which he believes truth depends; it is to nail truth down, to convert it into a mere sign of itself, like a crucifix: "What but a vain shadow else is the abolition of *those ordinances, that hand writing nayl'd to the crosse,* what great purchase is this Christian liberty which *Paul* so often boasts of" (563).

To bring Milton's radicalism on this point into sharper focus, it is useful to compare what would be excluded from Milton's free society, and why he would exclude it, with the exclusionary conditions required to ensure freedom in Mill's society. For Mill's society, the ideology of progressivism has already itself become an idol so canonic that even its libertarian spokesman is betrayed by it into a tyrannous lapse of empathic imagination:

It is, perhaps, hardly necessary to say that this doctrine is meant to apply only to human beings in the *maturity of their faculties* . . . we may leave out of consideration those *backward states of society* in which the race itself may be considered as *in its nonage.* The *early difficulties in the way of spontaneous progress* are so great, that there is seldom any choice of means for overcoming them; and a ruler *full of the spirit of improvement* is warranted in the use of any expedients that will attain an end, perhaps otherwise unattainable. Despotism is a legitimate mode of government in dealing with barbarians, provided the end be their *improvement,* and the means justified by actually effecting that end. Liberty, as a principle, has no application to any state of things anterior to the time when mankind have become *capable of being improved* by free and equal discussion. Until then, there is nothing for them but implicit obedience to an Akbar or a Charlemagne, if they are so fortunate as to find one. ("On Liberty," 136; my italics)

The talisman for modern European orthodoxy is not of course religious reformation, but "progress" itself. Thus Mill's open society may well have no right to require a complacent member of that society to better himself, but if self-satisfaction happens to afflict another society, or worse, a whole nation, then the open society shall by all means be obliged to root it out. Whereas Milton had merely excluded from England those who would actively interfere with the light that might aid English reformation, Mill boldly defends the right of progressive nations ("full," no doubt, "of the spirit of improvement") to *force* salvation on the barbarians.

The question of force in *Areopagitica*, on the other hand, is of particular concern because of its effect on the individual imagination. The society of readers and writers that Milton envisions in his portrait of London is markedly a collective of *individuals*. These are individuals engaged in the common enterprise of reform, but they are necessarily sequestered in their activities, separated from one another by the processes they are engaged in, processes which must be carried out, not in public, but in the private arena of the imagination. In the scene that begins "Behold now this vast City; a City of refuge, the mansion house of liberty," the opening words lead us to anticipate a portrait of communal life characterized by the sorts of cooperative group activities that might indeed fashion armaments in "the shop of warre." But when the scenario focuses on the actual conduct of this communal life, the activities are notably individual:

There be pens and heads there, sitting by their studious lamps, musing, searching, revolving new notions and idea's wherewith to present, as with their homage and their fealty the approaching Reformation: others as fast reading, trying all things, assenting to the force of reason and convincement. (554)

Not only do these reformists operate quietly and privately as *thinking* individuals, their apparent interests are not even necessarily circumscribed by the cause of reform: they muse, they search, they revolve new notions and ideas "wherewith to present, as with their homage and their fealty the approaching Reformation." According to the syntax, what these pens and heads actually intend to present with their notions and ideas could either be their homage and fealty to the Reformation (which suggests that they may have other items on their agenda as well); or it could be the Reformation itself that they will present (in an attitude of homage and fealty) as Reformation's very architects. Milton's phrasing allows for either reading, because the pens and heads that simultaneously *write* Reformation *and celebrate it* can in themselve be said to *be* the Reformation. As such they cannot be contained by the enforced terms of any reified ideological program. And there can be little doubt that, whatever else it might require, "a Nation of Prophets, of Sages, and of Worthies" engaged in this kind of activity would hardly need a devil's advocate to defend itself against ideological stasis.

THE SELF-AUTHORING VITAL TEXT

If oppression of the imagination is the most dangerous effect of ideology, what remains most compelling about *Areopagitica* is the fecund variability and sensory richness of the imaginative acts that Milton enlists in the name of "reading" and "writing" to wage battle against that oppression. Notwithstanding the particular appearances of the activities to be observed within the "mansion house of liberty," the materials of reading and writing in *Areopagitica* reach infinitely beyond such accidental effects as books, pen, and paper. The activities of reading and writing in *Areopagitica* encompass every aspect of individual imaginative life. Integral to the tract's argumentative process is the evolution of "books" into a metaphor for the entire spectrum of sensory experience—the same spectrum that conventional metaphor theory, as I suggested at the beginning of this study, has erroneously neglected. *Areopagitica*'s imagerial reconfiguration of "books" enacts the sensory inclusiveness of iconoclastic metaphor theory in such a way as to claim for carnal rhetoric not just the written word but every form of imaginative expression. Finally, as it breaks down the barriers between ideas and their manifestations, between words and things, the carnal rhetoric of *Areopagitica* invests not books but the individual imagination with a primacy that it would be unwilling to accord either ideology or any other reified form of the idea, regardless of how it might be manifested to the senses.

We have seen how *Areopagitica*'s image sequences liberate the idea by means of the articulate insufficiencies of affective language, as in "old good authors" whose essence may be discovered neither by the act of dissecting bodies nor by the act of anatomizing books. Midway into the tract, the idea of the book itself gets liberated, as Milton expands the reified form "book" to encompass everything on which we exercise our "freedom to choose, for reason is but choosing":

Wherefore did he creat passions within us, pleasures round about us, but that these rightly temper'd are the very ingredients of vertu? . . . what ever thing we hear or see, sitting, walking, travelling, or conversing may be fitly call'd our book, and is *of the same effect* that writings are. (527–28, my italics)

The fitness of any "thing" (object or activity) to be "call'd our book" lies not in its incidental outward form (not in food, nor in the eating of it; not in music, nor in the playing of an instrument), but rather in the "effect" of that "thing" on our creative imaginations. Through our reasoned choices and our imaginative responses to "what ever thing we hear or see," we not only read but simultaneously write the lively text of our being. As the moral indifference of external texts places the burden of moral judgment on the inward chooser, so choosing itself makes "readers" (by now the equivalent of "life-authors") into the only moral (or immoral) texts.[20] What is rhetorically most remarkable about the passage I have just quoted, however, is that by making the entire spectrum of sensory experience "our book" ("what ever thing we hear or see, sitting, walking, travelling, or conversing"), Milton sets up the iconic conditions necessary to generate in the imaginations of ourselves, Milton's readers, the ruling metaphor that actually informs all of *Areopagitica*'s argument. Significantly (and unlike, for instance, the empyreal coupling metaphor that rules the argument of *The Doctrine and Discipline of Divorce*), *Areopagitica*'s ruling metaphor may be expressed not as a depictive image but only as an *interactive principle*. By superimposing "our book" on "what ever thing we hear or see," Milton causes us imaginatively to construct another image of the unimageable, an imaginative act similar to that required by the "image of God in the eye." In this case an interactive principle, the fusion of book and life that sees "book-as-life-as-book," enables us to formulate the underlying thesis of the tract: As our daily lives are the books that we read, we ourselves are the books that we write.

The sensory dimension opened onto by Milton's conception of all life as "the book that we read" is a world limitless in its capacity for transformation. Its limitlessness may be intuited from the sense-transformations of the extended imagerial sequence in which he surveys what print licensers would actually have to regulate in order to embark on their mission to "rectifie manners":

We must regulat all recreations and pastimes, all that is delightfull to man. No musick must be heard, no song be set or sung, but what is grave and *Dorick*. There must be licencing dancers, that no gesture, motion, or deportment be taught our youth but what by their allowance shall be thought honest; for such *Plato* was provided of; It will ask more then the work of twenty licencers to examin all the lutes, the violins, and the ghittarrs in every house; they must not be suffer'd to prattle as they doe, but must be licenc'd what they may say. And who shall silence all the airs and madrigalls, that whisper softnes in chambers? The Windows also, and the *Balcone's* must be thought on, there are shrewd books, with dangerous Frontispices set to sale; who shall prohibit them, shall twenty licencers? The villages also must have their visitors to enquire what lectures the bagpipe and the rebbeck reads ev'n to the ballatry, and the gammuth of every *municipal* fidler, for these are the Countrymans *Arcadia's* and his *Monte Mayors*. Next, what more Nationall corruption, for which England hears ill abroad, then houshold gluttony; who shall be the rectors of our daily rioting? and what shall be done to inhibit the multitudes that frequent those houses where drunk'nes is sold and harbor'd? Our garments also should be referr'd to the licencing of some more sober work-masters to see them cut into a lesse wanton garb. Who shall regulat all the mixt conversation of our youth, male and female together, as is the fashion of this Country, who shall still appoint what shall be discours'd, what presum'd, and no furder? Lastly, who shall forbid and separat all idle resort, all evill company? (523–26)

To read this passage is to experience a gradual breaking down of the sense discriminations by which we ordinarily distinguish between the human activities of music and speech; between the human artifacts that are buildings and those that are books; between the sensory experience of hearing and being heard; and even between the capacity for willful agency that is available to persons, as opposed to that available to abstract concepts or inanimate objects. From this manifold breaching of customary sense discriminations there arises an affectively rich and compelling domain for the free play of the senses, and as a consequence, for the free exercise of choice and reason, taste and desire. It is the domain of the imagination, affectively rich yet morally and rationally indeterminate, in which the possibilities for restraint and exquisite delectation are put forward, and allowed to intermingle indiscriminately, with the possibilities for overindulgence, corruption, and satiety. As if they themselves could reason and speak, lutes, violins, and guitars "prattle" and therefore, according to the censors, must be examined, "must be licenc'd what they may say." Similarly, airs and madrigals "whisper softnes in chambers"; the bagpipe and the rebeck must be inquired into, for they "read lectures." To carry the breakdown of ordinary distinctions even further, "dangerous Frontispices" etymologically conflates the windows and balconies of houses with the marketing tactics of booksellers. Backed by "dangerous Frontis-pices," the moralized epithet "Shrewd books," in the action "set to sale," commodifies equally the outward material signs both of private household life and the life of the mind.[21] Moreover, England's repu-tation for "houshold gluttony," in a striking moment of grammatical self-reflexivity, "*hears* ill abroad." And, not just drink but "drunk'nes" is sold to the "multitudes that frequent" such houses, where drunk-enness itself becomes a "harbour'd" permanent guest. Garments too are capable of being referred, like wayward apprentices, to "some more sober work-masters" who might oversee their being chastened "into a lesse wanton garb."

By the end of the "recreations and pastimes" scenario, it is clear that the multiple inroads made by sensory experience on our imagi-native lives are so complexly interconnected that no single category of experience or sensation can be isolated from the rest: "who shall still appoint what shall be discours'd, what presum'd, and no furder?" What we speak or hear or read or do is the substance of what we live. It is the very *copiousness* of the sensory experience from which we choose to shape our faith and manners that gives moral significance to the reasoning choices on which our self-authorship depends. That race from which, earlier in *Areopagitica*, Milton had spied a "fugitive and cloister'd vertue" slinking ignominiously away notably lacked any sensory depiction of virtue's "adversary"; but about the character of the race itself, there can be little doubt. The race involves full commit-ment of and confrontation with the senses, precisely what a "fugitive" virtue would "cloister" itself to avoid: "that immortall garland is to be *run* for, not without *dust and heat*" (515, my italics).

Given the copiousness of sensory experience on which self-author-ship must draw, perhaps we might expect *Areopagitica* to provide ex-emplary guidance for making the moral determinations needed to write the kinds of books that Milton, and possibly we ourselves, would want human beings to become. But, if *Areopagitica* were now to provide a prescriptive image of the books our lives should write, it would mean that Milton had surrendered to the requisites of ideology exactly the independent imaginative exercise that he writes his progressivist tract to defend. As an argumentative strategy, Milton's avoidance of pre-scriptive demonstration exemplifies the way in which, as Stanley Fish puts it, the argument "offers itself as the occasion for the trial and exercise" of our judgment.[22] *Areopagitica*'s image constructs work to liberate, rather than prescribe to, individual imagination. The principle articulated by Susanne Woods with reference to the later tracts thus applies equally well to *Areopagitica:* "He who would be among the elect must choose liberty, and in so choosing exercise the liberty his calling requires."[23] That is how the tract promotes the self-authoring of our own individual lively texts without dictating how, once completed, our texts ought to appear.

What *Areopagitica*'s images can display, however, is an exemplum of the commodifying sensory and moral fragmentation that results when a person relegates to a prescriptive formula the work that properly belongs to the individual imagination. The "commodity" metaphor in *Areopagitica* develops an idea that Milton had first introduced in *Of Reformation*, where the prelates would have us "commit to their dispose the whole *meaning* of our salvation," thus making a vendible ware of our beliefs.[24] "Meaning," as we saw at the beginning of this study, is exactly what the carnal rhetoric of metaphor cannot deliver. The carnal rhetoric of *Areopagitica* now makes it possible, however, to explicate the "meaning of our salvation" as that which the vital text cannot "commit to the dispose" of another without reducing it to a commodity, thereby abrogating the indeterminacy on which creative self-authorship depends. In contrast with *Of Reformation*, blame for the commodifying disposition of the "meaning of our salvation" in *Areopagitica* is fixed not upon the executors of civil or ecclesiastical authority but upon the fragmented life of the "heretic in the truth" himself. This is the individual who, in his seeming efficiency and businesslike dispositions, subverts the creative and original composition of his own vital text. By subcontracting his own "meaning"—that is, the personal authorship of his spiritual and intellectual life—the "wealthy man addicted to his pleasure and to his profits" actually converts his vital act of self-composition to a "staple commodity":[25]

A wealthy man addicted to his pleasure and to his profits, finds Religion to be a traffick so entangl'd, and of so many piddling accounts, that of all mysteries he cannot skill to keep a stock going upon that trade. What should he doe? fain he would have the name to be religious, fain he would bear up with his neighbours in that. What does he therefore, but resolvs to give over toyling, and to find himself out som factor, to whose care and credit he may commit the whole managing of his religious affairs; som Divine of note and estimation that must be. To him he adheres, resigns the whole ware-house of his religion, with all the locks and keyes into his custody; and indeed makes the very person of that man his religion; esteems his associating with him a sufficient evidence and commendatory of his own piety. (544)

Because the wealthy man is "*addicted to* his pleasure and to his profits," pursuit of either pleasure or profit precludes his own imaginative indeterminacy. That is, instead of imaginatively determining, according to his free and independent reasoning, what might vitally be either pleasurable or profitable, the man himself is *addictively determined* by his pleasure and his profits. Thus determined, every aspect of his being may be parceled out and "disposed." The indeterminate truths of faith and manners that might contribute to the constituting of his religion are converted, like broadcloths and woolpacks, to a determinate "stock," a manipulable "trade," and yet a "traffick so entangl'd, and of so many piddling accounts" as to require warehousing and consigning to "som factor." So consigned, the now quantified and determinate stock acquires a figural vitality that at first seems independent of the wealthy man, but that in fact remains so in outward appearance only. The "factor" who, instead of facilitating it actually *becomes* the wealthy man's "religion" is only a "dividuall movable," a piece of household furniture that sleeps and eats and is capable of no greater imaginative indeterminacy than is the carnally addicted and conclusively determined man on whom this parasite feeds:

So that a man may say his religion is now no more within himself, but is becom a dividuall movable, and goes and comes neer him, according as that good man frequents the house. He entertains him, gives him gifts, feasts him, lodges him; his religion comes home at night, praies, is liberally supt, and sumptuously laid to sleep, rises, is saluted, and after the malmsey, or some well spic't bruage, and better breakfasted then he whose morning appetite would have gladly fed on green figs between *Bethany* and *Jerusalem,* his Religion walks abroad at eight, and leavs his kind entertainer in the shop trading all day without his religion. (544–45)

A literalist of the imagination, the wealthy man (as "implicit" a believer "as any lay Papist of Loretto") carnalizes and commodifies his religion by paying the priest to mind truth for him. Piecing together a faith that will secure himself both from the *possibility* of self-transformation and from the *desire* for it, he feeds his self-determining addiction with a construct of faith and manners that he fashions out of his concern for an assemblage of reified externals, the forms that "are duly observed," as Milton notes of hypocritical worship in *Of Christian Doctrine*, "but without any accompanying affection of the mind; which is a high offence against God."[26] These external forms include reputation ("he would have the name to be religious"), impressive appearances ("som Divine of note and estimation that must be"), luxurious provision ("He entertains him, gives him gifts, feasts him"), and mercantile profits ("his Religion . . . leaves his kind entertainer in the shop trading all day"). The religion that has become a "dividuall movable" is thus not only operatively identical to the man's other trade commodities, such as broadcloths and woolpacks and things materially separable from their corporate sponsor; his religion is also a sign that the man himself has become a commodity, the determinate product of his own carnal addictions. The imaginative indeterminacy of a self-composing vital text would for him be only one more "mystery" of entangled traffic and untraceable "piddling accounts": he "cannot skill to keep a stock going upon that trade"; the text he would compose must register fully on a balance sheet.

Finally, by hiring out the authorship of his "image of God" instead of composing it himself, the man addicted to his pleasure and profits does with his life what Milton had done in the antiprelatical tracts with his rhetoric: he uses carnal affect in such a way as to separate practical task from spiritual ideal, reason from truth. The implied retrospective critique is not lost on Milton: "It is not the unfrocking of a Priest, the unmitring of a Bishop, and the removing him from off the *Presbyterian* shoulders, that will make us a happy Nation" (550). The ultimate futility of such symbolic undoings was a lesson Milton's earliest carnal rhetoric had learned well. Yet the self-composing vital text that *Areopagitica* urges us to write also reaches beyond a mere concern for the cooperative union of body with spirit. This, as we have seen, had been the affective enterprise of *The Doctrine and Discipline of Divorce*. By contrast, the affective enterprise articulated through *Areopagitica*'s "image of God in the eye" supports an imaginative and independent self-authorship that is capable of *aspiring* to perfection without necessitating the idolatrous and, more important, the *unimaginative* pretense that one might actually *achieve* it. With this development in Milton's thinking, both idolatry and unimaginativeness in self-authorship crystallize into a decisive new exploratory theme, as he launches his inquiry into the carnal rhetoric of the king's book in *Eikonoklastes*.

5

"UNIMPRISONABLE UTTERANCE"

Imagination and the Attack

on *Eikon Basilike*

When Henry VIII first displaced the roodloft crucifix of a medieval English cathedral with his own coat of arms, his pointed act of iconoclasm shattered a symbolic and powerfully felt material connection between the worshiper's sense of divinity and the earthly spiritual prerogative of Rome.[1] What lay behind this iconoclastic act was a profound psychological insight into the nature of iconic illusion. The Tudor reformists knew that religious icons shared with every iconic representation the affective capacity to focus powerful, yet otherwise often diffuse, miscellaneous, and even objectively unrelated feelings. The iconic associations of a religious symbol can collapse into a single overwhelming emotional experience such diverse and intense feelings as the worshiper's hope for a better life (or fear of a worse one), his or her sense of unique personal significance in the bewildering plethora of lived experience, and subconscious association of the experience of primal nurturing with that of primal dependence on figures of power and authority. The coalescence of these and countless other natural, yet potentially ungovernable, feelings into the affective focus provided by a single iconic representation like a crucifix may be the function of mere illusion, but the Tudor reformists intuited that affective illusions are the realities of the mind.

For the believer, the "iconic as felt" inspires ontological vehemence, what Ricoeur calls our experience of "the deep structures of reality to which we are related as mortals who are born into this world and who *dwell* in it for a while."[2] But for the Tudor reformists, the "iconic as felt" also provided something more, something attributable directly to the phenomenon Ricoeur describes. The "iconic as felt" provides practical, working access to the affective resources of popular will. Because affective illusions are the realities of the mind, they are also the ultimate instrument of human power. That is, access to the affective resources of the individual will provides a measure of power to manipulate that will. The icon itself is not independently invested with power, nor does it independently exercise it: the icon itself is nothing more than a picture, a representation, an illusion. But when individual or collective imaginations invest the affective resources of their own transformative desires in the sensible lineaments of a given icon, that icon becomes an external means of tapping into those desires, and the individual or collective imaginations respond to the icon accordingly. Individual and collective imaginations thus invest the religious icon with a specific power of access—access both to their own sense of self and to their will toward self-transcendence. We may recall the nexus of transformative desires whereby, through metaphor, consciousness is iconoclastically reconstructed: the writer desires transformation and has the power to effect it in art; the reader desires transformation and has the power to will it in himself.[3] The iconoclastic nexus of desires becomes an instrument of almost unlimited power when the skillful icon-manipulator perceives and undertakes to maneuver, by means of appropriate icons, the affective reality of people's imaginations. Thus, when King Henry VIII displaced the medieval crucifix with his Tudor coat of arms, he did more than just expropriate and transfer to the English monarchy Rome's spiritual claims over the individual worshiper. His program aimed to redelineate, at the very core of their being, his subjects' entire imaginative blueprint, the pattern of affective intention, desire, and response whereby, as mortals born into the world, they *dwelt* in it for a while.

The Tudor reform program was designed specifically, of course, to facilitate renegotiations of political power and wealth in the institutions of the ecclesiastical and governmental establishment. For the Defender of the Faith, this meant reinterpreting the character of that which he would defend as a new and exclusively English national faith, represented by the Tudor coat of arms. By exploiting the worshiper's sacramental habit of using icons as a bridge between sensory experience and spiritual truth, divine right monarchy could now claim its divinity not only by the traditional means of ecclesiastical sanction, but also by the monarch's symbolic presence amid, and *iconic* participation in, the activity of ordinary religious worship.

Reiteration of King Henry's skillful image management by subsequent Tudor and Stuart monarchs further habituated the sacramentally inclined worshiper to iconic associations of Christian symbols with English heads of state. Henrician and Edwardian reformers symbolically and literally quarried the ecclesiastical edifice, in order to reinforce and sanctify the monarch's secular one.[4] Elizabethan and Jacobean portrait artists converted the symbolic two-dimensional medieval icon to a dazzling emblematic and allegorical costume-piece that heralded the monarch's spiritual as well as political supremacy.[5] And finally, the Caroline publicists saw to it that the frontispiece of *Eikon Basilike,* with its king kneeling in prayer for the people and grasping a crown of thorns, emblematically identified Charles I with Jesus Christ. Owen Felltham's extravagant epitaph for the martyred King Charles must be recognized not as a singular or blasphemous outburst but as the emotionally predictable response of a devout believer: "Here Charles the First and Christ the Second lies."[6]

Yet royal advisors had uneasily sensed at least as early as during the reign of Edward VI that icon manipulation entails great risks. On a purely practical level, once the iconoclast succeeds at rupturing "conceptual peace and rest"—the habituated affective response to the icon—no rationale and no substitute icon can be assumed to recapture the same quality of response. If the worshiper can witness the king's demolition of the crucifix, he or she can conceive as well destruction of the king's own sign, and ultimately, destruction of the king himself. But even more fundamental is the impact of the iconoclastic act on the individual sense of self, and on the felt transformative powers of the self, as experienced through the affective imagination. Much as the nexus of transformative desires links the writer or artist to the reader or partaker of art, so the primacy of the icon in each imagination links inextricably the iconoclast to the iconophile. Creation of images and destruction of images testify alike to the iconic power of the imagination. They both testify, indeed, to the essentially iconoclastic nature of imaginative self-transformation. To the affective imagination, experience of the iconoclastic act is simultaneously an invasive experience of *being acted upon,* and a revelatory, potentially empowering experience of *autonomous acting.*

Because illusions are the realities of the mind, illusions are also what empowers the imaginative, transformative dimension of our being. To experience the iconoclastic act—to experience the radical disruption of the familiar, of "conceptual peace and rest"—is to experience as well an incitement (possibly alarming) to the radical freedom of self-authorship. Ultimately for Milton, therefore, the call to reform meant restructuring not just icon-manipulating institutions and their agents, such as icon-exploiting kings and bishops and royalist propaganda. Even more than these it meant radical restructuring of the imaginative dynamics of individual faith. When John R. Knott points out that with *Eikonoklastes* Milton "had to destroy the image of a suffering church as well as that of a suffering king,"[7] the "suffering church" to which he refers must be taken to indicate the stricken believers themselves. The sacramental symbolism that instantly transferred to the dead King Charles the affective aura of a Christlike martyr also operated to consecrate into a vicarious martyrdom the bereavement of the king's subjects. For example, since the frontispiece of the king's book *Eikon Basilike* is a devotional rather than a representational instrument, says Ernest Gilman, the image "intends to engage the viewer in a kind of sacred vision, *clarior é tenebris,* analogous to the king's own. . . . Raised by his humility, we ourselves can say with him, and because of him, *Coeli Specto.*"[8]

But the vision in which the viewer might thus share was in Milton's view constructed by intentions neither sacred nor heavenly but political; and the exploitativeness of the vision so constructed could easily be exposed by dismantling piece by piece the pictorial and verbal affective rhetoric on which *Eikon Basilike*'s spectacular case for Christlike martyrdom rested.[9] The affective power of martyrdom was a force Milton had had to reckon with once before, in the equivocal rhetoric of his own treatment of the Marian martyrs Cranmer, Latimer, and Ridley as he wrote *Of Reformation.*[10] But now the political stakes were even higher. The force to be reckoned with was once again a rhetorical construct, but this time the emotional foundation for the construct was historically immediate and even palpable: relics of the king's martyrdom had multiplied as the blood-dipped handkerchiefs of spectators were supplemented by the auctioning off of bloody chunks of execution scaffolding. In addition, the king's embalmed body was put on display for a time at St. James's, admission fee required.[11] As for the rhetorical form of this martyrdom's spectacle, the challenge of *Eikon Basilike* differed from Milton's previous task in that its affective power was not at all beholden to Milton's own argumentative or stylistic inadvertence. *Eikon Basilike* was rather a royalist propaganda piece into which a politically calculated infusion of martyrdom's affective appeal breathed anarchic and proliferating independent life—a life to be reified in the imaginations of the English people, who drawn by their feelings into the emotional turbulence of the historical moment, could more readily be induced by those same feelings to resist reform than contribute to it.[12]

In Milton's denunciations of the English masses—of the "inconstant, irrational, and Image-doting rabble"—Keith Stavely reads an admission of "rhetorical defeat, testifying to the reformer's inability continuously to sustain his cold rational poise in a world that has replaced reason with superstition."[13] But superstition in Milton's view has always replaced reason in the realm of politics, and his polemical response to that enduring situation has always been to explode his own rhetoric of rationalism with a rhetoric of emotional outburst. Rather than "grandiosely" portraying himself as "a moral hero, steadfastly affirming the truth in a hostile world," or else merely retreating into an attitude of "cold rational contempt for a nation that has neither eyes to see nor ears to hear,"[14] Milton in *Eikonoklastes* applies his affective rhetoric to the specific political task of inducing imaginative self-transformation in the pamphlet-reading public. The defamatory outbursts cited by Stavely operate directly to assault the affective dispositions of the English people for whom those very dispositions are what make them receptive to the rhetorical strategies of the royalist faction. To dismantle the overwhelming symbolic authority of church and monarchy, an authority whose affective power had soared precisely *because* its practical power had been cut off with the monarch's head, Milton mounts an attack designed explicitly to dismantle the elaborate structures of affective rhetoric in *Eikon Basilike*, structures that Milton judged more dangerous by far than any of the book's political justifications.[15] Paradoxically, however, in order for his iconoclastic attack ultimately to succeed, his most crucial weapon would have to be none other than Milton's real target: not the royalists' propagandistic document itself but the icon-loving affective imagination of each of its readers. David Loewenstein comments perceptively on the extent to which Milton understood that breaking with royalist tradition required a forceful act of the imagination. Citing a phrase from *Tetrachordon*, Loewenstein characterizes the iconoclastic act as an "art of powerfull reclaiming."[16] Milton knew that to forestall the resurgent institutional power of church and monarchy required tracing that power to its true source in the iconic responsiveness of the individual imagination, and demonstrating that the iconoclastic and transforming imagination itself is the only possible means of reclaiming iconic power to its rightful place: in the autonomous will of the independent, self-authoring individual. Moving beyond his preceding cause of creative independence for the transforming imagination, a cause implicit in Milton's entire artistic career but explicitly championed in *Areopagitica*, Milton now extends his affective polemic in *Eikonoklastes* to attack the most fundamental kind of idolatry. This is the idolatrous abdication of self-authorship that he finds at work both in the composition of *Eikon Basilike* and in the testimony rendered by its astounding popular reception.

BREAKING THE VERBAL ICON

Milton's attack on abdication of self-authorship, and on the idolatry such imaginative indolence implies, begins with his own iconoclastic expropriation, literalization, and consequent explosion of *Eikon Basilike*'s carefully selected affective building blocks—the king's metaphors, images, and symbols. According to Bruce Boehrer, the resulting subjection of Milton's own argument to the structural irregularities of *Eikon Basilike* was what guaranteed that *Eikonoklastes* would fail. Unavailable to the counterarguments of any ordinary mortal was the capacity of the king's book to transcend conventional form because it was a king's: "In responding to the King's Book [Milton] was seeking to use traditional rhetoric against an adversary for whom the rules of rhetoric simply did not apply."[17] Leaving aside Boehrer's apparent acceptance of the royalist premise that monarchs are somehow intrinsically elevated above mortal rule (a premise rejected not only by Milton but by the early modern revolutionary movement in general), Boehrer's rhetorical critique assumes that Milton's primary concern was in fact a mere rational rebuttal of *Eikon Basilike*'s argument—the kind of exercise one might see performed in a debating society. But the compelling force of *Eikonoklastes* lies not in its pressure to refute a rational argument: on such grounds, as Keith Stavely notes, the king sets himself up to be treated "as a trivial opponent, easily and carelessly refuted."[18] The force of *Eikonoklastes* lies rather in its will to destroy exactly those politically structured yet unthinking reflexes by which the English people from the Tudor period onward had been induced to incorporate into the figure of the monarch the conceptual and affective character of paterfamilias and deity. "The royalists' thesis was at heart a simple one," Boehrer remarks: "no bishop, no king; no king, no God; no God, no father"; and he concludes that "Milton could not bring himself to view the king as father and therefore chose not to view him as anything at all, at least not as anything credible."[19] That, of course, is the point: the traditional and popular iconic associations of king with father and God are the very associations that in Milton's view had facilitated tyranny. To break down such associations therefore required an attack on precisely those iconic structures in *Eikon Basilike* that so depended, as Boehrer demonstrates, on the affective elements of intimate family relations, on private emotions, and on select glimpses of the royal father-god's personal conduct. This masterly configuration of iconic structures Milton discountenances by fragmenting and literalizing the figurative whole into multiple constituent parts: the king's metaphoric icon in *Eikonoklastes* disintegrates into a miscellany of discrete body images, for instance, in which the elementary activities of feeding and excreting and procreating render the figure incapable ever again of being joined in a harmonious portrait of majesty.

For example, when the king defends his intrusion on the House of Commons as justified by such "motives and pregnant grounds" as the parliamentarians had no knowledge of, Milton first counters the argument with a five-paragraph rebuttal that overturns the king's rational justification point by point with the sort of cold rational contempt to which Keith Stavely has referred.[20] But before moving on to the next argument, he reaches back to the seemingly innocuous metaphor, at this juncture almost forgotten by the reader, that the king had employed to give an effect of weight and seriousness to his concerns—"pregnant." Charles *"wanted not such probabilities* (for his pregnant is come now to probable) *as were sufficient to raise jealousies in any Kings heart.* And thus his pregnant *motives* are at last prov'd nothing but a Tympany, or a Queen *Maries* Cushion."[21] Milton's literalizing extension of the king's metaphoric "pregnant" to a pretense of actual bodily pregnancy makes the king's jealous motives appear not only false and mistaken but also, because of the derogatory historical associations with Mary Tudor, simultaneously insidious, ludicrous, and rather pathetic. The tumor that deceived the childless queen into thinking she was pregnant actually contributed to her death. But "tympany" also conveys a psychological morbidity: "pride, arrogance, self-conceit, etc., figured as a disease; a condition of being inflated or puffed up" (*OED*). By compounding the charge of self-delusion with the additional charge of arrogant self-inflation, Milton's "tympany" metaphor exposes the king's "jealousies" as paranoiac delusion and his rhetoric as puerile and incompetent. In an argument designed to sabotage *Eikon Basilike*'s triumph of affective style over historical substance, it is the latter revelation that damages most.

On a visually unrelated but rhetorically comparable occasion, Charles later employs the trope of a storm-tossed ship to embellish his withdrawal from Westminster, and Milton derides the "Simily" as "a garb somwhat more Poetical then for a Statist." But then he connects this particular royal effort at figurative language "with many straines of like dress" to cover the entire work: "I begun to think that the whole Book might perhaps be intended a peece of Poetrie. The words are good, the fiction smooth and cleanly; there wanted onely Rime, and that, they say, is bestow'd upon it lately" (406). Since Milton's metaphors "garb" and "dress" at this point convert the entirety of Charles's rhetorical effort to mere costuming, the king's book becomes on the affective level nothing but an insubstantial stage show, a contrived entertainment that is easily reducible to rhyme.[22]

But few of the king's figurative passages are dismissed quite so lightly. When Charles observes, on the militia's having seized his military power, that the "chiefest Armes" left him had been only his "Praiers and Teares," Milton fires back, with an oath, a vivid itemization of the king's preparatory arsenal-building and other martial maneuvers:

> O sacred Reverence of God, Respect and Shame of Men, whither were yee fled, when these hypocrisies were utterd? Was the Kingdom then at all that cost of blood to remove from him none but Praiers and Teares? . . . Were they Praiers and Teares that were listed at *York*, muster'd on *Heworth* Moore, and laid Seige to *Hull* for the guard of his Person? Were Praiers and Teares at so high a rate in *Holland* that nothing could purchase them but the Crown Jewels? Yet they in *Holland* . . . sold them for Gunns, Carabins, Morters-peeces, Canons, and other deadly Instruments of Warr. (452)

The phrase "Praiers and Teares" tellingly summarizes both the rhetorical cause and the far-reaching practical effect of the pathetic appeal that is implemented by the affective language of *Eikon Basilike*. The book is itself a compilation of prayers interspersed with tearful exculpatory lamentation. Moreover, "Praiers and Teares" accurately describes the way the book was instantly received by an emotionally shattered public. It is easy to see why the affectively loaded words "Praiers and Teares" should provoke Milton to obliterate the king's figurative phrase "chiefest armes" by maneuvering into position the king's arsenal of real military arms, along with the weapons deals and military exercises by which, in Milton's view, Charles had actually provoked the militia's seizure. As Milton had argued in *Areopagitica*, "books are not absolutely dead things."[23] The affective appeal of *Eikon Basilike* was designed not merely to arouse sympathy for its putative author or his party. It was also designed substantially to rewrite, after its completion, the not absolutely dead "book" that the king's life—his own individual choices, activities, and personal character—had in fact written. In Charles's *true* book—in the life authored not by propagandistic affective appeal but by the "efficacie and extraction" of the king's own "living intellect"—his "chiefest armes" had clearly signified the strategic manipulation of military weaponry, not rhetorical effects.

Not all of *Eikon Basilike*'s metaphoric arguments require such dismantling, however; some, when examined closely enough, seem to run aground almost of their own accord. Milton creates the effect of merely narrating their self-destruction. When Charles characterizes parliamentary government as a Hydra-headed monster, for instance, he starts out promisingly enough. If we admire such a government because it has more eyes to see, the king argues, we must also acknowledge that it has many more mouths to feed. But as Milton focuses on it, the king's body metaphor starts to flounder. Parliamentary government "hath rather a monstrosity than anything of perfection beyond that of right monarchy, where counsel may be in many, as the senses, but the supreme power can be but in one, as the head" (*EB* 49). With these words, Milton drily remarks, Charles "grounds his argument upon two or three eminent absurdities: First by placing Counsel in the senses, next by turning the senses out of the head, and in lieu therof placing power, *supreme* above sense and reason; which be now the greater Monstrosities?" (455). Whether, in this case, bad style leads to nonsensical thinking, or the reverse, does not particularly interest Milton: "Furder to dispute what kind of Government is best, would be a long debate, it sufficeth that his reasons heer for Monarchy are found weake and inconsiderable" (455). "Reasons" whose validity depends solely on metaphor require only destruction of the metaphor to render them invalid.

In some cases, the king's metaphors require only a shade of literalizing, in order for Milton to expose the supercilious thinking that lies underneath: "*But he must chew such Morsels as Propositions ere he let them down.* So let him; but if the Kingdom shall tast nothing but after his chewing, what does he make of the Kingdom, but a great baby" (468–69). Here, the line grows fine indeed between the king's incompetent metaphor and his deliberate contempt. His affective terms reduce his subjects to helpless dependents, toothless as infants, unable to consider governmental propositions according to the merits of those propositions rather than as minced and partially digested by the king.

But argument by metaphor, especially organic and body metaphor, carries other hazards as well. When metaphor tempts Charles to claim seriously the intellectual and political magnificence implied in the Renaissance trope of the king-as-sun, Milton carries that logic to a grotesque conclusion. Charles considers "*the concurrence of his reason . . . necessary to the begetting,* or bringing forth of any one *compleat act*

of public wisdom as the Suns influence is necessary to all natures pro-
ductions. So that the Parliament, it seems, is but a Female, and without
his procreative reason, the Laws which they can produce are but wind-
eggs" (467). An inherent and natural generative beneficence is claimed
by Charles's idea that the sun-king's influence is a necessary force
in bringing to fruition "all nature's productions." But Milton aborts
this claim by bringing forth instead a Rabelaisian travesty, legislative
"wind-eggs." Moreover, if King Charles, eyes on the sun, overlooks
the explicitly sexual and reproductive implications of "begetting" and
"bringing forth," Milton does not. Since the king claims his right by
law, itself no more than the "Counsel of a Nation," then by Charles's
own metaphor, he must acknowledge Parliament not conventionally
as the king's wife, but rather as the entity who gave birth to monarchy:
"He ought then to have so thought of a Parlament, if he count it not
Male, as of his Mother, which, to civil being, created both him, and the
Royalty he wore" (467). By probing the affective dimension of the con-
flicting imagery with which Charles articulates his relationship with
Parliament, Milton traces the king's authoritarianism to origins that
he finds comparable to the perversions of Nero: "And if it hath bin an-
ciently interpreted the presaging signe of a future Tyrant, but to dream
of copulation with his Mother, what can it be less then actual Tyranny
to affirme waking, that the Parlament, which is his Mother, can neither
conceive or bring forth *any authoritative Act* without his Masculine
coition" (467).[24] From this portentous explication of the king's lesser
metaphors "beget" and "bring forth," Milton derives the material he
needs finally to explode the king's major symbol, the sun: "Nay that
his reason is as Celestial and life-giving to the Parlament, as the Suns
influence is to the Earth: What other notions but these, or such like,
could swell up *Caligula* to think himself a God" (467). The uncon-
scious and overt impulses toward tyranny that Milton finds at work in
the king's lesser metaphors are now shown to be working as well in
Charles's use of the sun symbol. This image that equates "the Suns in-
fluence" to the king's "Celestial and life-giving" reason is no longer an
elegant rhetorical device, nor is it a conventional application of monar-
chic symbolism. It is rather malignant and idolatrous self-deification,
such a notion as "could swell up *Caligula* to think himself a God."

Hypothesizing from the above examples, we might be tempted to
conclude that *Eikon Basilike* carelessly sets itself up for Milton's at-

tack by its injudicious rhetorical application of metaphor and symbol. But we would be mistaken on several counts. First, the book's affective language was calculated to achieve specific emotional responses, in order to strengthen its political impact and also maximize any collateral returns. Its multiple editions testify to the strategy's resounding success: it not only got rhymed, it actually got set to music (360, n. 33). Second, Milton himself is perfectly capable of using the same metaphors that *Eikon Basilike* had used, and of using them in much the same way. Charles's hackneyed storm-tossed ship, for example, shows up again only two paragraphs after the point at which Milton had ridiculed it as "poetical garb": "he left the City; and in a most tempestuous season forsook the Helme, and steerage of the Common-wealth" (408). Elsewhere, notwithstanding his own critique of Charles's self-idolizing claim to the sun image, Milton attacks the king for applying that royal trope to an inferior personage: "with Scolastic flourishes beneath the decencie of a King, [he] compares [the Earl of Strafford] to *the Sun*, which in all figurative use, and significance beares allusion to a King, not to a Subject" (372).

Moreover, despite the regard for rhetorical convention that he seems to acknowledge by his phrase "in all figurative use," Milton's own figuration in *Eikonoklastes* answers to little rule beyond what will achieve *his* desired immediate effect. In an imagerial tour de force near the end of the tract, we can watch Milton's metaphoric construct rise literally from "nothing," shift mediums, collapse, and reconstruct itself with the breathtaking fluidity of Mulciber's Pandaemonium. The occasion in *Eikon Basilike* which gives rise to this construct is one of many concluding statements by the king, complacent in tone, but not otherwise intrinsically offensive: "Nothing can be more happy for all than in fair, grave, and honorable ways to contribute their counsels in common, enacting all things by public consent without tyranny or tumults" (*EB* 168). At this point Milton, having delivered to his own satisfaction the strictly rational substance of his rebuttal, arbitrarily converts the claim made by the statement into its logically opposed and negative form. Then he proceeds to build variations on the theme of "no." First, the negation:

The conclusion therfore must needs be quite contrary to what he concludes; that nothing can be more *unhappy*, more dishonourable, more unsafe *for all*, then when a wise, *grave*, and *honourable Parlament* shal have labourd, de-bated, argu'd, consulted, and, as he himself speakes, *contributed* for the public good *all thir Counsels in common*, to be then frustrated, disappointed, deny'd and repuls'd by the single whiffe of a negative. (579)

Milton's seemingly arbitrary conversion of the king's "happy" to "un-happy" waits syntactically suspended in its arbitrariness, while the character and activities of an "honourable Parlament" are also negated ("dishonourable . . . unsafe"), and the Parliament's experience of having "labourd, debated, argu'd, consulted, and . . . *contributed*" is rehearsed. The arbitrary conversion remains still suspended through the tension-building participles that express Parliament's further experience of being "frustrated, disappointed, deny'd and repuls'd." Only at the end of this rehearsal is the cause of the suspension, and of the conversion from "happy" to "unhappy," finally revealed. The accumulated weight of all that has been suspended—the legislative burden sustained by a frustrated Parliament and the syntactic burden sustained by the sen-tence which describes it—is at last explained and, at the same time, vaporized by the power of a mere word from the king: "the single whiffe of a negative." From this synaesthetic fragment, the very ghost of an image, Milton then shapes a complex and changing scenario:

Nothing can be more *unhappy* [than to be repulsed] by the single whiffe of a negative, from the mouth of one wilfull man; nay to be blasted, to be struck as mute and motionless as a Parlament of Tapstrie in the Hangings; or else after all thir paines and travell to be dissolv'd, and cast away like so many Naughts in Arithmetick, unless it be to turne the o of thir insignificance into a lamentation with the people, who had so vainly sent them. (579)

From the immaterial sound-scent "whiffe of a negative" proceed dev-astating effects. At the mere breath of a king, a king whose book now promotes and depends on the power of the affective image, a coun-seling and reasoning Parliament is not just silenced but transformed to a purely decorative image, a "Parlament of Tapstrie." But even that identity shrinks numerically and evaporates, as their no longer mea-surable substance dissolves to wordless lamentation, "dissolv'd, and cast away like so many Naughts in Arithmetick . . . the o of thir in-significance . . . a lamentation with the people." Then, permutations of volatile "nothing" gradually shape a palpable image of "stifleing and obstructing evil":

For this is not to *enact all things by public consent*, as he would have us be perswaded, this is to enact nothing but by the privat consent and leave of one not negative tyrant; this is mischeif without remedy, a stifleing and obstructing evil that hath no vent, no outlet, no passage through: Grant him this, and the Parlament hath no more freedom then if it sate in his Noose, which when he pleases to draw together with one twitch of his Negative, shall throttle a whole Nation, to the wish of *Caligula* in one neck. (579)

The "nothing" enacted by a "not negative tyrant" takes multiple forms, all patterned on the "naught," the "o," that had transformed parliamentary insignificance into lamentation. Remediless mischief, the rank "whiffe of a negative" from the tyrant's mouth, stifles and smothers by stopping even the exclamatory "Oes" of wailing mouths, allowing "no vent, no outlet, no passage through." In its final transformation, the stifling "whiffe" becomes a strangling "twitch," with the power to throttle an entire nation by the synaesthetic potency of "one twitch of his Negative." This is the last permutation of "naught"—the twitch that snaps tight the knot in the "o" of a Caligulan hangman's noose.

NAILING TRUTH TO THE ICON

In Milton's tactical metaphor-demolition and reconstruction, the iconoclastic assault on *Eikon Basilike*'s carnal rhetoric exposes the deceptive maneuvers of affective language in a singularly influential piece of royalist propaganda. But the key to *Eikon Basilike*'s extraordinary influence lies not simply in its own rhetorical constructs. For these to have their desired effect requires a predictable affective response. What links the propagandistic affective maneuver to the affective responses of those whom it manipulates is a common readiness on the part of both sender and receiver to treat representations of truth as truth itself. The coalescence in the icon of affective intention, desire, and response thus accords the sanctified primacy of truth not to Milton's cause of imaginative independence and righteous self-transformation, but rather to the icon itself. In the end, it is not the manipulative propagandist but the imaginatively passive responder whose affective assent sanctions the icon's claim to truth and makes the icon into an idol. Yet because sender and receiver, propagandist and consumer, participate simultaneously in their sanctioning of carnal claims to truth, the idolatries of both are reciprocally anatomized by a single act of analysis. This reciprocal act of analysis repeats itself every time Milton exposes the king's idolatrous abdication of individual responsibility for imaginative and independent self-authorship: not just the king but his worshipers as well abdicate their spiritual autonomy.

The idols *Eikonoklastes* pulls down with the king's image include prayers and covenants, liturgical forms and governmental policies, clerical offices and political reputations. In the context of *Eikon Basilike*, what these all have in common—what in Milton's view makes them idols—is the way they are used and intended to be received: in every case, their words, pictures, and outward forms are both proffered and accepted as actual truths, requiring implicit faith in their claims to truth rather than supporting inquiry into truth or bearing witness to it. The reciprocal complacencies of the proffered idol and the accepting idolater bear witness instead to their common investment in imaginative stasis, the affective comforts of conceptual peace and rest.

For Milton, the principle of distinguishing between a true image and a false idol had never depended on the icon's mere external or sensible characteristics. We have seen how readily he can appropriate for his own purposes icons whose similar use by others he criticizes. His satirical jibe at Charles's "poetical garb" hints at one aspect of imagery that can lead to idolatry—the image's capacity to delude or mislead through costuming or impressive shows. As Loewenstein points out, "one consequence of this kind of theatricalization . . . is that it renders meaning and motive equivocal."[25] Theatrics alone will not make an image into an idol, however. Spectacular shows by their very nature may indeed lend themselves to exposing falseness: Milton credits "the general voice of the people" with "almost hissing [King Charles] and his ill-acted regality off the Stage" (355). If the spectacle is poorly performed, there is always the chance that it may self-destruct. But even a self-destructing idol requires, for its accidental iconoclasm to be noticed, a measure of critical sophistication on the part of the audience. Given a sufficiently credulous responder, on the other hand, any image may become an idol—even, as Milton notes in *Christian Doctrine*, if it is an image of God: "Idolatry means making or owning an idol for religious purposes, or worshipping it, whether it be a representation of the true God or of some false god."[26] The truth or falsity that is actually tested by these words is not that of the idol itself but of the idolater, whose purposes define the artifact.

If idolatrous "purposes" are what determines religious idolatry, the same is true for what Milton terms "civil idolatry." Since *Eikon Basilike*'s spectacular shows demand worship, not applause, any distinction the book might make between true and false gods becomes a meaningless pretense. At the same time, Milton's portrayal of the king's book and style as a gallimaufry of religious sentimentalism and gaudy theatrics is complemented by his disdain for those who let themselves be manipulated by impressive shows: "Quaint Emblems and devices begg'd from the old Pageantry of some Twelf-nights entertainment at *Whitehall*, will doe but ill to make a Saint or Martyr. . . . But the People, exorbitant and excessive in all thir motions, are prone ofttimes not to a religious onely, but to a civil kind of Idolatry in idolizing their Kings" (343). The king's book appears as a "Tragedie" containing an "Antimasque"; his prayers are deceitful "trumpery" and "painted feathers"; the king himself is a weak player in a "Saints vizard" whose courtiers and prelates strive to "imitate him exactly" (362, 533, 364–65, 408, 361, 351). But the "miserable, credulous, deluded . . . vulgar" bear the brunt of Milton's contempt: their king "presumes a more implicit Faith in the people of *England*, then the Pope ever commanded from the Romish Laitie; or els a natural sottishness fitt to be abus'd and ridd'n" (426, 355).[27] A presumption of "implicit Faith" exposes the king's spiritual arrogance, but "a natural sottishness" places the burden of idolatry on English backs "fitt to be abus'd and ridd'n" because of the willing servility of their king-worship. It is not doctrinal identification with Rome that makes an icon into an idol for Milton; it is the believer's own proneness to idolatry that stamps his worship Roman, regardless of its accidental components: "If the People resolve to take him Sainted at the rate of such a Canonizing, I shall suspect thir Calendar more then the Gregorian" (343). Milton's doubts about the faith of the English people arise not from what they might call their religion (be it "Protestant," "Presbyterian," "Episcopal," or "Roman"). His doubts arise from what, by their conduct and demonstrated manner of receiving icons, the English people imagine religion to *be*.

Still, from the perspective of the icon worshiper, the icon must somehow satisfy the desire to worship *worthily*. The individual imaginative pattern of intention, desire, and response decrees the terms of the world to which the mortal is willing to lend affective assent and thereby "*dwell* in it for a while." Thus the sacrificial and sacramental character of Charles's publicly acknowledged piety had already prepared the way for *Eikon Basilike*'s imagerial exploitation of the suffering and death of Christ.[28] The king regrets that he should be sold off to Parliament by the Scots at a rate higher than that earned by Judas; he compares his settling with Parliament to Christ's permitting himself to be tempted by the devil on the pinnacle; he asks God to forgive the people for "they know not what they do"; in his frontispiece portrait, the kneeling king forsakes his earthly crown, gazes toward his heavenly crown, and in his right hand grasps the crown of thorns (*EB* 137, 23, 46).[29] Even if the people had not been predisposed to a "civil kinde of Idolatry," *Eikon Basilike* was equipped to expropriate from an iconically charged style of Christian worship a sufficient quantity of verbal and visual images to insure that the reflexes conditioned by that style of worship would automatically transfer to Charles. In Milton's view the intentionality of such martyrdom corrupts it:

If I beare witness of my self, saith *Christ*, my witness is not true. He who writes himself *Martyr* by his own inscription, is like an ill Painter, who, by writing on the shapeless Picture which he hath drawn, is fain to tell passengers what shape it is; which else no man could imagin: no more then how a Martyrdom can belong to him, who therfore dyes for his Religion because it is *establisht*. (575)

To die for a religion "because it is *establisht*" exposes not only the self-witnessing intent of the martyr but also the vacuousness of his claim to a *religious* cause. An established religion, Milton gibes, hardly needs martyrs. Moreover, since the strategies of the king's defense are clearly designed to promote *civil* idolatry, they bear witness of the royalist political party's intentions, desires, and responses in addition to those of the king.

Inevitably, however, all such witnesses betray themselves. To defend the king, *Eikon Basilike* uses strategies that mirror the wrongs of which the king has already been condemned. A case in point is the king's expressed regret for having consented to the execution of the Earl of Strafford.[30] The legitimacy of the charges against Strafford, which historians agree are questionable at best, is not for Milton an issue. He clearly agrees with Parliament's finding of treason. But what is at issue is *Eikon Basilike*'s exploitation of the dramatic Strafford case to create a public *perception* of royal remorse over one death that can in turn deflect perceptions of royal remorselessness over many others. As the king's "facile conscience" had first rejected and then later agreed to the treason charge against Strafford for reasons of policy, now his display of sorrow for the act of agreeing to it also has a political motive: "And we may well perceave to what easie satisfactions and purgations he had inur'd his secret conscience, who thaught, by such weak policies and ostentations as these, to gaine beleif and absolution from understanding Men" (376). The belief and absolution acquired by such "ostentations" neatly separate *the image of the act* of agreeing from the agreement itself, thus placing the act's meaning, its claim to "truth," not in what actually happened but in how it is made to appear. The image thus bears witness only of itself. Moreover, the king bewails

the blood of one man, his commodious Instrument, . . . that we might think him too tender to shed willingly the blood of those thousands, whom he counted Rebels. And thus by dipping voluntarily his fingers end, yet with shew of great remorse in the blood of *Strafford,* wherof all men cleer him, he thinks to scape that Sea of innocent blood wherin his own guilt inevitably hath plung'd him all over. (376)

Now since the king's "shew of great remorse" depends for its success on the credulity of the dazzled gazer, the calculated stagework of blood-dipped fingers might have been simply exposed by Milton as sensationalist propaganda. But the king's intended audience is not in fact merely the English public: "*He hop'd it would be som evidence before God and Man to all posteritie that he was farr from bearing that vast load and guilt of blood* layd upon him by others" (376). By offering to prove his innocence before God with the same display of "evidence" as depends on credulous men and posterity, the impressive show bears witness to the truth of its own self-idolizing intentions and desires.

The key to success in strategic ostentation is the "image-doting rabble," who fail to see that the image they worship requires their credulity. Milton argues this point explicitly as he rejects the king's claims to protection under the Solemn League and Covenant. As Merritt Hughes points out, exclusive adherence to the covenant's clause providing for protection of the king's person would have meant neglect of other more important provisions. Moreover, the covenant had already been variously broken, both by the king and by the Parliament. In any case, the king himself had never agreed to the covenant's terms.[31] The strategy of *Eikon Basilike* therefore consists in requiring that the covenant be honored, not for the sake of its terms (which would demand inquiry into whether or not its terms have actually been met), but for the sake of its *being a covenant*. By this strategy, in Milton's words, it "shall prevaile at last, over men so quell'd and fitted to be slaves by the fals conceit of a Religious Covnant" (595). Since a covenant by definition exists only according to its agreed terms, to detach it from these is to make it no longer a vital agreement. Thus the "Religious Covenant" idolized by *Eikon Basilike* serves merely in its own formal and titular capacity, bearing witness only of itself. And this, too, as a political expedient, is designed to foster the growth and expansion of "civil idolatry." Instead of seeking to earn from the king's subjects a reverence that they would freely grant to a reasonable and wise secular ruler, the "Religious Covenant" simply expropriates to the self-idolizing king the reverence that would otherwise be paid by covenant keepers to the covenant itself. But even covenant-keeping reverence turns out to be no more than the superstition of those who have forgotten that the icon they worship, the unexamined "truth" of their covenant, is an idol of their own making:

For so long as a King shall find by experience that doe the worst he can, his Subjects, *overaw'd by the Religion of thir own Covnant*, will only prosecute his evil instruments, not dare to touch his Person, and that whatever hath bin on his part offended or transgress'd, he shall come off at last with the same honour as for well doing, he will not faile to finde them worke. (595, my italics)

The "religion of their own covenant" can "overawe" only subjects who have abdicated their capacity for critical thought and imagination, and it is this self-abdication that ultimately empowers a people's tyrant. The king's showy book could not by itself have made an idol of the Solemn League and Covenant; it could only exploit the idol that the covenanters had already made by worshiping the devitalized icon of an already forsaken agreement. With that act of idolatry, they leave themselves open to continuing abuse: "For so long as a King shall find by experience . . . that whatever hath bin on his part offended or transgress'd . . . he will not faile to finde them worke." But even more important, by making a religious idol of the very covenant that they themselves had authored, they nail to that icon the vital truth of their own intentions, desires, and responses. Their idolatrous self-witness thus subverts their imaginative and reasoning capacity for witnessing truth.

SUCH EASY LITERATURE

Milton shatters the king's icon not only because it is a bad king's, but because it is a debased icon, an idol exploited and adored for purposes far removed from the apparent representations made by the image itself. But idolatry thrives as well on materials not overtly iconic. In its defense of personal chaplains, set prayers, and the liturgy; in the manner of its scriptural quotation; and most spectacularly in its plagiarism of the prayer offered by Pamela in Sidney's *Arcadia, Eikon Basilike* makes a showcase for what Milton could only regard as idolatry of words.[32] Words exploited for purposes alien to their original intent, words devitalized and dispirited by rote recitation, words distanced from the tensive impulses of thought and feeling that generated them, become, like their exploiters, slaves to idolatry. Such words are made by their misuse to signify, not human intention, desire, and response, as Milton would wish, but rather the cessation of these. Self-witnessing dead words thus travesty their vital origin in the divine Word.

That words may be the instruments of the most pervasive and subtle idolatry is suggested by Milton's remarks in the preface to *Eikonoklastes*. For *Eikon Basilike* to gain wide public approval, it is enough that it be merely inscribed with the king's name, "the gaudy name of Majesty . . . his Regal Name and Authority . . . a name, then which there needs no more among the blockish vulgar, to make it wise, and excellent, and admir'd, nay to set it next the Bible" (339). Under the aegis of the king's name, the king's book can be judged by "faction and the easy literature of custom and opinion," such easy literature as persuades its readers that they, too, may become "wise, excellent, and admir'd" by exerting as little imaginative, critical, and intellectual effort in reading the book as had gone into the writing of it (339). Like self-witnessing idols, "easy literature" depends on the cooperative servility, or more appropriately the cooperative indolence, of credulous readers and writers, word-speakers, and word-hearers.

Of the many offenses *Eikon Basilike* commits, none elicits from Milton more contempt than its intellectual, spiritual, and imaginative laziness. The king "had it not in him to make a prayer of his own, or at least would excuse himself the paines and cost of his invention" (367). He should "endeavour to have more light in himself: And not to walk by another mans Lamp, but to get Oyle into his own" (552). Milton's own strenuous religious and intellectual discipline made the act of praying one of a Christian's "Ecclesiastical duties," a vigorous "exercise of that Heav'nly gift" that is our "freedom of speech to the Throne of Grace" (506–7). The king's book, on the other hand, "unhallow'd, and unchrist'nd" the disciplined creative and spiritual freedom of prayer by succumbing to the easy sneak of facile borrowing. The dulcet orisons of the king's divines exude the sickly sweetness of unexercised morbidity: their "honycomb devotions" are supplied from the "*rheume* of thir Mellifluous prayers and meditations" (362, 365–66; my italics). Yet it is not the source of supply that makes borrowed prayers idolatrous. The king's prayers, and the claims made for them, are tainted not simply because they are borrowed, but because the act of borrowing words evinces the particular word-idolatry that would imprison vital truth in words themselves—words from heathen romance, hired priests, personal chaplains, the Common Prayer Book, Holy Scripture. To locate truth in set and circumscribed words, regardless of their origin, is to imprison the idea of truth in an incidental and temporal form.

What Milton demands instead, as we have seen in *Areopagitica,* is an activity of witness that, rather than presuming on truth itself, releases truth to the imaginative indeterminacy that is essential to the witness's being vital. This is a process that depends, significantly, on the unpremeditated impetus of feeling, of desire, of "affections":

They *who use no set forms of prayer,* have words from thir affections; while others are to seek affections fit and proportionable to a certain doss of prepar'd words; . . . so to imprison and confine by force, into a Pinfold of sett words, those two most unimprisonable things, our Prayers and that Divine Spirit of utterance that moves them. . . . He who prays, must consult first with his heart; which in likelyhood may stir up his affections. (505–6)

Prayer's truth resides not in the words but in the activity of *finding* the words—in the vital witnessing, the "unimprisonable . . . utterance," that brings the words into being. These words, if equated with prayer's truth and thus idolized, will imprison not only truth but natural "affections," the spontaneous feeling and desire that prompts them. To Milton, it is precisely the *effort* of original prayer, an effort subverted by liturgical forms, that gives initial impetus to the activity that constitutes prayer's worth. But the role played by "affections" in the process of prayer is most critical of all. Because of their vital generative capacity, and because of their mediatory province in body and soul, affective feelings are to be actively sought out and deliberately "stirr[ed] up," by consultation with the heart. For paradoxically, the believer with stirred-up, vigorous, and well-exercised affections finds that the effort of prayer becomes in fact supremely effortless—*easy*. The difference between the ease of "that Divine Spirit of utterance" and that of "the easy literature of custom and opinion" is measured by the vital engagement of a self-transforming imagination. On the other hand, for the worshiper who uses set prayers, "having both words and matter readie made to his lips, which is anough to make up the outward act of prayer, his affections grow lazy, and com not up easlie at the call of words not thir own." Lazy "affections" present God not with prayer but only with dispirited and meaningless forms, "a sett of stale and empty words" (506–7). Vital words stirred by the affections are like manna in the wilderness: "God every morning raines down new expressions into our hearts." But, like reserved manna, words idolatrously hoarded "will be found rather *to breed wormes and stink*" (505).

If affective indolence is the ultimate cause and consequence of idolatrous "easy literature," however, it is not the only contributing influence. To the combination of "ease" and "little . . . Christian diligence, or judgement" Milton attributes the imitative patchwork of *Eikon Basilike*'s devotional style, but he also tellingly links such "ease" to the consequent augmentation of the book's market value:

And this is the substance of his first section, till wee come to the devout of it, model'd into the form of a privat Psalter. Which they who so much admire, either for the matter or the manner, may as well admire the Arch-Bishops late Breviary, and many other as good *Manuals*, and *Handmaids of Devotion*, the lip-work of every Prelatical Liturgist, clapt together, and quilted out of Scripture phrase, with as much ease, and as little need of Christian diligence, or judgement, as belongs to the compiling of any ord'nary and salable peece of English Divinity, that the Shops value. (360)

"Till wee come to the devout of it" captures exactly the compartmentalizing effect created by *Eikon Basilike*'s division of each of its twenty-eight rather brief chapters into a section of political argument followed by a section of devotional meditations and prayer. The readily grasped, almost liturgical rhythms of the book's overall structure thus join its "clapt together, and quilted" devotions to make it a suitably easy-reading bookshelf companion to those other "as good *Manuals*," whose easy acquisition in the shops matches the equally easy "lipwork" of "the whole rosarie of his Prayers" (364).

Milton's association of "easy literature" with bought prayers is characteristic. From the beginning of his polemical career, his irony has targeted the business side of facile religion. We have seen how, in *Of Reformation*, the prelates desired to expand their task of spiritual relief into a burgeoning commercial enterprise by having us "commit to their dispose the whole managing of our salvation." Similarly, *Areopagitica*'s implicit believer gladly pays the caparisoned priest to mind his religion for him, because he finds it "to be a traffick so entangl'd, and of so many piddling accounts, that of all mysteries he cannot skill to keep a stock going upon that trade."[33]

But here, vendible "ease" is carried several steps further. The king in time of dire spiritual need discovers in himself such a "bankrupt devotion" that he is compelled not only to have "sharkd" his prayers "from the mouth of a Heathen worshiper" but to have "sould them to those that stood and honord him next to the Messiah" (367). The moral wrong in *Eikon Basilike*'s plagiarism of the Pamela prayer lies not just in its being inappropriately heathen, despite Milton's scathing characterization of it as "the polluted orts and refuse of *Arcadia's* and *Romances* . . . an ethnic Prayer" (364). Neither is it precisely in the plagiarism itself, which Milton treats ironically as an ingenious form of revenue enhancement: "Many Princes have bin rigorous in lay-ing taxes on thir Subject by the head, but of any King heertofore that made a levy upon thir witt, and seisd it as his own legitimat, I have not whome beside to instance" (365). For a spiritually bankrupt person to steal prayers might in itself be almost an object of pity: "he who wants a prayer to beseech God in his necessity, tis unexpressible how poor he is; farr poorer within himself then all his enemies can make him" (366). This bankrupt, however, steals prayers not to fill spiritual emptiness but to pawn the prayers "for hopes no less vain and presumptuous . . . then by these goodly reliques to be held a Saint and Martyr in opinion with the cheated People" (367). Proffered as an icon of Charles's piety, the prayer's success depends on thoughtless and spiritually indolent readers to buy up the icon as their truth: "How unhappy, how forsook of grace, and unbelovd of God that people who *resolv to know no more* of piety or of goodnes, then to account him thir cheif Saint and Martyr" (367, my italics). By resolving to limit their knowledge of piety and goodness to Charles's iconic representations, the people "forsook of grace" have in any event already forsaken themselves. Moreover, like these credulous and cheated worshipers, the would-be saint's impoverishment is both spiritual and intellectual: he "thought no better of the living God then of a buzzard Idol, fitt to be so servd and worship in reversion . . . *without being able to discern* the affront rather then the worship of such an ethnic prayer" (364, my italics). Inability to discern the difference between "affront" and "worship" suggests complete loss of human reason. Thus Sidney's prayer, in its fictional context the sign of a pagan character's piety, becomes in *Eikon Basilike* a sign of mental incapacitation, Christian piety's irrationally bartered demise.

Besides the test of intellectual and spiritual vitality, an additional test may be brought to bear on "easy literature." It is the simple test adduced by the life that is authored by the word-user himself. Throughout *Eikonoklastes* Milton challenges the king's words by pointing to the king's deeds:

But if these his fair spok'n words shall be heer fairly confronted and laid parallel to his own farr differing deeds, manifest and visible to the whole Nation, then surely we may look on them who notwithstanding shall persist to give to bare words more credit then to op'n deeds, as men whose judgement was not rationally evinc'd and perswaded, but fatally stupifi'd and bewitch'd. (346–47)

As with other truth tests, the test of deeds against words implicates those who read the words as well as those who write them. Any who would not be "fatally stupifi'd and bewitch'd" by these "fair spok'n words" must with open eyes read, not the book of the king's words, but the book of his life, the "farr differing deeds, manifest and visible to the whole Nation."

Yet it is the king's effort by words to expropriate the moral and spiritual justification that was authored by *someone else's life* that Milton finds most absurd. Charles seems to regard his personal suffering as itself sufficient claim on the mercies that were granted to King David: "I come far short of David's piety; yet since I may equal David's afflictions, give me also the comforts and the sure mercies of David" (*EB* 149). Just as sufferings cannot themselves make a martyr, in Milton's view, sufferings cannot by themselves sanctify a life of wrongdoing. "Had he borrow'd *Davids* heart," instead of borrowing the mere rhetoric of David's penitential psalms, "it had bin much the holier theft" (547). In the attempt to acquire David's self-authorship through David's words, however, the "easy literature" strategy backfires:

Transported with the vain ostentation of imitating *Davids* language, not his life, observe how he brings a curse upon himself and his Fathers house (God so disposing it) by his usurp'd and ill imitated prayer: *Let thy anger I beseech thee be against me and my Fathers house, as for these Sheep what have they don.* For if David indeed sind in numbring the people, of which fault he in earnest made that confession, and acquitted the whole people from the guilt of that sin, then doth this King, using the same words, bear witness against himself to be the guilty person; and either in his soule and conscience heer acquitts the Parlament and the people, or els abuses the words of *David,* and dissembles grossly eev'n to the very face of God. (555)

Words exploited as self-witnessing bearers of truth may thus betray the exploiter: "the same words, bear witness against himself," simultaneously deceiving the idolater and unmasking his idolatry. The example from David points both to the king's guilt and to his people's innocence. With this, the authorial imposture whereby King Charles attempts to rewrite himself as King David is also revealed as an effect both of carelessness in reading Scripture and of deceptiveness in self-authorship. Ultimately self-imprisoned by his idolatrous authorship of "the easy literature of custom and opinion," the king forfeits the liberating imaginative and affective capacity of his prayers to receive that "most unimprisonable" thing, the "Divine Spirit of utterance" that alone could move them.

Like every idol, "easy literature" fails and betrays because the idolater complacently accepts the literary icon as truth, rather than recognizing that all icons, verbal and otherwise, are themselves no more than finite mortal instruments—instruments to be used in the continuing search for immortal, and therefore inexpressible, truth. If we expect to locate truth *in* the icon, we may gratify our senses, but the "streaming fountain" sickens and dies. As a fitting parody of the vital "fountain of truth" that is represented in Scripture and alluded to in *Areopagitica*, Milton portrays the fountain of "ease" that he believes *Eikon Basilike* offers its readers. The king's book would have us hold "our *natural freedom* by meer gift, as when the Conduit pisses Wine at Coronations, from the superfluity of thir royal grace and beneficence" (486, my italics). The civil idolater, without whom the king's icon could never have turned idol, is set out by Milton's deft wine-transforming vulgarism to swill (under the guise of "royal grace and benevolence") the lifeless excreta of what once had been the subject's own vital freedom—now only superfluous urine, release of which provides the royal personage with nothing so much as his own "ease." Should the people desire to reject such a manifest, eminently expressible "truth," they need only exercise the natural freedom of their own unimprisonable imaginations, and cease their idolatrous imbibing. By thus retrieving to its rightful place the affective powers of imagination, they will transform themselves into autonomous individuals, whose self-authorship begins from the very moment that they "bethink themselves, and recover" (601).

For Milton, however, imaginative autonomy for the individual human being was not an end sufficient to itself. The subjective transcendental Individual, celebrated two centuries later in Romanticist criticism, would have been likened by Milton to the Satan whom the Romantics somewhat misleadingly equated with Milton's conception of imaginative will. Yet subjective and, in many ways, transcendent autonomy is still essential to Milton's understanding of the power by which affective imagination is able to serve the interests of truth. The truth served by Milton's affective imagination is a merging of the autonomous yet finite carnal self with the infinite autonomy of divine freedom. This freedom requires, above all, liberation from every carnal icon—liberation even, in the end, from the carnal icon of the subjective self. As we turn to Milton's iconoclastic hero, we find that the icons from which Samson must liberate his subjective self are not those created by someone else's affective imagination, but those created by his own. For Samson, ultimately to cast off every icon is to author himself finally as an autonomous, imaginative individual whose appalling perfect freedom lies beyond the capacity of any to interpret.

6

SAMSON'S TRANSFORMATIVE

DESIRE

To author the carnal self toward the autonomy of divine freedom is to undertake radical change and redefinition of all that pertains to the self and makes it recognizable to us. So when, as Manoa puts it, "Samson . . . quit[s] himself / Like Samson," we may question whether any such imaginative transformation has actually taken place. From his last words, we know that the renowned Nazarite of tricky heroics went down riddling:

> Hitherto, lords, what your commands imposed
> I have performed, as reason was, obeying,
> Not without wonder or delight beheld.
> Now of my own accord such other trial
> I mean to show you of my strength, yet greater;
> As with amaze shall strike all who behold.[1]

Samson's mocking double entendres sound like nothing so much as the old vaunting Samson, or like Milton's rebellious angel Satan "scoffing in ambiguous words" moments before mowing down the faithful with a burst of cannon fire: "Heaven witness thou anon, while we discharge / Freely our part; ye who appointed stand / Do as you have in charge, and briefly touch / What we propound, and loud that all may hear" (*PL* VI.564–68). Thus if Samson's eternal soul is saved, his outward conduct gives every sign that at least his temporal being remains unregenerate.[2]

Critical debate over *Samson Agonistes* has long centered on whether Milton's iconoclastic hero is to be understood as an instrument of divine justice, whose struggle against his own and his people's sinfulness makes him a prototype of the Christian hero; or if he is to be understood as a barbarously vengeful, tragically flawed tribal leader, doomed to the heroic constraints of Old Testament Law. If we follow the antiregenerationist readings of Irene Samuel or, more recently, Joseph Wittreich, Samson's benighted performance fulfills the Aristotelian requirement, as interpreted by Milton, that tragic poetry have the capacity for "raising pity and fear, or terror, to purge the mind of those and such-like passions, that is *to temper and reduce them to just measure* with a kind of delight, stirred up by reading or seeing those passions well imitated."[3] Samson becomes, in the antiregenerationist reading, the contrary of a model for imitation: simply stated, the unregenerate Samson's impressive doing of terrible things relieves us of the urge to do them ourselves.[4] Arguing that the negative ideological and behavioral representations of *Samson Agonistes* can justly be interpreted only in contrast with the positive representations of *Paradise Regained*, the tragedy's companion poem in the 1671 volume, Wittreich remarks: "As interpretive fictions, Milton's last poems are how-to-live and how-*not*-to-live poems."[5] The more orthodox reading of a regenerate Samson, on the other hand, salvages Samson's worthiness as a model to be admired and, if not imitated, at least recognized as mimetically representing psychological and ideological aspects of Milton himself.[6] Mary Ann Radzinowicz expands the regenerationist reading to a complexly unified portrait that "imitates and concludes Milton's own intellectual development; it demonstrates the necessity of mental labor for tempering of the mind and control of the passions."[7] Also arguing for the moral and spiritual worthiness of Milton's hero, Joan Bennett finds a Samson whose regeneracy depends on his having realized a higher definition of Christian liberty, according to which his act of sacrificial violence may only temporarily free his still-sinful compatriots, yet which nevertheless enables Samson in good faith to resign his cause to a stronger hand.[8]

The antiregenerationist and regenerationist arguments, seemingly opposed interpretations of *Samson Agonistes*, are in fact deeply united in a shared concern for the moral or doctrinal lessons to be drawn from the story. This is the same interpretive activity whose pressure to discover an explanatory "middle," a rational link between cause and effect, has been shown by Stanley Fish to absorb the minds of virtually everyone in the poem, whether friend or foe to the hero; and to absorb most notably, until moments before the crisis, the mind of Samson himself.[9] The interpretive certainty sought both by readers of the drama and by participants in it is notoriously elusive because of the ambiguity surrounding every sign that Samson or his interpreters might use as a guide to understanding the will of God. Uniquely in *Samson Agonistes*, Milton depicts the condition of the faithful in a world from which, to all appearances, God would seem to have withdrawn his influence: "Rather than representing some doctrine or truth," remarks Fish, Samson "represents the difficulty (not to say folly) of extracting doctrine from the diverse and multidirectional materials of a decentered world, that is, of a world in which God has so removed his ways from human sight that we are left to our own interpretive conjectures."[10] Such a world was that of the disillusioned, albeit temporally reconciled, former millennialist of 1671: a world in which the roots of modern political culture were fast putting forth new shoots. Confronting the decentered human condition of his contemporary world through the ancient tale from the Book of Judges, Milton pushes beyond interpretive conjectures with an iconoclastic poetics that answers, not to doctrine, but to the transformative desires that human efforts at extracting doctrine from the world are a carnal and ultimately futile attempt to satisfy. When Samson brings down the Philistine temple, his iconoclastic act not only puts an end to his own interpretive conjectures; it releases him as well from a sequence of iconoclastic self-transformations whose final truth can be known to his interpreters only as acts of true witness that manifest Samson's unimprisonable desire.

THE RHETORIC OF THE TRIBAL ICON

The distinction between truth and true witness is critical, for if truth is unknowable to Samson's interpreters, true witness is not. Efforts to extract doctrine from the world of *Samson Agonistes*, efforts which appeal both to regenerationist and to antiregenerationist interpretive bias, owe much of their disagreement to having overlooked this distinction. Precedent for that oversight is established, not surprisingly, by those eminently sincere, yet partial, first interpreters of Samson, the Chorus. As oppressed Hebrews and as friends of the national leader, their readiness to find benevolent providence in the Philistine disaster is to be expected. But their celebratory closing speech points to the epistemological hazards of extracting doctrine from the world, the hazards in this instance of religious partisanship and tribal nationalism.

> All is best, though we oft doubt,
> What the unsearchable dispose
> Of highest wisdom brings about,
> And ever best found in the close.
> Oft he seems to hide his face,
> But unexpectedly returns
> And to his faithful champion hath in place
> Bore witness gloriously. (1745–52)

From their perspective, the Chorus's sentiment that "All is best" following the apparent destruction of their enemy is easy enough to justify: "All is best" in the view of the Israelites because Samson's act of raining death on the Philistine aristocracy fits neatly into the prophecy of Israel's deliverance. Moreover, the shift from "unsearchable dispose" to "found in the close" points to the human interpreting that highest wisdom's "dispose" will inevitably be subjected to, "unsearchable" or not. But in the lines that follow, we see how readily such partial interpreting leads to deeper error. According to these tribal interpreters, "highest wisdom . . . unexpectedly returns" from hiding, and now "to his faithful champion hath in place / Bore witness gloriously." Yet we know that wherever there exists a concept of absolute truth, it is the faithful champion who bears witness to "highest wisdom," not the other way around. By reversing the terms, the Chorus put truth at the service of truth's witnesses, in effect subordinating truth to the doctrines of those who claim to serve it.[11] And that, of course, is exactly what the Chorus do when they celebrate Samson's destruction of the Philistines as an unambiguous triumph of truth over idolatry.

At the same time, however, this tribal God who bears witness to his champion is also the divine being who, in the final phrases of the Chorus, dismisses his servants "with new acquist / Of true experience from this great event"(1754–55). The exact content of this "true experience"—what there is in the experience that makes it true—is left unspecified, although from the words of the Chorus, we know that they believe *they* know. The content of the "true experience" which the Chorus believe they know can arguably be expanded from partisan tribal requisites to a more humanistically defensible public cause also known to Samson, a cause identified by Joan Bennett as "the right goal for a genuine governor: to free his people to live righteous lives." [12] Yet even this higher, seemingly nonpartisan (though in fact Miltonically Puritan) cause fails to justify the Chorus's belief that they are somehow privy to the "unsearchable dispose" of "highest wisdom." At the end of the tragedy, as Martin Mueller observes, "there remains some tension between the 'uncontrollable intent,' the 'unsearchable dispose,' and the quiet affirmation that 'all is best.' There may not be cause for lamentation, but there is no cause for the psalmist's joy and gladness either." [13] Nevertheless, from the perspective of the reader, the Chorus's claim that the catastrophic "great event" has given us "true experience" is not to be denied. For if truth itself cannot be interpretively specified, what finally is specified by the Chorus is something for which accounts *can* be presented: the *uninterpreted* affective measure among God's servants of "peace and consolation . . . / And calm of mind all passion spent" (1757–58).

In the triumphant interpretive postures of the Chorus's and Manoa's tribalism, then, we can recognize the *affective* bearing of conviction, metaphor's "conceptual peace and rest" come fully to fruition in the rhetoric of certainty that one's own cause, however defined, is the true cause. At the same time, in Samson's iconoclastic actions, we can also recognize the transformative desire that both sparks creative invention and distinguishes true witness—a struggle continuously to break out of the affective lineaments of conviction, the idols set up by conviction to *secure* the imagination (that is, to reassure it and also to put a stop to its restless activity) as the imagination strives toward an elusive ideal. In the course of the drama, the kind of doctrinaire thinking that Milton had attacked in *Areopagitca* and *Eikonoklastes* repeatedly presents itself in the rhetoric of tribal convictions—of Manoa, of the Chorus, of Dalila and Harapha, of the Philistine messenger, of Samson himself—the affective linguistic structures of belief according to which decisions are taken and actions are performed, and without some version of which the most ordinary proceedings of human life would be all but impossible. On the uninterpreted sensory level of response to these structures, then—on a level measured as "passion spent"—we are able to agree with the Chorus's claim that "this great event" has given us "true experience." We are able to agree because the *affective* truth of that experience depends not upon religious or other partisan assumptions but upon what we know of the ambiguities, the "multidirectional materials of a decentered world," to whose "unsearchable dispose" our own transformative desires act as true witness. Our assent to the "true experience" of *Samson Agonistes* is a function of Milton's insight into the very nature of spiritual and intellectual conviction confronted by such a world—his insight into the processes of confrontation played out among multiple interpreters in their efforts to extract doctrine, but played out especially in the dramatic private arena of the affective imagination.

Most importantly, *Samson Agonistes* concerns itself not with the question of what truth is: "truth" here, like "meaning" in metaphor, operates as the red herring that keeps interpreters distracted. Rather, through the experience of Samson, Milton's dramatic poem concerns itself with the question of what the effort toward *true witness* is *like*. To observe Samson is to gain insight into the very process by means of which, as Susanne Woods phrases it, "election as vocation and election as free choice come together" and enable the Nazarite to "seize control of his own destiny, and so fulfill it."[14] In seizing control of his own destiny, Milton's Samson becomes a metaphor for the paradox of bearing witness that is true *to transformative desire*, true to an impetus toward that which cannot itself be known. And, as might be expected from the intimate connection between metaphoric "truth" and the psychology of iconoclasm, mimetic representation of "true witness" requires an iconoclastic action.[15] But the iconoclastic action that articulates Samson's true witness is not in fact his violent destruction of the idolatrous Philistines. It is rather Samson's destruction of the graven images he has made of his own heroic and nonheroic career.

SAMSON'S ICONS OF SHAME AND GLORY

The affective measure to Samson of his dual career can be gauged from the speeches in which he articulates his sense of failure, disgrace, and loss. Among these speeches, what is most revealing is not Samson's lament over the miseries of his current condition—blindness, imprisonment, slavery at the mill. What reveals the affective value to him of his heroic and nonheroic past career is rather his vision of a possible future career should Manoa's efforts to ransom him succeed: he would become a pathetic sideshow attraction, a wasted symbol of a forsaken cause, a tarnishing trophy of his own lost glory-days:

> To what can I be useful, wherein serve
> My nation, and the work from heaven imposed,
> But to sit idle on the household hearth,
> A burdenous drone; to visitants a gaze,
> Or pitied object, these redundant locks
> Robustious to no purpose clustering down,
> Vain monument of strength; till length of years
> And sedentary numbness craze my limbs
> To a contemptible old age obscure. (564–72)

The affective burden of Samson's refusal to let Manoa ransom him points less to his sense of having failed in his service to God than to his dread of further public humiliation.[16] Indeed, even service to God looks in this speech not unlike service to the Philistines: as opposed to a freely willed undertaking, divine service is "work from heaven imposed." But far worse than this, and worse even than profane service rendered to Philistines, would be souvenir duty rendered to his own nation as "a burdenous drone; to visitants a gaze, / Or pitied object," his strength a "vain monument," his locks "Robustious to no purpose clustering down"—a service that would allow him neither to revitalize his carnal heroics nor to forget, in "a contemptible old age obscure," just how much he had once gloried in them. Manoa's solution of ransom would condemn Samson to a future that would be little different from what we have observed up to now of his present: the agony of endlessly rehearsing the best and the worst of his past—the history of his glory and the history of his shame. And yet, by the end of his upcoming confrontations with Dalila and Harapha, neither glory nor shame is any longer capable of exercising affective influence over Samson.

Samson's revitalization in response to the visits from Dalila and Harapha has long been acknowledged.[17] Before these two appear on the scene, his ruminations with the Chorus, with Manoa, and with himself have served to direct his tormented self-examinations more and more inward, so that what had begun as a primarily physical anguish over his external condition—blindness, imprisonment, degradation to the status of a draft animal or slave—has worsened to a consciousness of spiritual failure and self-betrayal that leave him prostrate and hopeless, longing only for death. But then Dalila comes along and arouses despair into anger. Next, Harapha; and anger is transformed into self-assured, outspoken belligerence that is nevertheless suspended, for one brief startling moment, by Samson's solitary and remarkably pure-toned declaration of faith: "My trust is in the living God" (1140). Somehow the visits of Dalila and Harapha, two hardly sympathetic figures, accomplish what the painstaking solicitude and well-intended, if not always tactful, discourse of Manoa and the Chorus cannot.[18] The enmity of Dalila and Harapha proves more useful than partisan support, even as the precise motivation of the Philistine visitors remains obscure.[19] Dalila seems to invent her love for Samson along with her excuses for betraying him. Harapha enters as the Philistine champion; and yet he declines to fight, on grounds that Samson is socially inferior and in need of a bath. The claims on Samson of both these characters seem to be made more intimate by their very alienation.

To discover what motivates these counter-partisan visits, I suggest that we look not to Dalila and Harapha, but to Samson himself. For Dalila and Harapha are not simply characters in the Old Testament story (indeed, Milton's invention Harapha is not even that). Rather, they are fetishistic images—icons fashioned by the interpretive phases through which Samson tracks his career to the present, where he languishes "eyeless in Gaza," imprisoned in the blind agon of unrealized witness.[20] From the depths of despair into which he has sunken shortly before Dalila's arrival, Samson epitomizes these two phases:

> So much I feel my genial spirits droop,
> My hopes all flat, nature within me seems
> In all her functions weary of herself;

> My race of glory run, and race of shame,
>
> And I shall shortly be with them that rest. (594–98)

By confronting Dalila, icon of his race of shame, and Harapha, icon of his race of glory, Samson confronts all there is for him to know, and more important, all there is for him to *feel*, about the alienated interpretations by means of which he has been securing imaginative conviction throughout his career. The Philistine visitors are able to torment Samson not as individuals in their own right, but only as they figuratively coalesce and thereby represent to him the personal and tribal idolatries of intention, desire, and response by which Samson has been delineating all that pertains to him: his prophesied mission, his phenomenal strength, his Nazarite vow, his magnificent hair, his "intimate impulse" to marry, God's "holy secret." In the process of confronting and dismantling the *affective* significance to himself of Dalila and Harapha, Samson shatters every sign he has been using to secure imaginative conviction of God's will. From the unimaginable idea of God's will, Samson strips away interpretive idol after idol, iconoclastically strips away glory, shame, appearance, expectation—every element of his affective consciousness, everything that is *not God*.[21]

"O WEAKNESS!"

Samson's confrontations begin with the icon of his race of shame. Dalila is the icon of Samson's shame not only because she is the temptress who has extracted his secret from him, but also because she now appears as a suppliant desirous of reconciliation.[22] Like a penitent Eve before Adam, Dalila before Samson presents an affective image of the peccant soul humbling itself to beg mercy from a wronged and wrathful God: "With doubtful feet and wavering resolution / I came, still dreading thy displeasure, Samson" (732–33). With the affective image of contrition before judgment thus displayed in the words of Dalila, Samson's carnal self-involvement, his obsession with his own shame and anguish, is forced into the open. His attack on Dalila thus begins to exorcise the "poisonous bosom snake" which has been Samson's own guilt-ridden gnawing at his vital self over his personal breach of faith with God: "Out, out hyaena; these are thy wonted arts, / And arts of every woman false like thee" (748–49). By reifying the "art" of betrayal into alienated images like "hyaena" and "every woman false," Samson affectively distances the act of faith-breaking from his own tormented bosom. Thus Samson begins to extricate his present suffering from the feelings that degrade suffering into paralysis.

Dalila is the first to bring to our attention the parallel between her own excuses for betrayal and Samson's. In his soliloquy and in his searching dialogue with the Chorus, Samson's contemptuous charge against himself had been effeminate "weakness": "She was not the prime cause, but I myself, / Who vanquisht with a peal of words (O weakness!) / Gave up my fort of silence to a Woman" (234–36). The affective burden of Samson's self-critique lies not with his having talked, but with his shame at the "weakness" of having been "vanquisht" by "a Woman." Appropriately, then, "weakness" is the term Samson's icon Dalila uses in her own defense:

> First granting, as I do, it was a weakness
> In me, but incident to all our sex, . . .
> Was it not weakness also to make known . . .
> Wherein consisted all thy strength and safety?
> (774–75, 778–80)

The icon of Samson's shame has become a speaking mirror: she tells him no more than what he already knows. His retort is *morally* just: "If weakness may excuse, / What murderer, what traitor, parricide, / Incestuous, sacrilegious, but may plead it?" (831–33). But more important, Dalila's defense of her "weakness" *affectively* reifies, hence makes subject to iconoclastic attack, an image of Samson's own obsessive self-accusations. Once he has shattered Dalila's excuse of feminine "weakness," Samson can no longer indulge in the egoistic self-flagellation that this particular excuse has up to now provided him. In his critique of Dalila's "weakness," the interpretive idol he had made of his own "weakness" disintegrates.

"INTIMATE IMPULSE"

Dalila's other excuse for betraying Samson moves from the private to the public sphere: she betrayed him, she claims, for the sake of her religion and her nation. Her argument mirrors Samson's own claims in a way that forces him to relinquish what had heretofore been another reliable self-defense. As Dalila phrases it:

> How honourable, how glorious to entrap
> A common enemy, who had destroyed
> Such numbers of our nation: and the priest
> Was not behind, but ever at my ear. (855–58)

The claims of nation and faith can justify the actions of either side. Perhaps sensing this, Samson dismantles Dalila's second excuse with less self-righteousness than he had her first. She should have placed her spouse above national enmity, he says, as he had her when "I before all the daughters of my tribe . . . chose thee . . . I loved thee, as too well thou knew'st" (876–78). Yet as we hear this, we ourselves remember something Dalila does *not* know, for Dalila is the one person to whom Samson would never repeat what we have heard him claim several times before: to Manoa, to the Chorus, and to himself, Samson insists that he married Philistine women to seek an "occasion" against Israel's oppressors. Why *did* Samson marry Philistine women? Was it love, was it God, or was it politics?[23] The Chorus's and Manoa's own ambivalence about Samson's "intimate impulse" to marry had perhaps cast doubts upon that impulse's reliability,[24] but Dalila's national vision actively *prohibits* Samson from using in her presence the claim that he married her in order to overthrow the Philistines. Samson gives no sign of recognizing that his present charges against his wife ("feigned religion, smooth hypocrisy") could thus apply equally well to himself, but he does not need to.[25] The *image* of his claim to "intimate impulse" has been displayed before him by his "country's enemy," and he has judged that image from the perspective of a correspondingly alienated vision. If not his religion, then Samson's love for Dalila had to have been "feigned . . . smooth hypocrisy": he cannot have it both ways.[26] To Harapha, Samson will still argue that his marriage choice proved him no enemy to his captors, but never again do we hear from him that he married Philistine women because God prompted him to do it. Perhaps God did prompt him; perhaps he didn't. Whatever the truth, during the exchange with Dalila, the interpretive idol that had been Samson's "intimate impulse" self-destructs.

GOD'S "HOLY SECRET"

But the idol central to Samson's race of shame is the one with which he has been most relentlessly flagellating himself, God's "holy secret." In an early bitter passage in which he rues his fate of being given strength without wisdom, Samson refers to the secret in terms that make God look like a practical joker: "God, when he gave me strength, to show withal / How slight the gift was, hung it in my hair" (58–59). But elsewhere the gift becomes "The Mystery of God" (378), a "holy secret" (497), a "hallowed Pledge" (535); and Samson terms his hair a "precious fleece" (539). The mystery and capriciousness of God's "holy secret" make the moral and spiritual quality of its betrayal particularly difficult for Samson (and thus ourselves) to assess:

> But I God's counsel have not kept, his holy secret
> Presumptuously have published, impiously,
> Weakly at least, and shamefully; a sin
> That Gentiles in their parables condemn
> To their abyss and horrid pains confined. (497–501)

Was betraying God's "holy secret" a presumptuous act? impious? weak? shameful? damnable? The Gentiles apparently know what to call it, but Samson doesn't. If the sum of Samson's present suffering is God's punishment for betraying His "holy secret," then that betrayal must be a heinous crime indeed. Like the apple in *Paradise Lost*, the seemingly trivial sign of kept faith in *Samson Agonistes* is broken with disastrous consequences: the "holy secret" thus seems invested with powers quite beyond what might have been humanly imaginable.[27] But is the comparison just? Is Samson's suffering truly God's punishment for a breach of faith? God's "holy secret," after all, consisted of making Samson's strength depend on the Nazarite vow not to cut his hair: logically, if the hair goes, the strength goes.[28] Samson suffers not because God is punishing him for revealing a precious secret; rather, he suffers because he wittingly told the Philistines exactly how to *make* him suffer.

The utter ignominy of Samson's self-betrayal is reflected in the abuse he heaps upon Dalila, whom he needs to see as a force whose powers of mystery or magic somehow correspond to those of the secret she has wrested from him: she is a "sorceress" (819); a "poisonous bosom snake" (763). Worst of all, Samson has betrayed God's "holy secret" to an *unworthy* woman, a "deceitful concubine" (537). His hissing, contemptuous rejection of Dalila—"such a viper"—draws *affective* attention away from Samson's autonomy in committing a crime against God, and transfers it to her who committed a crime against himself. Samson's animus begs some pertinent questions: would committing God's most sacred trust to a more respectable woman have mitigated the crime? And what if Dalila herself had actually *kept* God's "holy secret," thereby sparing Samson the suffering by which he measures his crime: would the crime have been thereby diminished? In Samson's search for "justice accessible to human understanding," Joan Bennett sees the Nazarite as being "forced to reason back from the magnitude of the punishment to what must necessarily have been the magnitude of the offense."[29] But therein lies the fallacy inherent in every mortal interpretation. Whenever Samson "reasons back" from his own suffering to what he thinks might be God's notion of an equivalent and justifying crime, he converts both his suffering and his supposed crime into interpretive idols, idols whose affective character reveals their true psychological nature. Samson's parting shot "to such a viper" shows that "reasoning back" has led him inexorably to the sexual humiliation from which his present sufferings took their origin. Neither his crime nor his punishment have been defined by God. Not only the blasphemy of the betrayal but also the mysteriousness of the "holy secret" itself lie exposed; hence both are destroyed, as interpretive idols. The next time Samson refers to what had previously been God's "holy secret," the subject is perfectly cleansed of the language both of mystery and of interpretation:

> I know no spells, use no forbidden arts;
> My trust is in the living God who gave me
> At my nativity this strength, diffused
> No less through all my sinews, joints and bones,
> Than thine, while I preserved these locks unshorn,
> The pledge of my unviolated vow. (1139–44)

The encounter with Dalila has forced him to discover—that is, to *reveal* as well as to locate—the "mystery" of God's secret and the "mystery" of its betrayal in the place from which the "mysteries" of both originated: the tangle of Samson's confused and sexually vulnerable relations with his Philistine wife. Illuminated by Samson's declaration of faith, God's "holy secret" turns out to have been one more false idol that Samson had desperately constructed from the carnal wreckage of his own failed attempt at true witness.

"THOU KNOW'ST ME NOW"

Before he can make his clear-minded declaration of faith, however, Samson has had first to confront the icon of his race of glory. Despite Harapha's declared enmity, the apocryphal giant is no alien. He is rather a distillation of Samson's own hubris, congealed into a form that is empowered by its unshared national vision—its philistinism—to mock him. Harapha is the icon not just of the tribal hero Samson once had been but of what, in his pride of strength and calling, Samson still remains.[30] As Harapha concludes his bombastic self-presentation—"I am of Gath, / . . . of stock renowned / As Og or Anak and the Emins old"—he proclaims "thou know'st *me* now / If thou at all art known" (1081–82). The last word of this sentence is normally glossed "possessed of knowledge."[31] But the passive construction "If thou at all *art known*" can also mean exactly what it says: "If you are in any way famous or renowned." To have been famed as Samson had once been famed demands indeed that Samson *know Harapha* now—now that the torment of self-inflicted impotence reveals to Samson the carnal delusiveness of heroic renown. To know Harapha now is for Samson to know his own famed acts from the perspective of his enemies, a condition that precludes the affective enthusiasms of partisan narrative. As confrontation with Dalila had identified, isolated, and demystified the self-idolatry that lay at the heart of Samson's excoriating self-punishment, so now confrontation with Harapha will isolate and deflate the equally idolatrous heroic pride that underlies Samson's agonizing self-analysis.

Samson's disdain for his own carnal hubris had been simultaneously expressed and belied at a point earlier in the poem, where he recollected a self who "like a petty god" strutted about "admired of all and dreaded / On hostile ground."[32] In the company of the Chorus, his fellow tribesmen, the very materials of self-critique lure Samson into momentary celebration of his "acts indeed heroic, far beyond / The sons of Anak, famous now and blazed, / Fearless of danger" (527–29). Despite his intention of self-criticism, the moment Samson favorably compares himself with "the sons of Anak," we find ourselves on the affective footing of Harapha country. But now Samson has a different audience. One of the sons of Anak demands a further account of Samson's acts, and Harapha's alienated vision defines them as acts not of a hero but of "A murderer, a revolter, and a robber" (1180). The Ascalon episode is difficult to justify by anybody's standards, regardless of partisanship: Samson makes a wager over his own riddle, loses it because he gives away the secret, then murders thirty uninvolved men and steals their clothes to pay off the winners. By insisting that the winners were "spies," Samson pieces together what might in an overwhelmingly partisan court pass for a defense. But the persuasive impact of Samson's current version of the episode is affectively pallid and even mechanical. We hear arguments that we've heard before, given to another Philistine, who is a different wife from the wife he refers to now: "Among the daughters of the Philistines / I chose a wife, which argued me no foe" (1192–93). When he argues for the right to overthrow an oppressive government, Samson reduces both conquered and conqueror to a single moral plane: "My nation was subjected to your lords . . . . force with force / Is well ejected when the conquered can" (1205–7). Finally, even Samson's claim to have received a divine command to free his country must now be qualified in light of apparent failure: "if their servile minds / Me their deliverer sent would not receive, . . . The unworthier they; whence to this day they serve" (1213–16).

The dry mechanicalness of Samson's present review of his heroic career results directly from the self-alienation imposed by a hostile audience. To know Harapha now is to recognize, and be forced to relinquish, the narrative embellishments that feed on tribal bias. As a son of Anak, Harapha embodies and alienates tribal renown, revealing it as no more than an idol—the very idol that Samson, in his race of glory, had always interpreted as a sign of his special favor in the eyes of God. Moreover, with the icon of his heroic renown fulminating before him, Samson's latest rehearsal of his race of glory is emptied not only of color and narrative interest but as well of the energy that conveys a sense of conviction. His deflated rhetoric negatively reformulates the affective principle "If it *feels strong*, it must be *true*."[33] Samson's affectively depleted final review of his race of glory not only *feels weak*; but because of that weakness, the race itself *feels false*. Thus when Samson blames the Israelites for failing to receive him as "their deliverer," he may in principle be right about their "servile" unworthiness ("The unworthier they"); but his own manifest blind servitude at the mill of the Philistines ironically drains affective conviction from his self-exonerating close "whence to this day *they* serve."

"WHOSE GOD IS GOD"

Yet the diminished sense of conviction that results from affective depletion does not make carnal authority intrinsically false. Samson's response to Harapha's taunting, for instance, shows that the Nazarite knows his command of the immediate situation depends on his capacity to meet Harapha on the giant's own, exclusively carnal terms. We learn this from the elemental sensoriness of Samson's threatening first words to Harapha: "The way to *know* were *not to see* but *taste*" (1091, my italics). Samson's true witness will require not that he renounce his own carnality: this would be impossible for any mortal, and for the heroic-bodied Samson it would mean denial of his essential divine gift. True witness requires instead that Samson no longer mistake his carnality itself for the affirmation that his carnality was given him to realize. Antiregenerationist and regenerationist readers alike observe with misgiving Samson's implicitly carnal leveling of Israel's God to a status equal with the Philistine idol Dagon. Samson offers to prove, by fighting Harapha, "whose God is strongest, thine or mine" (1155).[34] A few lines later he repeats the challenge:

> In confidence whereof I once again
> Defy thee to the trial of mortal fight,
> By combat to decide whose god is God,
> Thine or whom I with Israel's sons adore. (1174–77)

There is no escaping the carnal substance of Samson's imaginative construct for deity. But to hinge the question of Samson's *regeneracy* on the religious or doctrinal terms by which he or any other interpreter defines God is to rely on partisan definitions that are ultimately disallowed by the poem.[35] I see nothing inappropriate or troublesome, for Milton's argumentative purposes, in Samson's conception of a prizefighter-God—no more so than in any other believer's poet-God or fisherman-God. Neither is Samson entirely to be faulted for his assumption that mortal combat *can* "decide whose god is God." Samson is a fighter: overwhelming physical power is what has been given to him to know. The carnal terms that reify God to Samson, or to any mortal witness, have no necessary bearing on whether or not the witness may be true.

I say no *necessary* bearing, because this is not to say that true witness can be articulated without any regard whatsoever to the carnal terms that may be used for it. For example, Harapha's magical conception of Samson's strength is telling—both for its echo of where Samson's own thinking once had been and for its affective contrast with the simple clarity of the language it elicits from Samson in refutation. Following Samson's confident boast that he can demolish even heavily armoured Harapha with only an oaken staff (this is, we recall, the loquacious man who slew a thousand foreskins with the "jawbone of an ass"), the Philistine giant sneers:

> Thou durst not thus disparage glorious arms
> Which greatest heroes have in battle worn,
> Their ornament and safety, had not spells
> And black enchantments, some magician's art,
> Armed thee or charmed thee strong, which thou from heaven
> Feign'dst at thy birth was given thee in thy hair,
> Where strength can least abide. (1130–36)

As in less blatant terms Samson himself once had done, Harapha now obfuscates Samson's strength with the language of mystery—"spells / And black enchantments, some magician's art"—awed terms that manifest the mixture of fear and contempt with which the idolater of the flesh, the mentality of carnal superstition, regards whatever it does not understand. Samson's reply demonstrates the difference between, on the one hand, maintaining idolatrous presumptions about truth and, on the other, bearing true witness. The difference shows in the language he uses to characterize truths that are not understood: "My trust is in the living God who gave me / At my nativity this strength, diffused / No less through all my sinews, joints and bones, / Than thine" (1140–43). From this speech it is clear that Samson does not *understand* his strength any better than Harapha does. But what distinguishes between their respective attitudes toward that strength—what differentiates their *affective* postures toward its truth—is Samson's recognition (unavailable to him so long as he needed carnal "mystery" as an excuse) that where true witness is concerned, *not* understanding *does not matter.*

What does matter is that the servant of truth liberate himself from the idols by means of which he substitutes the security of carnal conviction for the imaginative restlessness of transformative desire. As Samson's final recitation of his career dwindles toward the present, unvarnished fact points to the conclusion that, whatever the conviction he had thought his heroics were upholding, that conviction no longer provides the affective force that would enable him to formulate for Harapha's benefit a heroic narrative finish:

> I was to do my part from heaven assigned,
> And had performed it if my known offence
> Had not disabled me, not all your force. (1217–19)

Harapha, the icon of his "race of glory," makes no longer accessible to Samson even the fugitive gratification that reflecting on past glories had hitherto momentarily permitted him. Samson is left at the end of his affectless exculpatory narration with nothing more nor less than what he is now:

> These shifts refuted, answer thy appellant
> Though by his blindness maimed for high attempts,
> Who now defies thee thrice to single fight,
> As a petty enterprise of small enforce. (1220–23)

What he is now is simply Samson: still strong, still boastful, still ironic, still shrewd in his assessment of his enemy. Most importantly, in retaining all of these qualities, both seemingly positive and seemingly negative, Samson is as capable as ever of acting on his desire to make true witness, a desire with which none of these attributes, not even those that seem unregenerate, need interfere. His confrontation with Harapha has forced Samson to discipline both corporal and verbal affect—to distinguish between his own carnal powers (physical, emotional, rhetorical) and the truth they enable him to serve. As subsequent events show, he can still exploit the affective rhetoric of heroic pride for purposes that lie beyond pride. But the bellicose verbal send-off with which he pelts the retreating giant shows that his imagination is no longer itself enslaved by the self-deluding potential of heroic conviction's affective bearing:

> Go baffled coward, lest I run upon thee,
> Though in these chains, bulk without spirit vast,
> And with one buffet lay thy structure low,
> Or swing thee in the air, then dash thee down
> To the hazard of thy brains and shattered sides. (1237–41)

The "baffled coward . . . Bulk without spirit vast," the affective icon of Samson's race of glory, makes an ignominious retreat because Samson's detached, mechanical, even bored recitation of his heroic career has demonstrated to Samson himself his own emotional disengagement from what had earlier dominated his painful recollections of his heroism: the affective appeal of the "race of glory" that the "petty god" Samson had once exploited to prove to his personal satisfaction just exactly "whose god is God." Before facing down Harapha, the affective appeal of glory had held Samson himself in idolatrous bondage to the assumption that it is God who bears witness to his champion instead of the other way around.

"HIS UNCONTROLLABLE INTENT"

The affective bearing of heroic conviction is what interpreters most seek in the final scenes of *Samson Agonistes*, and it is that which Samson's words and gestures most pointedly display only to overturn. To the Philistine messenger's concern that, by refusing to perform at the feast of Dagon, Samson may bring punishment on himself, Samson haughtily responds:

> Myself? my conscience and internal peace.
> Can they think me so broken, so debased
> With corporal servitude, that my mind ever
> Will condescend to such absurd commands? (1334–37)

The lines could almost have been spoken by Harapha, who in equally proud terms has rejected Samson's challenge to fight: "With thee a man condemned, a slave enrolled, / Due by the law to capital punishment? / To fight with thee no man of arms will deign" (1224–26). Harapha had even shown some of Samson's irony and personal fastidiousness: "To combat with a blind man I disdain, / And thou has need much washing to be toucht" (1106–7). Similarly, Samson's rudeness to the courteous Philistine messenger reminds us that civility was never counted among the hero's personal assets. His menacing "Perhaps thou shalt have cause to sorrow indeed" (1347) is perfectly in character for the man who had slain and stripped naked the innocent compatriots of those by whom he felt he had been wronged. When Samson's sufferings and his eloquence elicit our sympathy, they must do so despite a number of misgivings we are likely to have about his personality. Yet both our sympathy and our misgivings are a response to the same stimulus: the affective bearing of the hero that Samson's iconoclastic dismantlings have by the last scenes of the drama exposed. Neither our liking nor our disliking of Samson are relevant to the validity of his witness, which requires rather that Samson cast off all dependence on the affective bearing of heroic conviction.

In the end, this includes casting off the affective bearing even of "conscience and internal peace." When Samson finally accedes to the Philistine command, he directly contravenes the terms he has openly set forth as essential to keeping his "conscience and internal peace" intact. To enter the Philistine arena would require, as the hero in him had phrased it, that he "abuse this consecrated gift / Of strength, again returning with my hair":

> After my great transgression, so requite
> Favour renewed, and add a greater sin
> By prostituting holy things to idols;
> A Nazarite in place abominable
> Vaunting my strength in honour to their Dagon?
> Besides, how vile, contemptible, ridiculous,
> What act more execrably unclean, profane? (1354–62)

The heroic refusal neatly recapitulates all the carnal habits of thought Samson has been struggling against in his confrontations with Dalila and Harapha: phrases like "great transgression," "greater sin," and "prostituting holy things" fit directly into the pattern of carnal fear and mystery that had characterized his race of shame. And we hear echoes of his race of glory in "consecrated gift / Of strength . . . / Favour renewed . . . / A Nazarite . . . / Vaunting my strength in honour." Coupled with these is heroic disdain for a "place abominable," an act so "vile, contemptible, ridiculous / . . . execrably unclean, profane"—sentiments that echo Harapha's disdainful "thou hast need much washing to be toucht."

The affective dimension of Samson's "conscience and internal peace" (recognizable now by his itemization of the conditions that would disrupt it) corresponds directly with "conceptual peace and rest," the imaginative complacency that metaphor's iconoclastic impulse would also disrupt. We may recall metaphor's program for imaginative predication, whereby the visionary impetus depends for its anarchic power on the affective variables of human complacency: the anarchic element of affective indeterminacy both constitutes transformative power and is constituted by transformative desire.[36] The conflation of transformative power and transformative desire that links writer to reader in imaginative predication is now matched by the affective indeterminacy of Samson's final sequence of iconoclastic acts, whereby he manifests the full extent of his own power and desire for transformation. Samson's startling abjuration of his own declared requisites for conscience and internal peace indicates that he is prepared indefinitely to continue overturning the affective idols of secure conviction, of conceptual peace and rest, in the self-liberating desire to rid his consciousness of everything that is not God.[37] When he opens himself to the possiblity that God "may dispense with me or thee / Present in temples at idolatrous rites / For some important cause" (1377–79), Samson opens himself as well to the possibility that bearing true witness may have no connection with what his iconoclastic reversal now reveals to be merely another idolatrous affective disposition: the hitherto seemingly unimpeachable disposition of spiritual tranquillity.

Yet Samson's readiness to let God dispense with him as God chooses suggests another possibility as well—that his overturning of multiple idols has *infinitely expanded* his notion of "conscience and internal peace." The report that, before bringing down the temple, Samson had stood "as one who prayed, / Or some great matter in his mind revolved" (1637–38) could certainly be read as evidence that some new kind of peace is within him. Still, the riddling irony of Samson's last words reminds us that his pause could be, as Fish suggests, an acknowledgment "that even now his vision may be partial and his light 'delusive.' "[38] Therefore, when Samson's brief final speech reasserts, after his pause, the full affective measure of his heroic tricksterism, we are left knowing that, whatever else *can* be known of Samson, what *cannot* be known is whether his last act indeed fulfills the will of God. But we do know that it fulfills the will of Samson: "Now *of my own accord* such other trial / I mean to show you of my strength, yet greater; / As with amaze shall strike all who behold" (1640–45).[39] The "amaze" that strikes the spectacle-witnessing beholders and the "amaze" that strikes the doomed Philistines are subsumed under Samson's own sensory experience of the catastrophe—a sensory experience that we ourselves are explicitly denied.[40] By acting now of his own accord, Samson makes of himself alone both a victim of and a fully comprehending affective witness to his final iconoclastic act. And sensory amazement is also countered in Samson, by an opposing, radically self-determining force: the uncontrollable intent that restlessly drives his imaginative self-deliverance from the securities of worldly conviction. When the Chorus hear of the disaster, they rapidly generalize from the mourning of Gaza to the mourning that will inevitably befall "all that band them to resist / His uncontrollable intent" (1753–54). But the uncontrollable intent ascribed by the Chorus to "highest wisdom" and the uncontrollable intent of Samson himself have now become, by the drama's own affective witness, indistinguishable.[41] According to Christopher Grose, "the real victory" of *Samson Agonistes* "takes place onstage," as the choric commentary is displaced by "a dramatically more flexible, *freer*, Samson" who achieves "victory over himself and his own nation." In such a victory, "the ego is dismissed, the self here has become in its place the radical source of all value, and in this sense 'messianic.' "[42] Yet in the moment struck by "amaze," only the liberated imaginative impetus of Samson's own transformative desire can actually know, and it can know *without interpreting*, the "meaning" of that appalling perfect freedom.

Ironically, the "amaze" struck by Samson's final iconoclastic act is precisely what secures the Israelites in the affective bearing of tribal conviction, sealing them forever in conceptual peace and rest. As they absorb the catastrophe, we see that for them, nothing has changed. Manoa still interprets Samson's "life heroic" as one that is "Fully revenged on his enemies" (1711–12). Affectively for Manoa, Samson dead differs little from Samson alive—the adored icon sitting "idle on the household hearth," the trophy from lost glory-days that Samson had dreaded becoming, a "vain monument of strength" (566, 570). "There will I build him / A monument," Manoa proclaims, "With all his trophies hung, and acts enrolled / In copious legend, or sweet lyric song" (1733–37). Also unchanged is Manoa's ceaseless paternal disapproval. If Samson's heroic acts are to be apotheosized by "valiant youth" inflamed by example "To matchless valour, and adventures high," Samson's sins and errors are to remain durably untranscended, untransformed, and mercilessly unforgotten:

> The virgins also shall on feastful days
> Visit his tomb with flowers, only bewailing
> His lot unfortunate in nuptial choice,
> From whence captivity and loss of eyes. (1741–44)

Manoa's last words cling doggedly to the convictions he has held from the moment he first came upon the scene. Forever he will lament his son's refusal to find among the members of his own tribe a suitable woman and marry her. Forever the feastful virgins will bewail their loss of an opportunity to be made the object of an exemplary nuptial choice. In the conceptual peace and rest of Manoa's affective imagination, Samson's race of glory and his race of shame will run on into eternity.

Neither has Samson's iconoclastic agon with his two races changed anything for the affective imaginations of the faithful Hebrew Chorus. Their response to the news of Samson's death instantly absorbs grief over his loss into a cry of patriotic elation:

> O dearly-bought revenge, yet glorious!
> Living or dying thou has fulfilled
> The work for which thou wast foretold
> To Israel, and now li'st victorious

> Among thy slain self-killed
> Not willingly, but tangled in the fold
> Of dire necessity, whose law in death conjoined
> Thee with thy slaughtered foes in number more
> Than all thy life had slain before. (1660–68)

For the Chorus, not just solace but intense gratification comes with knowing that the death of their tribal hero is overmatched by the deaths of his and their "slaughtered foes *in number more* / Than all [his] life had slain before" (my italics).[43] The *quantifying* capacity of affective conviction both stimulates and satisfies the tribal hunger for revenge, a hunger that pretends to demand equal retribution of an eye for an eye, but that only a *greater* than equal measure of carnal retribution will truly satiate. To conviction's affective imagination, the blood feast *feels* like justice only because it gluts carnal voracity. Nothing has changed in the Chorus's national vision. Both the Chorus's understanding of the nature of Israel's servitude and their understanding of the nature of her liberation remain carnally defined by the affective terms that construct the iconic potency of their tribal leader.

Yet there remains an unintended truth in the terms by which the Chorus formulate their belief that Samson undertook self-destruction "not willingly, but tangled in the fold / Of dire necessity." The "fold of dire necessity" in which Samson died entangled was of a fabric woven from the uncontrollable intent of his own search for perfect freedom. The creative and iconoclastic principle of "articulate insufficiency" in carnal rhetoric finds in the whole of Samson's career a progressive seamlessness of impetus toward the appalling perfect freedom of the infinite divine. Each step in the sequence of Samson's "failures" to interpret correctly his divine mission to free the Israelites actually propels him affectively and imaginatively forward. The woman of Timna, the Ascalon episode, Dalila, the thousand foreskins slain with the jawbone of an ass: each of these steps has in fact been an iconoclastic movement toward positioning himself finally to relinquish affective conviction itself, in a single definitive iconoclastic bid for perfect freedom. At no point during the iconoclastic sequence could Samson know for certain what the outcome of his action would be: the predicative function of affective indeterminacy ever lags behind the anarchic function—and yet both functions constitute transformative power and are constituted by transformative desire. The iconoclastic action of *Samson Agonistes* performs a variation on the formula we have seen operating from the beginning of this book: Samson desires transformation, and he has the power to effect it through his iconoclasm; should his interpreters desire transformation, his iconoclastic pattern may be imaginatively traced within themselves. No doctrine, but only the means required to sustain imaginative impetus, is offered to the reader who seeks lessons from *Samson Agonistes*.

When Samson undertakes to author his carnal self toward the autonomy of divine freedom, his movement to liberate himself from carnal icons therefore carries his self-authorship beyond the individual acts that each, of their own accord, repudiate interpretation. As he departs from the scene of the prison yard, he reassures his countrymen:

> Happen what may, of me expect to hear
> Nothing dishonourable, impure, unworthy
> Our God, our Law, my nation, or myself,
> The last of me or no I cannot warrant. (1423–26)

This promise he fulfills: they hear of him nothing that in the view of *their* tribal God, law, nation, or hero would be considered dishonorable, impure, or unworthy. Neither, of course, do they hear anything to justify their conviction that by virtue of Samson's act, God "to his faithful champion hath in place / Bore witness gloriously" (1751–52). Yet the Chorus's interpretation does unwittingly confirm what the entire poem confirms about Samson: it confirms the truth of Samson's witness, a truth commensurate with Samson's, and their own, ontological longing. When Samson undertakes the radical change and redefinition of all that pertains to him and makes him recognizable to himself, nothing outwardly seems to change. But by disengaging himself, by detaching himself from the idolatries of conviction that are manifested by his carnal rhetoric, he liberates to indeterminacy his imaginative witness, and with that act he makes his witness true to his unimprisonable desire. Surely indeed, "Samson hath quit himself / Like Samson." Neither his tribal interpreters, nor we, nor Samson himself ("The last of me or no I cannot warrant") can frame carnal rhetoric sufficient to articulate exactly *what that means*. But as the iconoclastic argument of *Samson Agonistes* shows, such framing is not needed to affirm an ontologically driven true intent.

If a moral lesson were insistently to be extrapolated from Milton's last great poem, it would be that which Milton designed to meet anxieties he himself had known through the agon of his own political and religious battles, during which he evolved the iconoclastic medium of his carnal rhetoric. These anxieties were the existential alarms experienced by every European who was being confronted with the challenges to conviction produced by the increasingly decentered world of the early modern period. In such a world, Milton's poetics of desire affirms a principle that, as an artist of faith, Milton considered most humanly essential: an iconoclastic principle in which imagination, faith, and worldly experience converge. His poetics incorporates into the imaginative process a radical accommodation for necessary and inevitable change. In the iconoclastic affective pattern of *Samson Agonistes*—and finally in direct yet cooperative *contrast* with the tragedy's mimetic pattern of passionate catharsis—Milton equips the human imagination with a paradigm for *sustaining* (as opposed to "spending") its most precious asset and condition for survival: the ontological longing of transformative desire.

NOTES

INTRODUCTION

1. Book-length historicist studies of Milton especially pertinent to the concerns with iconoclasm of the present argument include those of David Loewenstein, *Milton and the Drama of History: Historical Vision, Iconoclasm and the Literary Imagination* (Cambridge: Cambridge University Press, 1990); Joan Bennett, *Reviving Liberty: Radical Christian Humanism in Milton's Great Poems* (Cambridge, Mass.: Harvard University Press, 1989); James Grantham Turner, *One Flesh: Paradisal Marriage and Sexual Relations in the Age of Milton* (Oxford: Clarendon Press, 1987); Joseph Wittreich, *Interpreting "Samson Agonistes"* (Princeton: Princeton University Press, 1986); Ernest B. Gilman, *Iconoclasm and Poetry in the English Reformation: Down Went Dagon* (Chicago: University of Chicago Press, 1986); and Mary Ann Radzinowicz, *Toward "Samson Agonistes": The Growth of Milton's Mind* (Princeton: Princeton University Press, 1978). James Turner makes the specific case for aesthetic and interpretive interdependence of Milton's poetry and his prose, arguing that Milton's epic vision is actively generated by his political engagement; see his "The Poetics of Engagement," in David Loewenstein and James Grantham Turner, eds., *Politics, Poetics, and Hermeneutics in Milton's Prose* (Cambridge: Cambridge University Press, 1990), pp. 257–75.

2. In *De Doctrina*, Milton delineates the role of *fiducia carnalis* (carnal reliance) along with three other opposites to trust in God: *diffidentia in Deum* (distrust of God), *praefidentia sive praesumptio* (overweening presumption), and *fiducia idololatrica* (trust in idols). For the role of *fiducia carnalis*, see *The Works of John Milton*, ed. Frank Allen Patterson et al. (New York: Columbia

University Press, 1934), vol. 17, pp. 56–57. John M. Steadman demonstrates the presence in *Samson Agonistes* of all four of these opposites to trust in God. In the poem, the opposites "serve, in varying degrees, as foils for Samson's faith"; see " 'Faithful Champion': The Theological Basis of Milton's Hero of Faith," reprinted in Arthur E. Barker, ed., *Milton: Modern Essays in Criticism* (London: Oxford University Press, 1965), pp. 467–83; originally published in *Anglia* 78 (1959): 12–28. The quotation is from the Barker edition, p. 475.

3. The abuse of the critical fiction "nonexistent text" is discussed further in Chapter 1 below.

4. *Iconoclasm and Poetry in the English Reformation,* p. 179.

5. See "Driving from the Letter: Truth and Indeterminacy in Milton's *Areopagitica,*" in Mary Nyquist and Margaret W. Ferguson, eds., *Re-membering Milton: Essays on the Texts and Traditions* (New York: Methuen, 1987), pp. 234–54.

6. *Interpreting "Samson Agonistes,"* p. xx.

7. Reading *Samson Agonistes* in conjunction with the controversial prose "provides a particularly sophisticated sense of history as dual spectacles," remarks Loewenstein: "There we witness the drama of God's 'horrid spectacle' (line 1642) in rivalry with the spectacle of Dagon. The spirit of iconoclasm . . . reminds us yet once more how closely interconnected the controversial prose and great poems truly are." See *Milton and the Drama of History,* p. 73.

1 METAPHOR AND "MEANING": TOWARD A THEORY OF CREATIVE ICONOCLASM

1. Contrasting but compatible versions of the literalist argument for metaphoric interpretation may be found in the essay by Donald Davidson, "What Metaphors Mean," in Sheldon Sacks, ed., *On Metaphor* (Chicago: University of Chicago Press, 1979), pp. 29–45, and the essay by F. C. T. Moore, "On Taking Metaphor Literally," in David S. Miall, ed., *Metaphor: Problems and Perspectives* (Brighton, Sussex: Harvester Press, 1982), pp. 1–13. Davidson's argument is critiqued by Nelson Goodman, "Metaphor as Moonlighting," in Sacks, pp. 175–80, and by Max Black, "How Metaphors Work: A Reply to Donald Davidson," in Sacks, pp. 181–92.

2. I use "proper" here to refer only to analysis of the experience of metaphor. Fully to account for all the enlightening and intellectually valuable critical domains of metaphor inquiry would be an undertaking well beyond the aims of the present study. A sense of the spectrum of concerns relevant to metaphor may be gained by consulting the ninety-five-page index prepared by Warren Shibles for his study *Metaphor: An Annotated Bibliography and History* (Whitewater, Wis.: Language Press, 1971). Concern with metaphor's affective

resonance can be found mainly in the work of critics disciplined in aesthetics, psychology, and literature as opposed to philosophy or structural linguistics. The first major attempt to move across disciplinary boundaries has been that of Paul Ricoeur, whose metaphor theory builds on these disciplines as well as on his abiding interest in speculative theological discourse. See Ricoeur, *The Rule of Metaphor*, trans. Robert Czerny with Kathleen McLaughlin and John Costello (Toronto: University of Toronto Press, 1975). More recently, an interdisciplinary perspective has informed Mark Turner's study *Death Is the Mother of Beauty: Mind, Metaphor, Criticism* (Chicago: University of Chicago Press, 1987), and that of Samuel R. Levin, *Metaphoric Worlds: Conceptions of a Romantic Nature* (New Haven: Yale University Press, 1988). Essay collections that bring to bear multiple, often conflicting views on the subject include Andrew Ortony, ed., *Metaphor and Thought* (Cambridge: Cambridge University Press, 1979); Sacks, *On Metaphor*; Mark Johnson, ed., *Philosophical Perspectives on Metaphor* (Minneapolis: University of Minnesota Press, 1981); Warren Shibles, *Essays on Metaphor* (Whitewater, Wis.: Language Press, 1972); David S. Miall, *Metaphor: Problems and Perspectives* (Atlantic Highlands, N.J.: Humanities Press, 1982).

3. Stephen Greenblatt, *Shakespearean Negotiations: The Circulation of Social Energy in Renaissance England* (Berkeley: University of California Press, 1988), p. 3.

4. See C. K. Ogden and I. A. Richards, *The Meaning of Meaning: A Study of the Influence of Language upon Thought and of the Science of Symbolism* (New York: Harcourt, Brace & World, 1959; first published in 1923), pp. 248–49, esp. chap. 8, "The Meaning of Philosophers," and chap. 9, "The Meaning of Meaning."

5. Stanley Fish, second preface to *Surprised by Sin: The Reader in "Paradise Lost"* (Berkeley: University of California Press, 1971; original publication, 1967), p. x.

6. That none of these issues is likely soon to be resolved is suggested by Constance Jordan's articulation in a recent issue of *PMLA* of "the vexed question of literary meaning—that is, where and how a reader apprehends meaning and what it means to us as creatures of culture to respond to these issues." Introduction to "Cluster on Reader-Response Criticism," *PMLA* 106, no. 5 (October 1991): 1037. Jordan's wordplay on her central term ("meaning . . . and what it means to us") highlights the debate's seemingly infinite capacity for sophisticated reformulation.

7. Experiences and interpretations vary; but so long as recorded words remain, texts remain. Where textual lacunae or textual variants raise unresolvable doubts about textual authority, as is often the case with a Shakespeare play, those doubts also remain. But it is intellectually careless to confuse the kinds of doubts that are generated by conflicting textual authority with those kinds of doubts that result from readers' conflicting interpretations of a text. And it

is intellectual sophistry to exploit such a confusion by using the term "text" ambiguously to refer at some times to words on a page, at others to what the author "meant," and at still others to the literary experience constructed by the interpreting reader. The distinctions I make here are apparent to most scholars, but even experienced critics have been known to blur them. Examples of the confusion's potential viciousness abounded during the furor that resulted from publication of *Satanic Verses*. When in casual conversation I once demonstrated that many who attacked Salman Rushdie had never read the book, or had read only those pages that contained a satiric fictional portrait of the prophet Muhammad, a widely published Marxist deconstructionist retorted that such people had indeed read the book, and that their reading was just as valid as any because there is no such thing as an uninterpreted text. What this argument does is to disallow the text itself as evidence that the text has not been read, which obviates both text and reading. The text is not the same as the reading of it. To play out the implications of equating a text with various readers' experiences of it may indeed generate volumes of critical polemic. But this is a practice which can tell us a great deal about contemporary academic politics without necessarily shedding any light on the work of art that is Rushdie's book.

8. The perplexity to which continued uncritical application of these terms can lead is illustrated by introductory remarks in an already cited book that I otherwise greatly admire for its brilliant insights and fresh historical perspective, Stephen Greenblatt's *Shakespearean Negotiations:* "Not only has a new generation of textual historians undermined the notion that a skilled editorial weaving of folio and quarto readings will give us an authentic record of Shakespeare's original intentions, but theater historians have challenged the whole notion of the text as the central, stable locus of theatrical meaning" (3). In a single sentence, Greenblatt slips his referent for the term "text" from the problem addressed by the Shakespearean textual scholar, to the problem of authorial intent, to the problem of theatrical experience. Since in the same paragraph he has also just stated that "the referent of the phrase 'the text itself' is by no means clear," his own shifting referents may be intended to illustrate this point. But his conclusion, that "it is impossible to take the 'text itself' as the . . . container of all of its meanings," once again begs the question implicit in Greenblatt's shifts of reference: exactly what is the *meaning* of "meaning"? And once again, the answer lies in the direction pointed by Ogden and Richards.

9. From an interview on the *Public Radio Book Show,* sponsored by the New York State Writers Institute, hosted by Tom Smith. The interview was aired October 10, 1991, on WAMC public radio station, Albany, New York.

10. Mark Johnson traces the troubled historical relations between figurative language and truth in the introductory essay to *Philosophical Perspectives on Metaphor*. The tradition that made metaphorical language cognitively inferior to literal language was well established by the seventeenth century and in fact

had its roots in Aristotle's *Poetics*. Although Aristotle credits metaphor with mimetic and affective powers, he at the same time destines such language to second-class status by treating it as a linguistic irregularity—an effective one in its proper place, but "deviant." With this, Johnson comments, "the fatal separation—figurative *vs.* literal—has been made." Moreover, Aristotle describes metaphor's operation as the transfer of meaning from one word or thing to another (never from a full sentence or context to another) that calls attention to a perhaps obscure but nevertheless perceived similarity. Thus Aristotle completes the "triad of half-truths" that determines the theory and philosophical understanding of metaphor for the ensuing twenty-three hundred years: "(i) focus on single words that are (ii) deviations from literal language, to produce a change of meaning that is (iii) based on similarities between things" (6).

11. William K. Wimsatt, *The Verbal Icon: Studies in the Meaning of Poetry* (Lexington: University of Kentucky Press, 1954), p. 279.

12. *Paradise Lost*, book III, lines 1–3. All quotations from Milton's poetry are taken from *John Milton: Complete Poems and Major Prose*, ed. Merritt Y. Hughes (Indianapolis: Bobbs-Merrill Educational Publishing, 1957; rpt. 1984).

13. I. A. Richards's terminology of "tenor" and "vehicle," current since their introduction, are explained in *The Philosophy of Rhetoric* (New York: Oxford Press, 1948 [1936]), Lectures 5 and 6. See also William Empson, *Seven Types of Ambiguity* (London: Chatto & Windus, 1930).

14. Sigurd Burckhardt, "The Poet as Fool and Priest," *English Literary History* 23(1956): 280.

15. *Symbol and Metaphor in Human Experience* (Princeton: Princeton University Press, 1949), pp. 59–60.

16. "If the conventional meanings of the terms drawn into the energy-tension were really destroyed, would not the tension cease to exist?" See Wheelwright, *The Burning Fountain: A Study in the Language of Symbolism* (Bloomington: Indiana University Press, 1968), pp. 107ff.

17. Wheelwright, *Metaphor and Reality* (Bloomington: Indiana University Press, 1962), chap. 4, "Two Ways of Metaphor," pp. 70–91.

18. *Metaphor and Reality*, p. 173.

19. *The Burning Fountain*, pp. 205 and 70.

20. Phillip Stambovsky justifies using the term "image" to cover the whole lot of metaphoric practice on the grounds that "visual perception is perhaps the most rationally accessible and comprehensive field of immediacy." See *The Depictive Image: Metaphor and Literary Experience* (Amherst: University of Massachusetts Press, 1988), p. 85. As my remarks in this paragraph show, our heavy reliance on visual metaphor is inevitable. That is why we should be particularly alert, in analytical applications, to our willingness (as shown here by Stambovsky) to ascribe to visual perception intellectual qualities like rationality and comprehensiveness. I will return to Stambovsky's phenomenological approach to metaphor later in this chapter.

21. According to Milton, trust and fear of idols (*idololatricus*) is the third of the means—after "slavish fear" (*timor servilis*) and "carnal security" (*securitas carnalis*)—by which we oppose reverence and fear of God (*timor Dei*). See *De Doctrina Christiana*, book II in *The Works of John Milton*, vol. 17 (New York: Columbia University Press, 1934), pp. 60–63.

22. W. J. T. Mitchell, *Iconology: Image, Text, Ideology* (Chicago: University of Chicago Press, 1986), p. 3.

23. Ibid., p. 6.

24. Quoted by Mark Johnson in *Philosophical Perspectives on Metaphor*, pp. 15–16.

25. See below in this chapter "Metaphor and Ricoeur's Psychologies of Imagination and Feeling" and "Metaphor and the Psychology of Creative Iconoclasm" for critical analysis of this idea and its role in development of the present metaphor theory.

26. Roman Jakobson, "Closing Statements: Linguistics and Poetics," in *Style and Language*, ed. T. A. Sebeok (Cambridge, Mass.: MIT Press, 1960), p. 371. Cited by Paul Ricoeur, *Rule of Metaphor*, p. 224. Jakobson sees this not as destruction or suppression of reference but rather as a provision for ambiguity: "The supremacy of poetic function over referential function does not obliterate the reference but makes it ambiguous. The double-sensed message finds correspondence in a split addresser, in a split addressee, and what is more in a split reference, as is cogently exposed in the preambles to fairy tales of various people, for instance, in the usual exordium of the Majorca storytellers: 'Aixo era y no era' (It was and it was not)."

27. *Rule of Metaphor*, p. 224.

28. I am grateful to Eshragh Motahar for providing this example from Iranian oral tradition.

29. The tradition that poetry is "a speaking picture" was founded, according to Lessing, by Simonides of Ceos. See *Laocoön*, trans. Ellen Frothingham (New York: Farrar, Straus & Giroux, 1969), p. vii. Cited by Mitchell in *Iconology*, p. 48. For the background to this paragraph's brief survey of lines of influence in aesthetics discourse, I am indebted to Mitchell's chapter 5, "Eye and Ear: Edmund Burke and the Politics of Sensibility," *Iconology*, pp. 116–49.

30. *Iconology*, pp. 125–31.

31. Edmund Husserl, *Ideas: General Introduction to Pure Phenomenology*, trans. W. R. Boyce Gibson (New York: Collier Books, 1962; rpt. 1972), p. 97. First published in English in 1931.

32. See Husserl's "Radical Alteration of the Natural Thesis 'Disconnexion', 'Bracketing,'" in *Ideas: General Introduction to Pure Phenomenology*, §31. Gibson renders Husserl's translation of the Greek term as "abstention"; I use the term "bracketing" based on Husserl's explanation, which follows: "In relation to every thesis and wholly uncoerced we can use this *peculiar εποχη, (epokhe—abstention), a certain refraining from judgment which is compat-*

ible with the unshaken and unshakable because self-evidencing conviction of Truth. The thesis is 'put out of action,' bracketed, it passes off into the modified status of a 'bracketed thesis,' and the judgment *simpliciter* into '*bracketed judgment*' " (98–99). For Husserl's transliteration "epokhe" I substitute the French form *epoché*, because it is more commonly used by Paul Ricoeur and others dealing with metaphor, as contrasted with Husserl's focus on phenomenology.

33. *Symbol and Metaphor in Human Experience*, pp. 59–60.

34. Ricoeur, "The Metaphorical Process as Cognition, Imagination, and Feeling," in Sacks, *On Metaphor*, pp. 141–157. Specific page references will appear in the text.

35. *Rule of Metaphor*, p. 249.

36. "To imagine, then, is not to have a mental picture of something but to display relations in a depicting mode." Ricoeur, "The Metaphorical Process," p. 148.

37. Sigurd Burckhardt, "The Poet as Fool and Priest," p. 280. The terms "dissociation" and "divestiture" later in this paragraph I adapt from Burckhardt: "Briefly put, the function of poetic devices is dissociative, or divestive" (281).

38. This analysis of the metaphoric process bears a superficial resemblance to that articulated by Paul Ricoeur as metaphor's "semantic sketch": "At the origin of this process . . . is what I shall call the ontological vehemence of a semantic aim, hinting at an unknown field that sets it in motion. This ontological vehemence cuts meaning from its initial anchor, frees it as the form of a movement and transposes it to a new field to which the meaning can give form by means of its own figurative property. But in order to declare itself this ontological vehemence makes use of mere hints of meaning, which are in no way determinations of meaning. An experience seeks to be expressed, which is more than something undergone. Its anticipated sense finds in the dynamism of simple meaning, relayed by the dynamism of split meaning, a *sketch* that now must be reconciled with the requirements of the concept" (*Rule of Metaphor*, pp. 299–300). The critical difference between Ricoeur's "dynamism of split meaning, a sketch that must now be reconciled" and my "suggestion of what satisfaction might look and feel like" lies in Ricoeur's location of metaphoric activity in the realms of meaning and representation of experience, as opposed to sensory affect. Despite the interpretive latitude provided by "hints of meaning, which are in no way determinations of meaning," Ricoeur's insistence on meaning as the final desideratum directs metaphor's activity into a rationalist channel. This suits Ricoeur's analysis of the procedures of speculative discourse, but it does not account for metaphoric activity that ranges beyond the rational or speculative.

39. Cf. Mitchell: "Iconoclasm is simply the obverse of idolatry . . . nothing more than idolatry turned outward toward the image of a rival, threatening tribe" (*Iconology*, p. 198).

40. Stambovsky, *The Depictive Image,* p. 90. Subsequent page references will appear in the text.

41. "The Metaphorical Process," pp. 146–47.

42. See Ernest B. Gilman, *The Curious Perspective: Literary and Pictorial Wit in the Seventeenth Century* (New Haven: Yale University Press, 1978), chaps. 1 and 2.

43. Ernest B. Gilman, *Iconoclasm and Poetry in the English Reformation: Down Went Dagon* (Chicago: University of Chicago Press, 1986). See also Christopher Grose, *Milton's Epic Process* (New Haven: Yale University Press, 1973), pp. 8 and 43, for discussions of Milton's distrust of the linguistic corporeality on which poetry depends. Grose characterizes Milton's poetic theory as "basically antipoetic, in the sense that if images are radically human (or 'natural') historically they have had a way of becoming more than images. Psychologically, indeed, they tend to harden into idols or icons; and though we cannot equate the terms 'poetry' and 'images' here, Milton all but formulated William K. Wimsatt's 'verbal icon.'" As Gilman shows, this ambivalence toward imagery is not peculiar to Milton, but is characteristic of virtually all English writers of the later sixteenth and the seventeenth centuries.

44. John N. King, *English Reformation Literature: The Tudor Origins of the Protestant Tradition* (Princeton: Princeton University Press, 1982), p. 266. See chap. 6, sec. 2, "The Banishment of 'Mistress Missa,'" for the stage dialogue tradition of this Reformation allegorical motif.

45. *Iconoclasm and Poetry in the English Reformation,* p. 45.

46. Neil Rhodes explores this thesis in rich and substantive detail; my comments in this section owe much to the valuable insights of his *Elizabethan Grotesque* (London: Routledge & Kegan Paul, 1980).

47. Rhodes, pp. 104–5.

48. Andrew Marvell, "A Dialogue between the Soul and Body," ll. 41–42, in Louis L. Martz, ed., *English Seventeenth Century Verse* (New York: W. W. Norton, 1973).

49. See *Renaissance Self-Fashioning: From More to Shakespeare* (Chicago: University of Chicago Press, 1980); also, essays by Greenblatt and others in *Reconstructing Individualism: Autonomy, Individuality, and the Self in Western Thought,* ed. Thomas C. Heller et al. (Stanford, Calif.: Stanford University Press, 1986).

50. *The Idea of the Renaissance* (Baltimore: Johns Hopkins University Press, 1989), p. 16.

51. For a Marxist critique of "The Ideology of the Individual in Anglo-American Criticism," see Lawrence Venuti, *Our Halcyon Dayes: English Prerevolutionary Texts and Postmodern Culture* (Madison: University of Wisconsin Press, 1989), chap. 1. Venuti defines the critical concept of the individual as follows: "the concept of the human subject as a free, unified consciousness that transcends the epistemological limitations of biography and history and is

the origin of meaning, knowledge, and action" (17). Venuti writes as if critics still felt bound by the precedent set by Eliot and the *Scrutiny* group, an assumption that seems inappropriate with regard to current Renaissance studies. Also, the terminology of popular Marxist criticism can create bizarre effects when applied to the field, as when Venuti alludes to critics who "ghettoize" the likes of Sir John Suckling and Richard Lovelace because of their Cavalier immorality. Nevertheless, Venuti's Althusserian "symptomatic reading" of Renaissance texts from Massinger's plays to Cavalier love poetry puts a wide variety of materials into an interesting historical and political light that does not, it seems to me, necessarily depend on the critical apparatus of his analysis of The Individual as promulgated by Eliot and Coleridge.

52. *On the Dignity of Man, On Being and the One, Heptaplus,* trans. Charles Wallis, Paul Miller, and Douglas Carmichael (New York: Bobbs-Merrill, 1965), p. 7. Quoted from the Wallis translation by Kerrigan and Braden, p. 120.

53. *An Apology for Poetry or The Defense of Poesy,* ed. Geoffrey Shepherd (London: Thomas Nelson & Sons, 1965), p. 112. Interestingly, for the present analysis, Sidney finds poetry's divinity in its power to move men to act: poetry changes men, it creates new beings of them.

54. The quoted phrase and its thesis allude to the fascinating study cited earlier, Gilman's *The Curious Perspective.*

55. *The Symbolism of Evil,* trans. Emerson Buchanan (New York: Harper & Row, 1967), p. 355.

2 "SHUFFLING UP SUCH A GOD": THE RHETORICAL AGON OF MILTON'S ANTIPRELATICAL TRACTS

1. *Complete Prose Works of John Milton,* vol. 1, ed. Don M. Wolfe (New Haven: Yale University Press, 1953), pp. 821–22. All quotations from Milton's antiprelatical tracts are from this edition, and subsequent page references will appear in the text.

2. See Keith Stavely, *The Politics of Milton's Prose Style* (New Haven: Yale University Press, 1975), pp. 23, 28: "Milton pretends that Armageddon has come. . . . We have . . . not political discourse or persuasion, not even political polemic, but a kind of millennial melodrama. . . . Returning again and again to denunciations of the fleshly corruptions wrought by popery and prelacy, Milton attempts to inflate these received Protestant attitudes and feelings into expressions of divine wrath. . . . Milton seeking no less than to make himself the voice of a nation of inspired prophets."

3. *Self-Consuming Artifacts* (Berkeley: University of California Press, 1972), pp. 301–2.

4. Ibid., p. 302.

5. In his detailed analysis of comparable imagerial progressions in *Reason of*

Church Government, Stanley Fish calls this the "zoom lens effect". See *Self-Consuming Artifacts*, pp. 265–302.

6. Richard M. Weaver has noted that Milton's "frequent use of pairs of words . . . give[s] the impression of thickness, which is in turn the source of the impression of strength . . . what the pairs create is the effect of dimension"; see *The Ethics of Rhetoric* (Chicago: H. Regnery, 1953), p. 158.

7. The image of the "radiant singing body" is one of the great unifying metaphors that Thomas Kranidas finds working to create a coherence throughout the prose. See *The Fierce Equation* (The Hague: Mouton & Co., 1965), chap. 2, passim.

8. Janel Mueller traces the troubling philosophical and religious implications of Milton's disjunctive time scheme to the influence of Thomas Brightman's *A Revelation of the Revelation* (1615). Like Milton and other apocalypticists after him, Brightman "worked to improve the fit between the times of prophecy and the times of history" by manipulating the rhetoric of "then" and "now": "England's dilatoriness greatly complicated the stock bifurcation between all other thens and the now of Reformation." See "Embodying Glory: The Apocalyptic Strain in Milton's *Of Reformation*," in David Loewenstein and James Grantham Turner, eds., *Politics, Poetics, and Hermeneutics in Milton's Prose* (Cambridge: Cambridge University Press, 1990), p. 19. I demonstrate Milton's particular rhetorical struggle with this complication by analyzing an apocalyptic passage from *Animadversions* in the section below titled "Saving Carnal Rhetoric."

9. See, in Chapter 4 below, "The Self-Authoring Vital Text."

10. See Kranidas, "Milton and the Rhetoric of Zeal," *Texas Studies in Literature and Language* 6, no. 4, (fall 1964): 423–32.

11. French's article "Milton as Satirist" is in *PMLA* 51 (1936): 414–29. See also Edward LeComte, "Milton as Satirist and Wit," in *Th' Upright Heart and Pure*, ed. Amadeus Fiore (Pittsburgh: Duquesne University Press, 1967), p. 51.

12. "The Structure of Milton's Prose," in *Language and Style in Milton*, ed. Ronald David Emma and John T. Shawcross (New York: Frederick Ungar, 1967), p. 329. Hamilton's comment is anticipated by Fred Emil Ekfelt in "The Graphic Diction of Milton's English Prose," *Philological Quarterly* 25 (1946): 66: "There are long concrete passages which not only do not advance the argument but often conceal it."

13. *Self-Consuming Artifacts*, p. 283.

14. *The Politics of Milton's Prose Style*, p. 33.

15. Ibid., pp. 33, 10.

16. French, "Milton as Satirist," p. 429.

17. Acknowledging the influence of Pauline thought and radical Presbyterianism on Milton's metaphoric intensity, Janel Mueller nevertheless attributes the particular sensory richness of his apocalyptic visions in *Of Reformation* to Milton's urge toward religious transcendence through poetry: "Ultimately . . . his first prose tract is driven towards apocalyptic innovation by his vatic im-

pressionability to glory, itself a symptom of his activist yearnings to fuse the polemical and rhetorical skills of the religious radical with the high ambitions of the poet" (Mueller, "Embodying Glory," p. 10).

18. Michael Lieb comments on the extent to which Milton's divergence from the established celebratory tradition regarding the bishops, as well as his similarly critical treatment of Constantine, shows that he "departed from views shared not only by the Anglican church but by many of his Nonconformist brethren as well," including the Smectymnuans. As Lieb points out, and as I further demonstrate in the argument that follows, Milton justifies this departure by appealing to the revelatory capacity of divine testimony. See "Milton's *Of Reformation* and the Dynamics of Controversy," in Michael Lieb and John T. Shawcross, eds., *Achievements of the Left Hand: Essays on the Prose of John Milton* (Amherst: University of Massachusetts Press, 1974), pp. 55–82. The quotation is on p. 58.

19. The philosophical and theological significance of this rhetorical split is explicated by Mueller as Milton's critique of the native apocalypticism that infuses *The Actes and Monuments,* which had been for Milton a major historical source on the bishops. See "Embodying Glory," pp. 23–24.

20. John R. Knott Jr. helpfully sorts out the doctrinal requisites and the implications for episcopacy of the distinctions that Milton makes between true and false martyrs in " 'Suffering for Truths sake': Milton and Martyrdom," in Loewenstein and Turner, *Politics, Poetics, and Hermeneutics in Milton's Prose,* pp. 153–70.

21. As Knott demonstrates, the specific argumentative point that is made by this kind of displacement applies to all the martyrs with whom Milton deals: "With Ignatius, as with Latimer and Ridley, Milton was less interested in the fact of suffering than in the truth of the position taken." See " 'Suffering for Truths sake,' " p. 156.

22. Lieb reviews the classical as well as contemporary theories of invective that place Milton "firmly in line with the radical Puritans of his time" while also justifying his practice according to well-established oratorical tradition. Of particular interest to the present argument is the observation from Quintilian that the orator should "move the affections through *visiones:* 'images by which the representations of absent objects are so distinctly represented to the mind, that we seem to see them with our eyes, and to have them before us. Whoever shall best conceive such images, will have the greatest power in moving the feelings.' " "Milton's *Of Reformation* and the Dynamics of Controversy," pp. 72–73.

23. See Kranidas, *The Fierce Equation,* for a definition of "decorum" rich enough to embrace such images as the foregoing.

24. Fish, *Self-Consuming Artifacts,* 290–91.

25. Svendsen, *Milton and Science* (Cambridge, Mass.: Harvard University Press, 1956), p. 223 and passim; Kranidas, *The Fierce Equation,* p. 52 and passim.

26. While it seems likely that, as Lieb suggests, the church-outed Milton

makes his antiprelatical tracts a surrogate "for the apocalyptic exhortation he would have otherwise thundered from the pulpit," the wavering of apocalyptic fervor in *Animadversions* raises interesting questions about how much of that fervor would have existed without the battle against the prelates in the first place. See "Milton's *Of Reformation* and the Dynamics of Controversy," pp. 76–77.

27. See the discussion in Chapter 1 above on the iconological fallacy.

3 "WAS SHE THY GOD?": THE COUPLING RHETORIC OF THE DIVORCE TRACTS

1. "Elective Poetics and Milton's Prose: *A Treatise of Civil Power* and *Considerations Touching the Likeliest Means to Remove Hirelings Out of the Church*," in David Loewenstein and James Grantham Turner, eds., *Politics, Poetics, and Hermeneutics in Milton's Prose* (Cambridge: Cambridge University Press, 1990), pp. 193–211. The present quotation is on p. 198.

2. *Complete Prose Works of John Milton*, vol. 2, ed. Ernest Sirluck (New Haven: Yale University Press, 1959), pp. 311 and 302. All quotations from the divorce tracts are from this edition, and subsequent page references will appear in the text.

3. Noting the double significance of "restor'd" in Milton's title—that it can signify either "return to an original state of self-identity, or to make good a loss (to re-store)"—Stanley Fish sees the ambiguity as one of many signs of Milton's contradictory intentions in *The Doctrine and Discipline of Divorce*: "What Milton wants is at once to put the force of interpretation into play and to arrest that play the moment it produces the configuration he desires." See "Wanting a Supplement: The Question of Interpretation in Milton's Early Prose," in Loewenstein and Turner, *Politics, Poetics, and Hermeneutics in Milton's Prose*, pp. 41–68. The present quotation is on p. 61.

4. Stephen M. Fallon, "The Metaphysics of Milton's Divorce Tracts," in Loewenstein and Turner, *Politics, Poetics, and Hermeneutics in Milton's Prose*, pp. 69–83. The present quotation is on p. 74; subsequent page references will appear in the text. For an expanded treatment of Milton's animist materialism and its place within the conceptual evolution of the materialist tradition, see chap. 3 of Fallon's *Milton among the Philosophers: Poetry and Materialism in Seventeenth-Century England* (Ithaca: Cornell University Press, 1991).

5. Although Fallon is concerned primarily with the metaphysical, as opposed to the rhetorical, principles that inform Milton's argument, he nevertheless hints at the significance of the latter: "For obviously polemical reasons, Milton zealously guards the Platonist division between matter and spirit that he will abandon later and that he had shown signs of abandoning in *Comus*." See

Milton among the Philosophers, p. 84. According to this comment, the "zeal" with which Milton "guards" the Platonist division might as readily be taken to indicate Milton's affective requisites as his philosophical ones.

6. Such an interdependence is accounted for by Fallon as the "materialism that allowed [Milton] to literalize Paul's figurative economy of the will and to eliminate the Platonists' ontological gap between soul and body." By materializing the soul, Milton enables it to "become carnal and fleshly in more than symbolic terms." See *Milton among the Philosophers*, p. 85.

7. *One Flesh: Paradisal Marriage and Sexual Relations in the Age of Milton* (Oxford: Clarendon Press, 1987), p. 205.

8. See Edward LeComte, *Milton and Sex* (New York: Columbia University Press, 1978), pp. 29–30. Turner also uses the language as a key to Milton's personal psychology, but recognizes this imagery as a sign of Milton's "horror equal to the delight of the true 'act of love,' and generated by the same intimacy of spirit and flesh." See *One Flesh: Paradisal Marriage and Sexual Relations in the Age of Milton*, p. 202. Analysis of Milton's sexual language purely as a rhetorical strategy in the tract appeared first in an earlier form of the present argument, "Coupling Logic and Milton's Doctrine of Divorce," in *Milton Studies XV*, ed. James D. Simmonds (Pittsburgh: University of Pittsburgh Press, 1981), pp. 143–59.

9. See Patterson, "No meer amatorious novel?" in Loewenstein and Turner, *Politics, Poetics, and Hermeneutics in Milton's Prose*, pp. 85–101.

10. "No meer amatorious novel?" p. 99.

11. See "Coupling Logic," p. 148.

12. "No meer amatorious novel?" p. 96.

13. Ibid., p. 98.

14. See my overview of W. J. T. Mitchell's findings in Chapter 1 above, in the section "The Iconological Fallacy."

15. Mitchell treats this issue primarily in chapter 5, "Eye and Ear: Edmund Burke and the Politics of Sensibility," in *Iconology: Image, Text, Ideology* (Chicago: University of Chicago Press, 1986). My observations in this paragraph are based on Mitchell's study.

16. *Answerable Style: Essays on Paradise Lost* (Minneapolis: University of Minnesota Press, 1953), p. 79.

17. "No meer amatorious novel?" pp. 96–97.

18. "The Metaphysics of Milton's Divorce Tracts," p. 81.

19. "Wanting a Supplement," p. 65.

20. Ibid., p. 66.

21. Ibid. In making this point, Fish elaborates on David Aers and Bob Hodge, "'Rational Burning': Milton on Sex and Marriage," in *Milton Studies XIII*, ed. James D. Simmonds (Pittsburgh: University of Pittsburgh Press, 1979), p. 19.

22. James Turner, *One Flesh*, p. 199, n.16.

23. See the above section "The Problem of Rhetorical Dualism."

24. "On the Morning of Christ's Nativity," lines 133–40. Subsequent line numbers will appear in the text.

25. "The Metaphysics of Milton's Divorce Tracts," p. 74. Fallon's quotation is from *De Doctrina Christiana* (Yale edition, *Complete Prose*, 6:318; Columbia ed., 15:40).

26. See above, chapter 1, subsections three and four, for the workings of cognition, imagination, and feeling in iconoclastic metaphor theory and in its psychology of self-transformation.

4 "THE IMAGE OF GOD IN THE EYE": *AREOPAGITICA*'S TRUTH

1. *Iconoclasm and Poetry in the English Reformation: Down Went Dagon* (Chicago: University of Chicago Press, 1986), p. 175.

2. See "Driving from the Letter: Truth and Indeterminacy in Milton's *Areopagitica*," in Mary Nyquist and Margaret W. Ferguson, eds., *Re-membering Milton: Essays on the Texts and Traditions* (New York: Methuen, 1987), pp. 234–54.

3. See above, in Chapter 1 "Carnal Rhetoric and the Poetics of Desire" for exploration of the iconoclastic impetus in transformative desire; see also "The Semantic Fallacy" for Wheelwright's argument regarding the creative value of "changing, from time to time, our ways of being wrong."

4. *Complete Prose Works of John Milton*, vol. 3, ed. Merritt Y. Hughes (New Haven: Yale University Press, 1962) p. 584.

5. *Complete Prose Works*, vol. 2, p. 526. Subsequent page references to this volume will appear in the text.

6. See above, in Chapter 1 "The Iconological Fallacy."

7. See above, in Chapter 3 "Coupling Rhetoric and Its Transformations."

8. See above, in Chapter 1 "Metaphor and Ricoeur's Psychologies of Imagination and Feeling."

9. See above, in Chapter 1 "Metaphor and the Psychology of Creative Iconoclasm," for metaphor's interception of the assimilation that would constitute conceptual peace and rest.

10. "Driving from the Letter," p. 242.

11. "Elective Poetics and Milton's Prose: *A Treatise of Civil Power* and *Considerations Touching the Likeliest Means to Remove Hirelings Out of the Church*," in David Loewenstein and James Grantham Turner, eds., *Politics, Poetics, and Hermeneutics in Milton's Prose* (Cambridge: Cambridge University Press, 1990), pp. 193–211. The phrase quoted is on p. 208.

12. Ibid.

13. "*Areopagitica*: Voicing Contexts," in Loewenstein and Turner, *Politics, Poetics, and Hermeneutics in Milton's Prose*, pp. 103–22. The quotations appear on pages 103 and 104.

14. Ibid., pp. 106, 105, 109.

15. Willmoore Kendall, "How to Read Milton's *Areopagitica*," *Journal of Politics* 22 (1960): 439–73.

16. "On Liberty," in *The Six Great Humanistic Essays of John Stuart Mill*, ed. Albert Levi (New York: Washington Square Press, 1963), p. 160. Subsequent page references will appear in the text.

17. See above, in Chapter 1, "The Iconological Fallacy."

18. See above, Chapter 2, closing arguments.

19. "How to Read Milton's *Areopagitica*," p. 442.

20. Fish elaborates on Milton's case for moral indifference of the outward text: "Once again, then, books are declared to be absolutely essential to the maintenance of truth and virtue, not, however, because truth and virtue reside in books . . . but because it is by (the indifferent) means of books that men and women can make themselves into the simulacrums of what no book could ever contain." See "Driving from the Letter," p. 242.

21. Ernest Sirluck makes the eytmological point about "Frontispices": "This orthography . . . is more strictly accurate than that now standard, which derives from a false popular etymology connecting the final syllable with 'piece,' whereas it actually is from *specio*, to behold, and comes to English by way of medieval *frontispecium*, the front-look or facade of a building." The effect of commodification is amplified if we accept Sirluck's suggestion that there is a further allusion here to "the display methods of brothel-keepers" (*Complete Prose Works of John Milton*, 2: 524, n.139).

22. "In short, if the *Areopagitica* is to be faithful to the lesson it teaches, it cannot teach that lesson directly; rather it must offer itself as the occasion for the trial and exercise that are necessary to the constituting of human virtue; it must become an instrument in what Milton will later call 'knowledge in the making' " ("Driving from the Letter," p. 242).

23. "Elective Poetics," p. 209.

24. *Complete Prose Works of John Milton*, 1: 548; the italics are mine.

25. John X. Evans has used the same appropriately commercial terms for his comment on this passage: "The man in the metaphor, by subcontracting his moral responsibilities, has forfeited his prospects of salvation, and all the world's licensers cannot redeem this loss for him." See "Imagery as Argument in Milton's *Areopagitica*," *Texas Studies in Literature and Language* 8 (1966): 199.

26. "Et cultus hypocriticus: cum externus quidem cultus rite observatur, sed sine interno animi affectu; id quod Deo graviter offensum est"; from *De Doctrina Christiana*, book II, in *The Works of John Milton*, vol. 17, ed. Frank Allen Patterson et al. (New York: Columbia University Press, 1934), pp. 76–77.

5 "UNIMPRISONABLE UTTERANCE": IMAGINATION AND THE ATTACK ON *EIKON BASILIKE*

1. The earliest known example of such displacement is the royal arms of Henry VIII at Rushbrooke in Suffolk. See John Phillips, *The Reformation of Images: Destruction of Art in England, 1535–1660* (Berkeley: University of California Press, 1973), p. 205, n.4. Phillips points to the role of Reformation iconoclasm in the development of human consciousness, pp. 201ff, where he discusses the extended historical implications of Tudor icon manipulation, in addition to the more immediate effects discussed in chapters 3 and 4. See also Ernest B. Gilman, *Iconoclasm and Poetry in the English Reformation: Down Went Dagon* (Chicago: University of Chicago Press, 1986), for a study of Renaissance literary iconoclasm that gives particular attention to Milton's poetics.

2. Paul Ricoeur, *The Rule of Metaphor*, trans. Robert Czerny with Kathleen McLaughlin and John Costello (Toronto: University of Toronto Press, 1975), p. 151. For discussion of the iconic stimulation of "ontological vehemence" and its role in contemporary metaphor theory, see above, in Chapter 1, "Metaphor and Ricoeur's Psychologies of Imagination and Feeling."

3. See above, in Chapter 1 "Metaphor and the Psychology of Creative Iconoclasm."

4. By appropriating ecclesiastical building materials for secular use, the Tudor reformists in many instances created irreversible material facts. Phillips notes that attempts by the Marian regime to reestablish Roman Catholicism in England were blocked in part by numerous destructive alterations such as those worked on the priory church of St. John of Jerusalem. Having first been converted by King Henry to an armory which also housed royal hunting paraphernalia, the church and bell tower were subsequently blown up under Edward VI and the stone used to build the house of the Lord Protector Somerset in the Strand. See *The Reformation of Images*, p. 107.

5. Roy Strong, *The English Icon: Elizabethan and Jacobean Portraiture* (New Haven: Yale University Press, 1969), p. 29.

6. The line comes from Felltham's "Epitaph to the Eternal Memory of Charles the First . . . Inhumanely Murthered by a Perfidious Party of His Prevalent Subjects." William Lamont and Sybil Oldfield collect and discuss representative contemporary views on the public image of the executed king in chapter 5, "Charles I: Royal Martyr or 'Popish Favourite'?," of *Politics, Religion, and Literature in the Seventeenth Century* (London: Dent, 1975).

7. " 'Suffering for Truth's sake': Milton and Martyrdom," in David Loewenstein and James Grantham Turner, eds., *Politics, Poetics, and Hermeneutics in Milton's Prose* (Cambridge: Cambridge University Press, 1990), p. 161.

8. *Iconoclasm and Poetry in the English Reformation*, p. 156.

9. David Loewenstein comments on the specifically theatrical quality of *Eikon Basilike*'s "spectacle of martyrdom": "By assuming the part of saint and martyr in *Eikon Basilike*, the king displays his power to assume a starring part

in the drama of history." *Milton and the Drama of History: Historical Vision, Iconoclasm, and the Literary Imagination* (Cambridge: Cambridge University Press, 1990), pp. 55–56.

10. For rhetorical analysis of this treatment see above, in Chapter 2 "The Seducer Seduced."

11. See Bruce Boehrer, "Elementary Structures of Kingship: Milton, Regicide, and the Family," *Milton Studies XXIII*, ed. James D. Simmonds (Pittsburgh: University of Pittsburgh Press, 1987), pp. 97–98.

12. Steven Zwicker sheds revealing light on *Eikon Basilike*'s popular reception by showing how the book's multifaceted participation in royalist aesthetic culture establishes its iconic precedence. See chapter 2, "The King's Head and the Politics of Literary Property," in *Lines of Authority: Politics and English Literary Culture, 1649–1689* (Ithaca: Cornell University Press, 1993), pp. 37–59.

13. *The Politics of Milton's Prose Style* (New Haven: Yale University Press, 1975), p. 90. The quotation from *Eikonoklastes* appears in *Complete Prose Works*, vol. 3, p. 601.

14. Stavely, *The Politics of Milton's Prose Style*, pp. 85–86.

15. As Zwicker sees it, *Eikon Basilike*'s consciously constructed iconic authority is what necessitates Milton's specific attack on "the authority of the aesthetic" in the king's rhetorical construct: "Milton understood that to combat the book and its legacy he would need to deny its capacity as literature and its imaginative authority." While I fully agree with this part of Zwicker's argument, I am less comfortable with the inference he draws from it—that Milton "aimed altogether to deny the authority of the aesthetic within political discourse" (*Lines of Authority*, p. 39). Milton's attack on the aestheticism of *Eikon Basilike* may sometimes appear to vilify thief and booty alike, such as when he mocks the theft of a heathen prayer from Sir Philip Sidney's *Arcadia*. But the object of this rhetorical assault is not the aesthetic authority within political discourse (an authority on which, as I have demonstrated throughout this book, Milton makes himself entirely too dependent to deny). Rather, he attacks the appropriation of aesthetic authority as a delusive cover for what he sees as political mischief—in this instance, the specific mischief of rewriting political history.

16. *Milton and the Drama of History*, p. 65.

17. "Elementary Structures of Kingship," p. 105.

18. *The Politics of Milton's Prose Style*, p. 86.

19. "Elementary Structures of Kingship," pp. 104, 115.

20. The quotation is from *Eikon Basilike: The Portraiture of His Sacred Majesty in His Solitudes and Sufferings*, ed. Philip A. Knachel (Ithaca: Cornell University Press, 1966), p. 11. Subsequent page references (abbreviated *EB*) will appear in the text. Although *Eikon Basilike* was compiled and largely written by John Gauden, I discuss the book in the terms according to which Milton himself approached it: as a rhetorical construct, a document that was publicly received as it was intended to be received, and as a testimony composed entirely

by its putative author, King Charles I. For a review of the authorship question and of Gauden's actual role, see Hugh Trevor-Roper, "Eikon Basilike: The Problem of the King's Book," *History Today* 1 (September 1951): 7–12. In *Stuart England* (London: Allen Lane, 1978), J. P. Kenyon characterizes *Eikon Basilike* as "a mixture of pietistic moralizing and shrewd historical revisionism" and regards it as a "seriously undervalued" book, second only to the Bible and Foxe's *Acts and Monuments* in its influence during the century (165).

21. *Complete Prose Works*, vol. 3, p. 379. Subsequent page references to this volume will appear in the text.

22. For a detailed discussion of theatricality and representation in *Eikonoklastes*, see David Loewenstein's *Milton and the Drama of History*. Emphasizing the historical dimension of Milton's iconoclasm, Loewenstein argues that shattering the king's equivocal image and recasting it to display underlying corruption is itself an imaginative and theatrical gesture by which Milton intends to influence and dramatically reshape the course of English history. By his iconoclastic action, Milton "attempts to free history from the tyranny of the king's image" (51).

23. *Complete Prose Works*, 2:492.

24. Milton's bawdry in this passage seems only compounded by efforts to treat it with critical solemnity. Apparently not noticing that Milton's gross imagerial expansion is made possible only by the fact that the king has garbled his metaphors, Boehrer remarks that "the king, after all, could act reasonably like a father to his people, but who could believe for a moment that the gentlemen of the Rump might be anyone's mother? . . . The result [of Milton's pressing the maternal identity of Parliament] is this bemusing vision of incest-by-committee, with King Charles committing his rape upon the Rump" ("Elementary Structures of Kingship," p. 113).

25. *Milton and the Drama of History*, p. 57.

26. *Complete Prose Works*, vol. 6, pp. 690–91.

27. Zwicker remarks on the extent to which Milton's attack on a "mad multitude" possessed by vulgar idolatry enables him as well to make "a social argument that echoes and inverts, perhaps as well mocks, the conventional royalist charges against the Elect." See *Lines of Authority*, p. 48.

28. Florence Sandler elaborates on the sacramental tradition in Anglican piety in "Icon and Iconoclast," in *Achievements of the Left Hand: Essays on the Prose of John Milton*, ed. Michael Lieb and John T. Shawcross (Amherst: University of Massachusetts Press, 1974), pp. 160–84. See also chapter 1 of John Phillips, *The Reformation of Images*, for definition of the medieval Christian use of the arts as a "bridge" to the divine. A related perspective is offered by J. J. Scarisbrick, *The Reformation and the English People* (Oxford: Blackwell, 1984), p. 68.

29. Analyzing the emblematic details of the frontispiece portrait, Gilman remarks that "with such motifs clustered around the pious figure of the king, the

frontispiece becomes a rich pictorial synopsis of Charles's Christlike virtues." See *Iconoclasm and Poetry in the English Reformation*, pp. 154–56; the quotation is on p. 156. The frontispiece portrait has recently been reprinted in David Loewenstein and James Grantham Turner, eds., *Politics, Poetics, and Hermeneutics in Milton's Prose* (Cambridge: Cambridge University Press, 1990), p. 160.

30. The Strafford case is for Loewenstein a prime example of *Eikon Basilike*'s theatricalizing equivocation: "Milton's point is not only that the king is as guilty as the earl, but that Charles's actions and motives are staged in such a way that they remain highly ambiguous." See *Milton and the Drama of History*, p. 57.

31. See Hughes's comments on this issue in the introduction to volume 3 of *Complete Prose Works*, pp. 80–88.

32. Gilman comments insightfully on Milton's mocking reinterpretation of the Latin tag with which *Eikon Basilike* concludes. The Latin tag is *Vota dabunt quae Bella negarunt*, which Milton converts from "What he could not accomplish by war, he should achieve by his meditations" to a claim that Charles is "a politic contriver to bring about that interest by faire and plausible words, which the force of Armes deny'd him." Says Gilman, "As this tiny confrontation between the image and the words demonstrates, . . . the king's language is no less idolatrous than his portrait." See *Iconoclasm and Poetry in the English Reformation*, p. 157.

33. These passages have been studied in Chapters 2 and 4 above. The quotation from *Of Reformation* is in *Complete Prose Works*, vol. 1, p. 548; that from *Areopagitica*, vol. 2, pp. 543–44.

6 SAMSON'S TRANSFORMATIVE DESIRE

1. *Samson Agonistes*, lines 1640–45. All quotations from the poem will be from *The Poems of John Milton*, ed. John Carey and Alastair Fowler (London and New York: Longman, Norton, 1968). Subsequent line numbers will appear in the text.

2. An interesting argument has been made, however, for Samson's riddling as a key to his nascent prophetic role. See Daniel T. Lochman, " 'If there be aught of presage': Milton's Samson as Riddler and Prophet," *Milton Studies XXII*, ed. James D. Simmonds (Pittsburgh: University of Pittsburgh Press, 1987), pp. 195–216.

3. From Milton's prefatory epistle to *Samson Agonistes*, "Of That Sort of Dramatic Poem Which Is Called Tragedy"; the italics are added. Some of the most influential antiregenerationist readings of Samson have been those of Irene Samuel, "*Samson Agonistes* as Tragedy," in *Calm of Mind*, ed. J. R. Wittreich (Cleveland: Case Western Reserve University Press, 1971), pp. 235–57;

Joseph Wittreich, *Interpreting "Samson Agonistes"* (Princeton: Princeton University Press, 1986); and Kenneth Burke, "The 'Use' of *Samson Agonistes*," *Hudson Review* 1 (1948):151–67.

4. John M. Steadman articulates and thoroughly analyzes the interpretive difficulties that are created by Milton's reading of Aristotelian poetics in terms of Aristotle's and Milton's own ethical requisites. See Steadman, " 'Passions Well Imitated': Rhetoric and Poetics in the Preface to *Samson Agonistes*," in Joseph A. Wittreich, ed., *Calm of Mind*, pp. 175–207.

5. *Interpreting "Samson Agonistes,"* p. 379. Out of context, this statement of course misrepresents Wittreich's rich interweaving of parallels and constrasts that make Milton's final two poems into a complementary pattern for interpretation. But as I will continue to demonstrate, the model-seeking ideological assumptions that underlie such a statement contradict the iconoclastic enterprise of Milton's poetics.

Patrick Cullen also reads *Samson Agonistes* as structurally parallel to *Paradise Regained*, with the temptations presented by Manoa, Dalila, and Harapha schematically reiterating those of the world (Dalila: avarice/lust/glory), the flesh (Manoa: intemperance/despair), and the devil (Harapha: pride/might). The difficulty with such a reading, in my view, is that it tends to locate the problem of sin in external conditions to be rejected rather than internal conditions to be redefined. The externality of sin in Cullen's *Samson Agonistes* is suggested by the externality of the reward for its overthrow: "Just as Christ in *Paradise Regained* receives as His reward fruits from the *arbor vitae*, . . . so Samson receives his reward after a similar pilgrimage, a monument planted round 'with shade / Of Laurel ever green, and branching Palm.' " The kind of God who, for such triumphs, would dole out such rewards is in fact defined for us by Cullen's tempter of the flesh, Manoa. See chapter 5, "*Samson Agonistes*: Milton's Christian Redefinition of Tragedy," in *Infernal Triad: The Flesh, the World, and the Devil in Spenser and Milton* (Princeton: Princeton University Press, 1974); the quotation is on p. 236.

6. Gary Hamilton summarizes this perspective in the image with which he concludes his case for Milton's self-portrait in *The History of Britain* as an unsuspected "tugging at the pillars" of Stuart monarchy: "For all of the complicated things that Milton may be trying to convey through this story and this character, few would refuse to acknowledge that the blind and haughty Samson is there to project and reject and modify various images of Milton himself." "*The History of Britain* and Its Restoration Audience," in *Politics, Poetics, and Hermeneutics in Milton's Prose*, ed. David Loewenstein and James Grantham Turner (Cambridge: Cambridge University Press, 1990), p. 253.

7. *Toward "Samson Agonistes": The Growth of Milton's Mind* (Princeton: Princeton University Press, 1978), p. 7. Although I would give far greater weight to the affective than to the rational dimension of Samson's self-critique, Radzinowicz gains valuable insights by portraying Samson as endowed with psycho-

logical elements drawn from an earlier Milton: wounded, beleaguered, the victim of a bad marriage. Compare, however, David Loewenstein's view of Samson as the enraged and derisive victim of a Circean seduction, in *Milton and the Drama of History* (Cambridge: Cambridge University Press, 1990), see chap. 6, "Spectacle of Power," esp. pp. 133–34. In Loewenstein's view, Samson's continued intermittent rages that culminate in the violence of his final theatrical gesture necessarily complicate any argument for his rational regeneration. Earlier influential regenerationist readings include those of Joseph Summers, "The Movements of the Drama," in *The Lyric and Dramatic Milton*, ed. Joseph Summers (New York: Columbia University Press, 1965), pp. 153–75; Arnold Stein, *Heroic Knowledge: An Interpretation of "Paradise Regained" and "Samson Agonistes"* (Minneapolis: University of Minnesota Press, 1957); and Anthony Low, *The Blaze of Noon: A Reading of "Samson Agonistes"* (New York: Columbia University Press, 1974). Low's reading absorbs the negative aspects of the tragedy into the regenerationist perspective by articulating Milton's complex synthesis of classical form and Christian belief.

8. See *Reviving Liberty: Radical Christian Humanism in Milton's Great Poems* (Cambridge, Mass.: Harvard University Press, 1989), chap. 5.

9. See "Spectacle and Evidence in *Samson Agonistes*," *Critical Inquiry* 9 (1989): 556–86; and also its predecessor "Question and Answer in *Samson Agonistes*," *Critical Quarterly* 9 (1969): 237–64. My reading of Samson's iconoclasm is deeply indebted to Fish's insights in both of these articles.

10. "Spectacle and Evidence," p. 580, n.18.

11. Regenerationist critics regularly support the Chorus's reversal even as their arguments point out the error of such a practice. For example, having shown that Samson "has learned by experience . . . not to glory in his strength," John M. Steadman nevertheless describes the destruction of the Philistine temple in terms that have a tribal God glorifying and "bearing witness to" Samson exactly as the Chorus wishes God to do: "It is at this moment that God intervenes to 'vindicate the glory of his name,' to destroy the idolators, and to bear witness to his faithful Champion." See " 'Faithful Champion': The Theological Basis of Milton's Hero of Faith," reprinted in Arthur E. Barker, ed., *Milton: Modern Essays in Criticism* (London: Oxford University Press, 1965), pp. 467–83; originally published in *Anglia* 67 (1959): 12–28. The quotations are from the Barker edition, pp. 477–78.

12. *Reviving Liberty*, p. 141.

13. "*Pathos* and *Katharsis* in *Samson Agonistes*," in *Critical Essays on Milton from ELH* (Baltimore: Johns Hopkins University Press, 1969), p. 252; originally published in *ELH* 31, no. 2 (June 1964): 156–74.

14. "Elective Poetics and Milton's Prose: *A Treatise of Civil Power* and *Considerations Touching the Likeliest Means to Remove Hirelings Out of the Church*," in Loewenstein and Turner, *Politics, Poetics, and Hermeneutics in Milton's Prose*, p. 197.

15. The connection is delineated in the present study in Chapter 1 under the subhead "Metaphor and the Psychology of Creative Iconoclasm."

16. There is much truth in Irene Samuel's comment that "no peaceable life, however attained and however full of opportunity to instruct or judge or in any other nonviolent way deliver Israel, could recompense the Samson of this tragedy for the indignity of having to continue in life knowing himself to have been physically defeated by the Philistines" (*"Samson Agonistes* as Tragedy," p. 244). But as my argument for Samson's iconoclastic impetus will show, I am not convinced that the tragedy's procedure of *defining* Samson through his violence ("the Samson of this tragedy") necessarily constitutes the kind of *judgment* of his violence that Samuel hands down. Neither condemnation nor celebration of any specific violent act is implied by recognizing the psychological truth of the iconoclastic impetus.

17. Burton Weber helpfully reviews the modern interpretive record on Samson's visitors in the course of his own bipartite structural reading of the poem. See "The Schematic Design of the *Samson* Middle," *Milton Studies XXII,* ed. Simmonds, pp. 233–54. As will become apparent in the argument that follows, however, I cannot agree with Weber's argument that Dalila and Harapha contribute to Samson's regeneration by enabling him to see that, in comparison with their reprobate characters, his own moral and spiritual state is not as depraved as he had thought.

18. The irony of this sequence is referred to by Fish as a critical commonplace: Samson's "would-be consolers succeed only in reinforcing his despair, while the taunts of Harapha and Dalila rouse him from his lethargy and lead him once more to look to 'the living God' whose 'ear is ever open; and his eye / Gracious to re-admit the suppliant' (1172–73)." "Question and Answer in *Samson Agonistes,*" p. 250.

19. Irene Samuel's argument that Dalila comes to Samson for exactly the reason she says she does ("in some part to recompense" her deed) seems to me both perfectly reasonable and beside the point. The woman to whom such an excuse could, under the appalling circumstances, make sense is necessarily the "birdbrain" that Samuel makes Dalila out to be ("Dalila is surely the most birdbrained woman ever to have gotten herself involved in major tragedy"). But as Samuel seems to recognize ("In context, of course, Dalila is not comic"), this reading cannot finally prove aesthetically satisfactory. Like Harapha, Dalila is a two-dimensional figure whose flatness is a function of iconic, not mimetic, requisites. See "*Samson Agonistes* as Tragedy," p. 248–49.

20. The assumption that Dalila and Harapha are images, reflections, or at least reminders of Samson's own past weakness is well established as a critical perspective for dealing with these characters. What is not so clearly agreed upon is the nature of the psychological process that is actually induced by the two visits. The present argument is concerned explicitly with the affective and iconoclastic dimension of this process. For an interesting psychological study

based on Renaissance humoural theory, with particular analytical focus drawn from the period's fascination with melancholy, see Raymond B. Waddington, "Melancholy against Melancholy: *Samson Agonistes* as Renaissance Tragedy," in Wittreich, *Calm of Mind*, pp. 259–87. Anthony Low finds in Samson's satire against Dalila and Harapha an aggression that in its effects resembles the self-critical phase of iconoclastic psychology: "The satire . . . is no more bitter or powerful than what he turns against himself. In his own case, it helps to work his cure." Although this "cure" as Low sees it, accords with a regenerationist reading of Samson that I cannot accept, I do think that for Milton the iconoclastic *pattern* of Samson's action traces the psychological and cognitive requisites to a progressive "journey of mankind as a whole . . . if only they would seize hold of the proffered opportunity" (*The Blaze of Noon*, pp. 162, 173).

21. This stripping from Samson's consciousness of the interpretive idols of his affective inner being parallels the outward disempowering that Darryl Tippens has shown to be the necessary downward phase of the kenotic experience: "Depotentiation, the loss of power, is of course Samson's means to ultimate power; or, viewed from another perspective, it *is* power. God the great iconoclast brings down the rulers of this world through divine weakness." See "The Kenotic Experience of *Samson Agonistes*," *Milton Studies XXII*, ed. Simmonds, p. 181.

22. The possibility that Dalila represents as much a positive image of repentance as she does a negative reminder of Samson's moral degradation is argued by Heather Asals in "In Defense of Dalila: *Samson Agonistes* and the Reformation Theology of the Word," *Journal of English and Germanic Philology* 74 (1975): 183–94.

23. Since these are the only interpretive options offered by Samson himself to justify his marriage choices, the case that has been made against Dalila by Dayton Haskin seems moot. Dalila may indeed be unfit for marriage to Samson because she fails to provide him "genuine spiritual conversation," as Haskin argues. But while the marriage thus "can be seen as fulfilling the criteria Milton establishes [in the prose tracts] for warranting divorce," those criteria are made irrelevant by accepting, as Haskin does, the Chorus's position that the marriage is providential, part of God's scheme to deliver Israel rather than a means for mutual satisfaction: "[God] would not else who never wanted means, / . . . Have prompted this heroic Nazarite, / Against his vow of strictest purity, / To seek in marriage that fallacious bride, / Unclean, unchaste" (315–21). Haskin rightly articulates as Miltonic the principle that "freedom and salvation lies in moral rectitude and union with God, not in slavish adherence to either legal strictures or merely human values." But to argue that Milton particularly "exploits the metaphoric possibilities of [Samson's] unfit marriage" in order to support that principle is to make the institution of marriage central to Samson's regenerative potential on a doctrinal and disciplinary level denied by the poem. Whether regenerate or unregenerate at the close, Samson does not divorce Dalila; nor is

any movement toward divorce required for him to do what he does. In contrast to the case of the ill-wedded spouse in the divorce tracts, Samson's bad marriage operates in the poem neither as a block to the hero's efforts toward salvation nor as a foil to the kind of good marriage that might provide a more congenial route to the same goal. Haskin's claim that "divorce from Dalila is Samson's only road to harmony with God" carries with it the assumption that Samson had at one time seen marriage in the way Milton had seen it when he wrote the divorce tracts—as a means of realizing spiritual salvation in the flesh—and that fleshly disillusionment subsequently forced Samson to transcend the connubial vision: "Samson, finally, achieves a harmonious union with God that enables him, like the Christ of *Paradise Regained*, to bypass married love in working out his salvation." But the contradictions that distinguish Samson's own stated reasons for marrying make Haskin's argument for the role of divorce in the Nazarite's salvation seem mistaken, if not irrelevant. See Dayton Haskin, "Divorce as a Path to Union with God in *Samson Agonistes*," *ELH* 38, no. 3 (September 1971): 358–76. The quotations I have used may be found on pages 368 and 369.

24. See lines 215–18, 420–24. In lines 315–25, the Chorus raise the issue and quickly move to dismiss it ("Down Reason then, at least vain reasonings down") in the course of acknowledging God's right to dispense with his own laws; yet in the process, they reveal too much uncertainty to allow this dismissal its intended effect. The term "intimate impulse" is Samson's: "The first I saw at Timna, and she pleased / Me, not my parents, that I sought to wed, / The daughter of an infidel: they knew not / That what I motioned was of God; / I knew / From intimate impulse, and therefore urged / The marriage on" (219–24).

25. Anne Davidson Ferry remarks, "It is *as if* we do not learn to understand his experiences by the same means as we learn about Adam and Eve or Satan— by what he says about himself, or by words spoken to him, or words spoken about him; the effect is as if we come to know Samson by what is *not* said." See "Samson's 'Fort of Silence,'" in *Milton and the Miltonic Dryden* (Cambridge, Mass.: Harvard University Press, 1968), p. 149.

26. Albert C. Labriola argues that Samson's "intimate impulse" (or in Manoa's terms, his "divine impulsion"), though it results in the sinful act of marriage to a Philistine, is just as much a prompting from God as are the "rousing motions" that later lead Samson to yield to the Philistine command and make the appearance that will result in his enemies' destruction. But despite their common divine origin, Labriola demonstrates that the two promptings nevertheless belong to opposed categories, the terms of which Milton sets out in his discussion of Providence and temptation in *De Doctrina Christiana*. Samson's "intimate impulse" is allied to the kinds of "evil" temptations— "occasions of sin"—that are designed by God to blind the understandings and harden the hearts of those who have already conceived evil. His "rousing mo-

tions," on the other hand, signal Samson's will newly liberated to doing good, having been restored to righteousness by resisting the equally providential "good" temptations represented by his confrontations with Manoa, Dalila, and Harapha. See "Divine Urgency as a Motive for Conduct in *Samson Agonistes*," *Philological Quarterly* 50 (January 1971): 99–107. For an argument based on comparing "intimate impulse" and "rousing motions" that leads to very different conclusions, see Helen Damico, "Duality in Dramatic Vision: A Structural Analysis of *Samson Agonistes*," *Milton Studies XII*, ed. James D. Simmonds (Pittsburgh: Pittsburgh University Press, 1978). Damico's article is discussed briefly in note 39 below.

27. The magical irrationality that links Samson's Nazaritic prohibition with the prohibition in *Paradise Lost* is learnedly contextualized by Michael Lieb in his study of the prohibition theme in the Jahwistic tradition; see *Poetics of the Holy: A Reading of "Paradise Lost"* (Chapel Hill: University of North Carolina Press, 1981), chap. 5.

28. The simplicity with which is here expressed the logical principle by which Samson retains or relinquishes his strength should in no way be taken to diminish the complex theological significance of that divine gift. For a richly detailed exploration of the nature of Samson's strength, as manifested both in the exegetical tradition and in Milton's poem, see the final chapter of Michael Lieb, *The Sinews of Ulysses: Form and Convention in Milton's Works* (Pittsburgh: Duquesne University Press, 1989), "The Theology of Strength."

29. *Reviving Liberty*, p. 128.

30. Joseph Wittreich remarks that "Harapha is not so much a foil to, as a revelation of, an equally blustering Samson who has more than a fair share of Goliath in him." *Interpreting "Samson Agonistes"* (Princeton: Princeton University Press, 1986), p. 310.

31. Carey and Fowler edition, 1082n.

32. Labriola notes the paradox inherent in Samson's sin of pride: Samson's "recognition that he was destined by God to liberate Israel" was itself the thing that "alienated him from God; rendered him unworthy to serve as God's champion; and made him vulnerable to evil temptation. . . . Much as David was impelled to take the census as a manifestation of pride, so also Samson was incited by 'intimate impulse' that 'was of God' . . . to display the sinful arrogance of mind that he had freely conceived." See "Divine Urgency as a Motive for Conduct in *Samson Agonistes*," p. 102.

33. Discussed in Chapter 1 and 2 above.

34. Contrasting the style of Samson's vengeful deity with that of Jesus' deity in *Paradise Regained*, "whose only law is love," Wittreich comments: "The sinister, squabbling gods of *Samson Agonistes* . . . are so personated as to make not only Dagon but Samson's 'God' seem ridiculous (cf. *PR* IV.342). In the face of Jesus are to be found 'glimpses of his Fathers glory' (I.93), is to be seen the 'True Image of the Father' (IV.596). In the figure of Samson, the Chorus discovers

only 'The Image of [God's] strength' (706), the image of a snarling, combative deity. That is, Jesus reveals the totality, is in every respect the similitude of deity, whereas Samson is but an aspect, a manifestation of the dark side of a deity; and it is a deity who produces through Samson the claims for justice which express themselves in vengeance and violence, the very qualities that the God of Milton's epics cannot brook." See *Interpreting "Samson Agonistes,"* pp. 350–51. In terms of Christian ideology, of course, Wittreich is quite right. But the Jesus of *Paradise Regained* cannot be said to reveal the totality even of the Son of God, much less of God Himself, if we take into account Milton's multiple portrayals of each in *Paradise Lost*. There we see, among many other views, a God whose sneer at the rebellious angels ("Nearly it now concerns us to be sure / Of our omnipotence" [V.721–22]) is heartily applauded by his only Begotten ("Mighty Father, thou thy foes / Justly hast in derision, and secure / Laugh'st at their vain designs" [V.735–37]). This is the same Son who later "into terror changed / His countenance too severe to be beheld / And full of wrath bent on his enemies" (VI.824–26). Such images suggest that Milton's epics brook whatever qualities in God their immediate affective thrusts require— a stylistic determination that is more clearly supported by Milton's expressed concepts of infinitude and omnipotence in deity than are other determinations by his presumed ideological boundaries.

35. Samson's reduction of God "to the Philistine scale of tribal deity" clinches the antiregenerationist case for Irene Samuel. See *"Samson Agonistes* as Tragedy," pp. 253–54. Although Samuel's essay is among the most cogent of many intelligent readings of *Samson Agonistes*, I do not find in it (or in Milton's poem) evidence to support an interpretation of God that would securely operate to correct or critique Samson's reduction.

36. See, in Chapter 1, "Metaphor and the Psychology of Creative Iconoclasm."

37. Fish sees Samson's preparedness at this point to relinquish dependence on Hebrew law as paralleling that of the reader: "With Samson [the reader] moves beyond the limits of choice dictated by the intersection of the situation and the Law, and accepts the awful responsibility of freedom." See "Question and Answer," p. 254.

38. "Question and Answer," p. 256. For Irene Samuel, "Everything must turn on whether Samson's final deed is to be read as 'service of God' and as showing Samson's 'tranquility of mind' " (*"Samson Agonistes* as Tragedy," p. 241). This is precisely what cannot be determined on the evidence of the poem.

39. For antiregenerationist critics, Samson's words define the deed they announce as aligned with his earlier unsanctioned deeds of killing, and also with his unauthorized second marriage. According to Joseph Wittreich, the words "Of my own accord" are no less than "code words, as it were, for 'A private, extrajudicial arrangement.' " A regenerate interpretation of any such arrangement is disallowed by Samson himself and also by Milton, says Wittreich; the

code words are a function of Milton's iconoclastic attack on the heroic image of Samson that had been promulgated during the height of the Civil War. See *Interpreting "Samson Agonistes,"* p. 143. Arguing along similar lines, Helen Damico juxtaposes the "rousing motions" that lead to Samson's entering the Philistine temple next to the inward promptings that led to his marriages. The analogous consequences of both make sufficient reason "to regard the ostensibly heroic act as the fulfillment of Samson's will rather than God's." See "Duality in Dramatic Vision," p. 107. That his final act fulfills Samson's will, there seems to me little doubt. But Damico's speculation that Milton took measures such as fusing comic and tragic forms "to ensure that Samson would be judged disobedient and a sinner" (111) rests on the questionable assumption that Milton's primary concern for his readers was that they should pass moral judgment—exactly the kind of interpretive certitude that the poem's iconoclastic movement undermines. For a regenerationist counterargument to the case made by Damico, see Albert C. Labriola, "Divine Urgency as a Motive for Conduct in *Samson Agonistes,*" pp. 99–107. This article is briefly discussed in note 26 above.

40. This denial of our own sensory witness to the catastrophe is essential to Milton's iconoclastic reconfiguration of the genre of tragedy from external spectacle to internal salvation, says Ernest Gilman: "By barring our direct entry into a violent spectacle, Milton at once succeeds in preserving the decorum of classical tragedy and in frustrating a desire, aroused by our forced confinement in the drama's blindness, to see the events of that tragedy. Like the Messenger's, our own salvation depends on an act of abstinence: in our role as readers or auditors we must stand 'aloof' (1611) from the temptation to see up close." See *Iconoclasm and Poetry in the English Reformation: Down Went Dagon* (Chicago: University of Chicago Press, 1986), p. 172.

41. Fish finds a like coalescence in God's and Samson's uninterpretability: "God and Samson unite only in being inaccessible, objects alike of an interpretive activity that finds no corroboration in the visible world. When Samson leaves off assuming that he can decipher God's will and resolves instead to go along with whatever that will might turn out to be, he becomes as mysterious—as difficult to read—as the God whose disposition he refuses to appoint." See "Spectacle and Evidence in *Samson Agonistes,*" p. 586.

42. "'His Uncontrollable Intent': Discovery as Action in *Samson Agonistes,*" *Milton Studies VII*, ed. James D. Simmonds (Pittsburgh: University of Pittsburgh Press, 1975), p. 63.

43. The sheer barbarousness of this exultation in bloody revenge can only too easily be passed over by the reader swept up in the heroic impetus of the Chorus's rhetoric of conviction. Fish comments trenchantly on "the extraordinary combination of blood lust and interpretive lust that takes up the last one hundred lines of the play." See "Spectacle and Evidence," p. 569.

INDEX

22, 130; iconoclastic, Milton's, 4–5
and throughout; metaphorical truth,
20; as mode of discovery, 118–19;
and the Osiris myth in *Areopa-
gitica*, 127–28; poetic truth, 18,
30–31, 47–48; and true witness in
Samson Agonistes, 173–76, 195–96;
truth-bearing capacity of language,
philosophical inquiry into, 14–19;
truth claims, 15, 24, 47, 123; truth-
effect, 15, 47; truth-value, 47, 124.
See also Affective language; Icono-
clasm; Metaphor; Transformative
desire
Turner, James, 105–6, 197 n.1, 206 n.8,
207 n.20, 208 n.1, 209 n.8, 209 n.22,
215 n.29
Turner, Mark, 199 n.2

Venuti, Lawrence, 204 n.51

Waddington, Raymond B., 219 n.20
Wallis, Charles, 205 n.52
Weaver, Richard M., 206 n.6
Weber, Burton, 218 n.17
Wheelwright, Philip, 16–17, 35, 201
n.16, 201 n.17, 210 n.3
Williams, Roger, 128
Wimsatt, William K., 15, 17, 19, 27, 201
n.11
Wittreich, Joseph, 8, 172, 197 n.1, 215
n.3, 216 n.4, 216 n.5, 221 n.30, 221
n.34, 222 n.39
Wolfe, Don M., 205 n.1, 214 n.21, 214
n.26
Woods, Suzanne, 90, 127, 140, 176

Zwicker, Steven, 213 n.12, 213 n.15,
214 n.27

*Lana Cable is Associate Professor
of English at the State University of
New York at Albany.*

Library of Congress Cataloging-in-Publication Data

Cable, Lana.
Carnal rhetoric : Milton's iconoclasm and the poetics of desire /
Lana Cable.
p.   cm.
Includes bibliographical references and index.
ISBN 0-8223-1560-2. — ISBN 0-8223-1573-4 (pbk.)
1. Milton, John, 1608–1674—Technique.   2. Modernism (Literature)—
England—History—17th century.   3. Iconoclasm in literature.
4. Desire in literature.   5. Rhetoric—1500–1800.   6. Metaphor.
I. Title.
PR3591.C33   1995
821'.4—dc20   94-38249   CIP

DATE DUE